Cross-Cultural Psychology

Hede Helfrich

Cross-Cultural Psychology

Hede Helfrich
Institute of Psychology
University of Hildesheim
Hildesheim, Germany

ISBN 978-3-662-67557-1   ISBN 978-3-662-67558-8 (eBook)
https://doi.org/10.1007/978-3-662-67558-8

This book is a translation of the original German edition „Kulturvergleichende Psychologie" by Helfrich, Hede, published by Springer-Verlag GmbH, DE in 2019. In addition, data and literature references were updated. The translation was done with the help of artificial intelligence (machine translation by the service DeepL.com). A subsequent human revision (by the author) was done primarily in terms of content, so that the book will read stylistically differently from a conventional translation. Springer Nature works continuously to further the development of tools for the production of books and on the related technologies to support the authors.

© The Editor(s) (if applicable) and The Author(s), under exclusive license to Springer-Verlag GmbH, DE, part of Springer Nature 2023

This work is subject to copyright. All rights are solely and exclusively licensed by the Publisher, whether the whole or part of the material is concerned, specifically the rights of translation, reprinting, reuse of illustrations, recitation, broadcasting, reproduction on microfilms or in any other physical way, and transmission or information storage and retrieval, electronic adaptation, computer software, or by similar or dissimilar methodology now known or hereafter developed.

The use of general descriptive names, registered names, trademarks, service marks, etc. in this publication does not imply, even in the absence of a specific statement, that such names are exempt from the relevant protective laws and regulations and therefore free for general use.

The publisher, the authors, and the editors are safe to assume that the advice and information in this book are believed to be true and accurate at the date of publication. Neither the publisher nor the authors or the editors give a warranty, expressed or implied, with respect to the material contained herein or for any errors or omissions that may have been made. The publisher remains neutral with regard to jurisdictional claims in published maps and institutional affiliations.

This Springer imprint is published by the registered company Springer-Verlag GmbH, DE, part of Springer Nature.
The registered company address is: Heidelberger Platz 3, 14197 Berlin, Germany

Preface to the Second Edition

In the course of globalisation, members of different cultures are increasingly coming together – think of economic relations, internet communication and migration movements. At times, it seems as if the different cultures are increasingly converging and cultural differences are fading more and more. Examples include forms of communication such as the use of emojis or the popularity of foods such as sushi, hamburgers and French fries.

At the same time, however, signs can be found that do not speak for a homogenisation of cultures, but on the contrary, for an emphasis on cultural differences, both the "speciality" of one's own culture and the "otherness" of foreign cultures are emphasized. The perception of otherness here moves between the poles of "tremendum" (frightening) and "fascinosum" (mysteriously delightful). Examples of the frightening "tremendum" and the associated desire for isolation would be the QAnon movement in the USA, the Pegida movement in East Germany and the change in policy in the USA beginning with the administration of Donald Trump. An example of the "fascinosum" would be the transfiguration of supposedly original ways of life combined with the longing for a "back to nature" in the form of the tradition of "archaic" cultures such as the inhabitants of the highlands of New Guinea.

Both positions are largely not based on personal experience or credible research results, but rather on projections of fear or wishful thinking onto the supposedly "familiar" and the supposedly "alien". Cross-cultural psychology represents the scientific attempt to shed light on this darkness. Scientific guiding questions are: Are people of other countries or other cultural origins different from us? Or are similar deep structures of thinking, feeling and acting hidden under the surface of the fascinatingly exotic or even threateningly foreign? But why do conspicuous differences in behaviour occur, and how can they be explained?

In contrast to the other sub-disciplines of psychology, cross-cultural psychology not only covers a specific subject area, but also sees itself as an interdisciplinary discipline. It subjects the psychological laws of perception, feeling and thinking that have been established in Western culture and are supposedly universally valid to critical scrutiny by broadening the perspective and thus revealing the relativity of some of the insights gained from a Western perspective.

I am pleased with the positive response to the first edition of this book. It has encouraged me to produce a new edition in which printing errors have been corrected, improvements have been made to the content and newer literature has been included.

In addition to the people already mentioned in the first edition, other people have contributed to the book in its present form. I would like to express my sincere thanks to Dr. Werner Faßmann, Prof. Dr. Geert Hofstede, Prof. Dr. Adelheid Kühne, Dr. Wolfgang Rechtien, Dr. Ibrahim Sari and Ms. Xiaomei Wang for their correspondence, discussions and inspiration. My very special thanks go to Ms. Dagmar Roseblade for her critical text comments and her concentrated support in the reprocessing of the galley proofs.

Any errors are of course the responsibility of the author. I would be very pleased if this book finds your interest and am always grateful for suggestions and criticism to helfrich@uni-hildesheim.de.

Dalian, China Hede Helfrich
March 2018

Preface to the First Edition

> Every person is similar in some ways to *all* other people, in other ways to *some* other people, and ultimately in certain ways to *no* other people. (Kluckhohn and Murray 1948)

Are people from other countries or other cultural backgrounds different from us? Or are similar deep structures of thinking, feeling and acting hidden under the surface of the fascinatingly exotic or even threateningly foreign? But why do striking differences in behaviour occur, and how can they be explained? Such questions are attempted by cross-cultural psychology. In contrast to the other sub-disciplines of psychology, it not only covers a specific subject area, but also sees itself as an interdisciplinary discipline. It subjects the psychological laws of perception, feeling, and thinking that have been established in Western culture and are supposedly universally valid to critical scrutiny by broadening the perspective and thus revealing the relativity of some of the insights gained from the Western perspective.

The book is primarily aimed at readers of bachelor's degree programmes not only in psychology, but also in other fields of study. It is intended to provide a basic insight into the most important contents, approaches and methods of cross-cultural psychology without expecting any special prior knowledge. In accordance with the character of an introductory book, suggestions are given after each chapter in the form of further reading recommendations. The selection of topics is essentially based on the classical canon of subjects in psychology. The questions raised there are considered from a comparative cultural perspective and thus at the same time have repercussions for established scientific psychology.

The book would not have come about in its present form without the assistance of many other people. The editor of the series "Basiswissen Psychologie" (Basic Knowledge Psychology), Prof. Dr. Jürgen Kriz, gave me numerous helpful hints for shortening and revising the manuscript. Ms. Julia Jürging and Ms. Jana Rumberger, from the perspective of potential readers, have subjected the book to critical scrutiny and provided fruitful suggestions for increasing its comprehensibility. Ms. Jürging also prepared important passages in the form of mnemonic boxes. My husband, Prof. Dr. Erich Hölter, was a great help not only in the design of the illustrations. Last but not least, the book has also benefited from many discussions in and outside of lectures with students of the Chemnitz University of Technology, the Nizhegorod State University of Architecture and Civil Engineering (NNGASU) in Nizhny Novgorod (Russia) as well as the Dongbei University of Finance and Economics (DUFE) in Dalian (China). I would like to express my sincere thanks to all of them.

Dalian, China   Hede Helfrich
March 2013

Contents

1		**Subject Area of Cross-Cultural Psychology**	1
	1.1	Aims of Cross-Cultural Psychology	1
	1.2	Different Research Directions	2
	1.3	Cross-Cultural Psychology in the Canon of Psychological Subjects	2
	1.4	Concept of Culture	4
	1.5	Historical Development	6
	1.6	Conclusion	9
	1.7	Questions of Understanding	10
2		**Methodological Considerations**	13
	2.1	Etic Versus Emic Approach	13
		2.1.1 Two Views	13
		2.1.2 Universality Versus Uniqueness	18
		2.1.3 Outside View Versus Inside View	19
	2.2	Comparability of the Objects of Investigation	20
		2.2.1 Object of Comparison and Standard of Comparison	20
		2.2.2 Equivalence Postulates	20
		2.2.3 Consequences for Cross-Cultural Comparison	24
	2.3	Methods of Data Collection and Analysis	25
	2.4	Selection of Suitable Study Units	33
		2.4.1 Selection of Cultures	34
		2.4.2 Selection of Individuals	35
		2.4.3 Selection of Situations and Instruments	35
	2.5	Statistical Testing of Hypotheses	36
	2.6	Conclusion	38
	2.7	Questions of Understanding	39

3	**Culture and Phylogenetic Development**	41
	3.1 Human Universals as a Result of Natural Selection	41
	3.2 Adaptation and Exaptation	43
	3.3 Conclusion	45
	3.4 Questions of Understanding	46
4	**Nature-Nurture Controversy from a Cross-Cultural Perspective**	47
	4.1 Universal and Differential "Nature"	47
	4.2 Genetic Make-Up and Cultural Influence	48
	4.3 Conclusion	51
	4.4 Questions of Understanding	52
5	**Description and Classification of Cultures**	53
	5.1 Cultural Factors	53
	5.2 Cultural Dimensions According to Hofstede	54
	5.3 Cultural Dimensions According to Schwartz	57
	5.4 Cultural Dimensions According to the GLOBE Research Group	58
	5.5 Cultural Dimensions According to the World Values Survey	59
	5.6 Cultural Dimensions According to Trompenaars	59
	5.7 Cultural Dimensions According to Hall	60
	5.8 Comparison of the Dimensional Approaches to Culture Description	62
	5.9 Context Factors: The Human Development Index (HDI)	62
	5.10 Conclusion	65
	5.11 Questions of Understanding	66
6	**Perception**	67
	6.1 Perception and Experience	67
	6.2 Brunswik's Theory of Transactional Functionalism	68
	6.3 Whorf's Principle of Linguistic Relativity	71
	6.4 Conclusion	75
	6.5 Questions of Understanding	75
7	**Cognitive Abilities and Performance**	77
	7.1 Deficit Versus Difference Model	77
	7.2 General Intelligence Versus Specific Abilities and Performances	78
	7.3 Antecedents of Cognitive Differences	81

		7.3.1	Individualist Versus Collectivist Mode of Thinking	81
		7.3.2	Confucian Dynamics	84
		7.3.3	Mother Tongue	84
		7.3.4	School Education	87
		7.3.5	Minority Status	88
		7.3.6	Poverty	89
	7.4	A Model for the Interaction of Culture and Cognition		90
	7.5	Conclusion		95
	7.6	Questions of Understanding		95
8	**Emotion**			97
	8.1	Feeling and Emotion		97
	8.2	Categorisation of Emotions		98
	8.3	Emergence and Expression of Emotions		99
		8.3.1	Emotion Theories	99
		8.3.2	Process Model of Emotion	100
		8.3.3	Situations that Trigger Emotions	101
		8.3.4	Appraisal of Emotion Triggering Situations	102
		8.3.5	Manifestation of Emotions	103
		8.3.6	Coping with Emotions	105
	8.4	Recognition of Emotions		105
	8.5	Conclusion		107
	8.6	Questions of Understanding		107
9	**Language and Communication**			109
	9.1	Language as a Means of Exchanging Information		109
	9.2	Language as a Species-Specific and Culture-Specific Characteristic		110
	9.3	Comparability of Verbal Utterances		112
	9.4	Linguistic Universals		114
	9.5	Linguistic and Communicative Relativity		115
	9.6	Communication Model According to Schulz von Thun		116
	9.7	Cultural Factors as Antecedents of Language Use		118
		9.7.1	Individualism-Collectivism and Power Distance	118
		9.7.2	Masculinity-Femininity	120
	9.8	Conclusion		121
	9.9	Questions of Understanding		121

10 Personality ... 123
- 10.1 Culture and Personality from a Psychoanalytical Point of View ... 123
- 10.2 Dimensional Description of Personality ... 125
  - 10.2.1 Cross-Cultural Validity of Personality Factor Models ... 125
  - 10.2.2 Cultural Differences in Single Personality Factors ... 128
- 10.3 Conclusion ... 129
- 10.4 Questions of Understanding ... 130

11 Sex and Gender ... 131
- 11.1 Universality and Culture-Specificity of Gender Differences ... 131
- 11.2 Biological Basis of Gender Differences ... 132
- 11.3 Gender Differences and Economic Development ... 133
- 11.4 Gender Differences and Cultural Values ... 134
- 11.5 Conclusion ... 136
- 11.6 Questions of Understanding ... 137

12 Development in Childhood and Adolescence ... 139
- 12.1 Maturation and Learning in Childhood and Adolescence ... 139
- 12.2 Role Expectations in Childhood and Adolescence ... 143
- 12.3 Testing the Universal Validity of Cognitive Development Models ... 144
  - 12.3.1 Piaget's Stage Model of the Development of Childrens' Thinking ... 144
  - 12.3.2 Cognitive Development as a Gradual Process ... 147
  - 12.3.3 Kohlberg's Stage Model of the Development of Moral Judgement ... 148
  - 12.3.4 Language Development ... 149
- 12.4 Achievement Behaviour in Childhood and Adolescence ... 149
- 12.5 Social Behaviour in Childhood and Adolescence ... 151
  - 12.5.1 Aggressive Behaviour ... 152
  - 12.5.2 Prosocial Behaviour ... 154
- 12.6 Conclusion ... 154
- 12.7 Questions of Understanding ... 155

13 Working World ... 157
- 13.1 Organisational Structure and Organisational Culture ... 158
- 13.2 Work Attitude and Work Motivation ... 159
- 13.3 Work Performance ... 162

	13.4	Leadership Behaviour	163
	13.5	Decision-Making Behaviour	164
	13.6	Work Behaviour	166
		13.6.1 Use of Time	166
		13.6.2 Incorrect Actions	168
	13.7	Group Work	170
	13.8	Conclusion	171
	13.9	Questions of Understanding	172
14	**Mental Disorders**		173
	14.1	Cross-Cultural Versus Culture-Specific Diagnostics	173
	14.2	Depression	174
	14.3	Schizophrenia	175
	14.4	Anxiety Disorders	175
	14.5	Suicide	176
	14.6	Conclusion	177
	14.7	Questions of Understanding	178
15	**Final Remarks**		179
	15.1	Possibilities and Limits of Cross-cultural Psychology	179
	15.2	Consequences for Intercultural Cooperation	182
	15.3	Conclusion	184
References			185
Index			201

About the Author

Prof. Dr. Hede Helfrich was Chair of Psychology and Intercultural Communication at the Universities of Hildesheim and Chemnitz (Germany) as well as Visiting Professor at the Dongbei University of Finance and Economics (DUFE) in Dalian (China). She is also Honorary Doctor and Honorary Professor at the Nizhny Novgorod State University of Architecture and Civil Engineering (NNGASU) in Nizhny Novgorod (Russia).

Subject Area of Cross-Cultural Psychology

Encounters with people from other countries or other geographical origins are increasingly part of our everyday lives. These encounters can be of a direct nature, such as in the form of economic joint ventures, scientific exchanges, internet forums, conversations with people travelling abroad or personal experiences with migrants in our own country. But they can also be indirect, for example when work structures that have been tried and tested are changed in order to survive in global competition, or when jobs that were previously considered secure are suddenly relocated abroad.

1.1 Aims of Cross-Cultural Psychology

Often, we find that people who do not belong to our culture behave differently than we do in many areas of life. They have other problems, and they also seem to think differently about the same problems. We may ask ourselves what these differences are like and where they come from. But we can also ask whether under the surface of what the respective otherness – be it fascinatingly exotic or threateningly alien – similar deep structures, i.e. similar principles of thinking, feeling and acting, can be discovered after all.

Cross-cultural psychology tries to answer such questions. It examines individuals in various cultures and makes a comparison, either explicitly or implicitly. Two goals are pursued: On the one hand, the question arises as to the psychological realities that are common to people all over the world, and on the other hand, the question to what extent individual actions, thoughts and feelings depend on the cultural environment. In the first case it is about so-called universals, in the second case it is about cultural conditions that shape human action, feeling and thinking in a decisive way.

1.2 Different Research Directions

Within cross-cultural psychology, "culture" forms either the context within which individual behaviour occurs (Munroe and Munroe 1997, p. 173), or the antecedent, i.e., a prior condition for individual behaviour (Lonner and Adamopoulos 1997). When "culture" is considered as a context, the question of "what" and "how" of similarities and differences arises. When "culture" is considered as an antecedent, the question of the "why" of differences is additionally asked, i.e. culture is explicitly examined as a factor influencing individual behaviour.

In addition to cross-cultural psychology, other research directions within psychology also deal with cultural issues (Table 1.1). They will be distinguished from each other in the following.

Cross-cultural psychology in the narrower sense ("cross-cultural psychology" or "culture-comparative psychology") examines the relationships between psychological variables on the one hand and cultural variables on the other. Implied is the assumption that there are universal mental structures and processes that may, however, exhibit culture-specific modifications.

Cultural psychology deals with the way in which cultural traditions and social practices are expressed in experience and behaviour. Implicit is the assumption of a fundamental culture-related diversity of psychological structures and processes.

The aim of *indigenous psychology* ("indigenised" or "local psychology") is the investigation of experience and behaviour on the basis of the premises, theories and methods developed in one's own cultural tradition.

Intercultural psychology ("psychology of intercultural action") is understood as the application-oriented study of encounters between members of different cultural backgrounds in the service of the practical management of communication and interaction problems.

1.3 Cross-Cultural Psychology in the Canon of Psychological Subjects

Cross-cultural psychology is not easily classifiable in the spectrum of the other disciplines of psychology. Similar to how social psychology examines social circumstances as factors influencing individual behaviour and experience, cross-

1.3 Cross-Cultural Psychology in the Canon of Psychological Subjects

Table 1.1 Research directions within psychology concerned with the topic of culture

Direction	Aim	Assumptions	Example
Cross-cultural Psychology in the narrow sense ("Cross-cultural psychology" or "Culture-comparative psychology")	Investigation of the relationship between psychological variables on the one hand and cultural variables on the other hand	Existence of universal mental structures and processes, which, however, may show culturally specific modifications	Examination of the extent of adolescent aggression (psychological variable) as a function of culturally influenced parenting style (cultural variable)
Cultural Psychology	Investigation of the ways in which cultural traditions and social practices are expressed in behaviour and experience	Fundamental cultural differences in mental structures and processes	Investigation of special forms of psychotherapy on the basis of a Buddhist conception of man
Indigenous psychology	Investigation of experience and behaviour on the basis of premises, theories and methods developed in one's own culture	Fundamental cultural differences in mental structures and processes	Investigation of intelligence on the basis of a local understanding of thinking
Intercultural psychology ("Psychology of intercultural action")	Application-oriented investigation of encounters between members with different cultural backgrounds in the service of practical coping with communication and interaction problems	Trainability of intercultural competence	Identification of key standards of behaviour in a foreign culture and development of training programmes to adapt to such standards

cultural psychology focuses on the extent to which cultural circumstances influence individual psychological events. Similar to differential psychology, cross-cultural psychology deals with the description and explanation of differences between different people. However, while differential psychology examines at the level of the individual what distinguishes a particular person from other people, cross-cultural psychology focuses on cultural differences. Moreover, cross-cultural psychology not only covers a specific subject area – like the other psychological disciplines – it also sees itself as a cross-disciplinary branch. From this point of view, it attempts to examine the extent to which psychological laws of perception, thinking or development, for example, can be generalised, i.e. applied to all people.

1.4 Concept of Culture

In everyday understanding, "culture" is often understood in the humanistic-educational-bourgeois sense as a higher way of life enriched with fine arts, literature and enlightened thinking. In cross-cultural psychology, on the other hand, "culture" is understood in the anthropological sense that originally goes back to Herder (1887, p. 4). Accordingly, "culture" does not form an antithesis to "nature", but belongs to the "natural" endowment of man as a consequence of the development of a phylogenetic tradition. All societies have a culture, However, they have devepoped different forms of culture. Thus, a *universal* aspect common to all societies must be distinguished from a *specific* aspect typical of a particular society (Box 1.1).

"Culture" as a typical manifestation of a particular society refers to the entirety of the lifeworld shared within this social community. The lifeworld includes both external conditions, such as geographical features, and the patterns of thought, feeling and action specific to the members of the community (cf. D'Andrade 1995, p. 212). The latter are assumed to have developed as a result of people's confrontation with their biological make-up, environmental conditions and traditionally grown behavioural patterns.

> **Box 1.1: Concept of Culture**
> In cross-cultural psychology, *culture* is understood as the consequence of the formation of a phylogenetic tradition, which is part of the "natural" endowment of man.
>
> However, the various forms of culture can vary. Culture understood in this sense refers to the totality of the *lifeworld* shared within a social community and includes both the external environmental conditions and the patterns of thought, feeling and action.
>
> In the course of his development, man grows into the cultural forms of life, whereby culture and individual interact.

(continued)

1.4 Concept of Culture

Box 1.1 (continued)

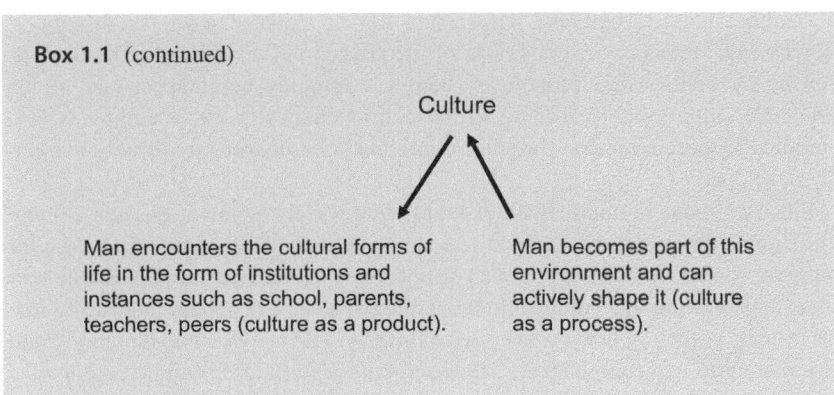

For the members of a culture, they are often not explicitly retrievable but provide implicitly as "self-evident facts" (Hofstätter 1966, p. 57) the basis for a meaningful, plausible and largely routine action.

In the course of his or her individual development, the so-called ontogenesis, the human being grows into the surrounding environment. This growing into is called *"enculturation"*. The same process is often referred to as "socialisation" in other sub-disciplines of psychology. However, while the focus there is on the generalisable aspects of this process, cross-cultural psychology goes beyond this to include the aspects that are typical of a particular culture. Enculturation must be seen as a dynamic process whereby culture and individual interact: On the one hand, the individual encounters the surrounding lifeworld in the form of institutions and instances such as school, parents, teachers, and peers; on the other hand, the individual himself becomes part of this lifeworld and can actively help shape it. "Culture" must therefore be viewed both as a "product" and as a "process". In cross-cultural psychology, the dominant view is that of culture as a product whose influence on individual thinking, feeling and behaviour is investigated.

Culture as a "lifeworld" can encompass different social communities, depending on how one looks at it: Examples are nations ("national culture"), geographical regions ("regional culture"), ethnic minorities ("minority culture"), language communities, ideological and religious-political communities as well as partial lifeworlds such as a certain youth scene ("subculture").

"Culture" in the outlined sense must not be equated with "civilisation".[1] *"Civilisation"* refers to the conditions of life created by science and technology as well as by politics and economy. These are certainly not independent of the respective culture, but according to the anthropological view, a culture is also attributed to those societies whose technical and scientific progress is only marginally developed.

Since everyone normally belongs to different social communities, their cultural affiliation is not necessarily limited to a single culture. This is particularly true for migrants, for example: In their case, a distinction is often made between a culture of origin and an admission culture. Growing into the latter, as opposed to growing into the former, is then referred to as *"acculturation"* (Box 1.2). "Enculturation" and "acculturation" can complement each other, but they can also run into conflicts.

> **Box 1.2: Enculturation and Acculturation**
> *"Enculturation"* is the term used to describe the process by which a person grows into the world around him or her as part of his or her individual development (ontogenesis).
> The process of growing into an admission culture, i.e. a culture that does not correspond to the person's culture of origin, is referred to as *"acculturation"*.

1.5 Historical Development

Even in ancient times, scholars were concerned with the question of whether the people of foreign cultures were fundamentally different from themselves. The Greek historian Herodotus (484–425 BC) described the customs and traditions of the Scythians, Egyptians and other "barbarians". Chinese scholars of the Han dynasty wrote monographs on the Hiung-Nus, a tribe that migrated along the northwestern border of China, and Tacitus (55–118 BC) contrasted the behaviour of the Germanic tribes with that of the Romans in his "Germania" (ca. 98 BC)

---

[1] It should be noted here that the terms "culture" and "civilisation" are used differently in German than in English and French (cf. Elias 1994). In his book "Clash of Civilizations" (Huntington 1996), for example, Samuel Huntington uses the term "civilization" in the sense of "culture" or "culture area", whereas he uses the term "culture" in the sense of the German term "civilization".

1.5 Historical Development

(cf. Kluckhohn 1949). Later on, the discovery of the "New World" stimulated the interest of the European conquerors in the otherness of the "primitive" peoples. The actual scientific preoccupation with the diversity of cultures did not begin until the late eighteenth and nineteenth centuries. The works of the linguistic philosophers J. G. Herder (1744–1803) and W. von Humboldt (1767–1835), Darwin's "Origin of Species" (1859) and the psychoanalysis of Freud (1856–1939) were decisive.

Starting with Darwin, the writings of Tylor (1865), Spencer (1876), and Morgan (1877) established social evolutionism as the predominant school of thought. According to it, the phylogenetic development of the human race inevitably leads from barbarism to civilisation, with individual societies following this path at different speeds. According to Ernst Haeckel (1834–1919), the phylogenetic development from "primitive" to "civilised" man is repeated in the ontogenetic development from childhood to adulthood – an idea that also influenced developmental psychologists such as Jean Piaget, Lev Vygotsky, Heinz Werner and G. Stanley Hall.

Although the French sociologist Lévy-Bruhl criticised the social-evolutionary point of view of Tylor and Spencer, he characterised the thinking of non-Western societies as "prelogical". In contrast to Tylor and Spencer, Lévy-Bruhl did not attribute the fundamental differences between "primitive" and "civilised" people to the biological endowment, but to the "social milieu" (Lévy-Bruhl 1910).

The German language philosophers Lazarus and Steinthal (1860) also pursue the idea of a historical development of mental abilities by postulating a universal sequence of stages in the development of the human mind. Wilhelm Wundt (1832–1920), the "father of experimental psychology", criticised the ideas of Lazarus and Steinthal as being too vague and speculative, but shared their belief that the "higher mental processes" emerge from historical development and cannot be investigated by experimental methods. So he writes, in the introduction to his book "Elemente der Völkerpsychologie",[2] that "Völkerpsychologie[3] is an indispensable supplement to the psychology of individual consciousness in the analysis of higher mental processes" (Wundt 1913, p. 3).

The German cultural anthropologist Franz Boas (1858–1942), a disciple of Wilhelm Wundt, on the one hand emphasises the unity of the human race, which has "the possession of language, the use of tools and the power of reason" and thus differs from all other living beings. On the other hand, he questions the claim to universality of knowledge gained in the Western world – for example, about human

---

[2] Sometimes (inaccurately) translated as „Elements of folk psychology".
[3] An English translation would be „cultural-historical psychology"(cf. Wong 2009, p. 230).

intelligence or the course of child development – and instead points out the environmental dependence and cultural determinacy of human behaviour.

The ideas of Franz Boas, who was intensively involved in the study of Native American languages, were taken up in America by the linguists Sapir (1844–1939) and Whorf (1897–1941). As the "Sapir-Whorf hypothesis" they have left a lasting mark on comparative cognition research across cultures (Sects. 6.3, 7.3, and 9.7).

The disciples of Franz Boas – Ruth Benedict (1887–1948) and Margret Mead (1901–1978) – are considered the founders of the "culture and personality school". Their core thesis was that a specific culture was also associated with a culturally typical personality, which was later referred to as "basal personality" (Kardiner 1939), "modal personality" (DuBois 1944) or "national character" (cf. Kluckhohn 1949). The application of psychoanalytic thought led to two theses regarding the dynamics of cultures: on the one hand, the social practices mediated by culture should produce a culture-typical personality; on the other hand, conversely, specific sociocultural systems should emerge as a product of the dynamics of personality-specific adaptations. Margaret Mead's book "Coming of Age in Samoa" (1928) caused a great stir. In the bookshe describes a society in which children and young people enjoy a carefree lifestyle and in which aggression is virtually unknown. Mead blames this on an upbringing that is characterised by the avoidance of a close mother-child bond and by sexual permissiveness. Statistical data on the frequency of murder and bodily harm, as well as the strictness of social rules in Samoa established by other researchers (cf. Kornadt 2003, p. 352 f.), however, stand in stark contrast to Mead's assertions.

The cultural anthropologist and psychoanalyst Kardiner (1939) emphasised the interaction between personality and culture: On the one hand, a culturally typical personality structure ("basal personality") emerges as a result of primary institutions such as family structure and economic form; on the other hand, this personality structure forms the basis for the formation or modification of secondary social institutions or forms of life such as religion or art.

The considerations of the culture and personality school were further developed in the "ecological" (Whiting 1963) as well as in the "ecocultural" approach (Berry et al. 2011; Bronfenbrenner 1979). Milestones include the "Six Cultures Study" (Whiting 1963; Whiting and Edwards 1988) as well as the study by Barry and co-workers (1959) on the relationship between preferred economic form and child rearing in non-industrialised cultures. In the latter, secondary data from 100 societies were used to show that education in peasant cultures emphasises cooperation and responsibility, while hunter cultures tend to value initiative and creativity.

In another form, the ideas of the culture and personality school have been taken up by "indigenous" and "cultural psychology" (Shweder and Sullivan 1990). Both directions do not view "culture" as an independent variable acting from outside, but radicalise the assumption of an intertwining of culture and personality. In their view, "culture" forms an integral part of personality with the consequence that scientific research on personality is not at all possible independently of the cultural context (cf. Poortinga and Van Hemert 2001, p. 1036 f.).

In the 1950s and 1960s, cross-cultural psychology was largely dominated by Skinner-style American behaviourism. Accordingly, it limited to currently observable and measurable behaviour, while the discussion of the socio-historical conditionality of behaviour was largely left to anthropologists, ethnologists, and sociologists. It was not until the "cognitive turn" in the 1970s and 1980s that Wundt's ideas found their way back into the field, for example in the form of the "social representations" of the French social psychologist Moscovici (1981). Although current cross-cultural psychology is still strongly influenced by the behaviourist approach, in that it strives for the objective measurement of cultural and psychological variables, it nevertheless tries to include the perspective of historically grown traditions.

1.6 Conclusion

Cross-cultural psychology studies individuals in different cultures. On the one hand, it asks for commonalities in human thinking, feeling, and acting despite cultural diversity, and on the other hand, for differences in human thinking, feeling, and acting depending on the respective cultural environment. "Culture" here forms either the context within which human behaviour occurs or the antecedent condition for human behaviour. In addition to cross-cultural psychology in the narrower sense, other areas of research in psychology are also concerned with the topic of culture: cultural psychology, indigenous psychology and intercultural psychology. They are based on the assumption of a fundamental, culturally conditioned difference in psychological structures and processes.

Within the individual disciplines of psychology, cross-cultural psychology occupies a dual position: On the one hand, as a sub-discipline of psychology – just like the other psychological sub-disciplines – it covers a specific subject area; on the other hand, however, it also sees itself as an interdisciplinary discipline that puts the psychological insights gained in the Western cultural sphere to the test of universal validity.

To paraphrase a saying by Hermann Ebbinghaus (1908), cross-cultural psychology has a "long past" but a "short history". Already in ancient times, scholars wondered whether people of foreign cultures, often called "barbarians", were fundamentally different from themselves. The question was often answered to the effect that there were different stages in the development of being human in the manner of social evolution. This view is shared by Wilhelm Wundt (1832–1920), who is generally regarded as the founder of scientific psychology. He distinguished between "experimental psychology", which investigates basic perceptual processes, and "peoples psychology", which considers "higher mental processes" as the result of a historical development. Wundt's thoughts were continued in different ways by cultural anthropologists, linguists, and psychoanalysts. After World War II, a break with tradition occurred, as now cross-cultural psychology was largely dominated by Skinnerian behaviourism. Only recently has there been a renewed attempt to incorporate the perspective of the historically developed tradition.

1.7 Questions of Understanding

1. Describe the difference between *cross-cultural psychology* and *cultural psychology*.
2. Characterise the ambiguity of the term "*culture*".
3. Outline similarities and differences between the psychological subdisciplines of *differential psychology* and *cross-cultural psychology*.

Further Reading

Jahoda, G. (2011). Past and present of cross-cultural psychology. In F. J. R. Van de Vijver, A. Chasiotis, & S. M. Breugelmans (eds.), *Fundamental questions in cross-cultural psychology* (pp. 37–63). Cambridge: Cambridge University Press.

Kroeber, A. L., & Kluckhohn, C. (1952). *Culture: A critical review of concepts and definitions*. Vol. 47, No. 1, Cambridge, MA: Peabody Museum.

Marsella, A. J., Dubanoski, J., Hamada, W. C., & Morse, H. (2000). The measurement of personality across cultures. *American Behavioral Scientist, 44,* 41–62.

Smith, P. B. (2010). Cross-cultural psychology: Some accomplishments and challenges. *Psychological Studies, 55,* 89–95.

(continued)

Straub, J., & Thomas, A. (2003). Positionen, Ziele und Entwicklungslinien der kulturvergleichenden Psychologie. In A. Thomas (ed.), *Kulturvergleichende Psychologie* (2nd ed., pp. 29–80). Göttingen: Hogrefe.

Wong, W. (2009). Retracing the footsteps of Wilhelm Wundt: Explorations in the disciplinary frontiers of psychology and in Völkerpsychologie. History of Psychology, 12 (4), 229–265.

Methodological Considerations 2

In principle, the same requirements are placed on the methods used in cross-cultural psychology as in other psychological disciplines. But these requirements are sometimes much more difficult to meet in cross-cultural psychology than in other psychological disciplines. Above all, the comparability of psychological phenomena between societies with different ways of thinking, different languages, and different value systems represents a challenge for psychology.

2.1 Etic Versus Emic Approach

2.1.1 Two Views

There are two major approaches within psychological cultural research: the *etic*[1] and the *emic* approach. With the etic approach, the researcher tries to take a standpoint outside of the cultures under consideration and thus to conform to the scientific ideal of "objectivity". The emic approach, on the other hand, attempts to look at the phenomena through the eyes of those affected and thus to correspond to the ideal of "perspectivity" in the humanities. Table 2.1 and Box 2.1 illustrate the distinction.

The distinction originally comes from linguistics: *Phonetics* focuses on sound features that can be used to describe the phonetic inventory of all languages, while *Phonemics* is the study of sounds used in a particular language. Transferred to the comparison of cultures, this means that the etic approach tries to apply universally

---

[1] It must be noted that "etic" is not to be confused with „ethic" that refers to moral behaviour.

© The Author(s), under exclusive license to Springer-Verlag GmbH, DE, part of Springer Nature 2023
H. Helfrich, *Cross-Cultural Psychology*,
https://doi.org/10.1007/978-3-662-67558-8_2

Table 2.1 Etic versus emic approach

Etic (nomothetic) approach	Emic (idiographic) approach
The researcher takes a standpoint outside of the cultures under study ("objectivity")	The researcher takes a standpoint within the culture under study ("perspectivity")
The researcher him/herself creates the structure to be investigated	The researcher uncovers a pre-existing structure
The investigation categories are cross-cultural, i.e. the same for all cultures	The investigation categories are based on the respective culture
The researcher tries to capture general regularities ("universality")	The researcher tries to capture the cultural specificities ("uniqueness")
The aim is the scientific explanation of cause-effect relationships	The aim is the holistic understanding of contexts with the help of hermeneutics
Quantitative methods dominate	Qualitative methods dominate

valid standards of comparison, while the emic approach aims to uncover the functionally relevant aspects within a specific culture.

In part, the distinction corresponds to the dichotomy between the "nomothetic" and the "idiographic" approach, as is particularly evident in personality psychology. The nomothetic approach describes the differences between individuals as different expressions of general characteristics, whereas the idiographic approach emphasises the uniqueness of each individual. Applied to psychological cultural research, the etic approach focuses on universally applicable variables, while the emic approach emphasises the uniqueness of a culture.

The aim of cultural comparison from an etic view is to examine the susceptibility or resistance of individual actions and thoughts to cultural influences. In most cases, the "culture" factor is operationalised in the form of certain cultural characteristics such as school conditions, educational styles or social value orientations. Culture is thus viewed as a set of "independent" variables lying outside of the person, whose impact on individual cognition, learning and action is examined in the form of "dependent" variables (Box 2.2).

> **Box 2.1: Etic and Emic View**
> In psychological cultural research there are two views: the etic and the emic.
> Under the *etic* view, a position outside of the cultures is taken (external view). Universally valid descriptive systems and standards of comparison are used to examine the phenomena.

(continued)

2.1 Etic Versus Emic Approach

Box 2.1 (continued)

Under the *emic* view, culture is viewed from the eyes of the respective people concerned and described with categories that are specific to the culture (internal view). The focus is on emphasizing the uniqueness of the culture.

The two approaches are not mutually exclusive, but can complement each other.

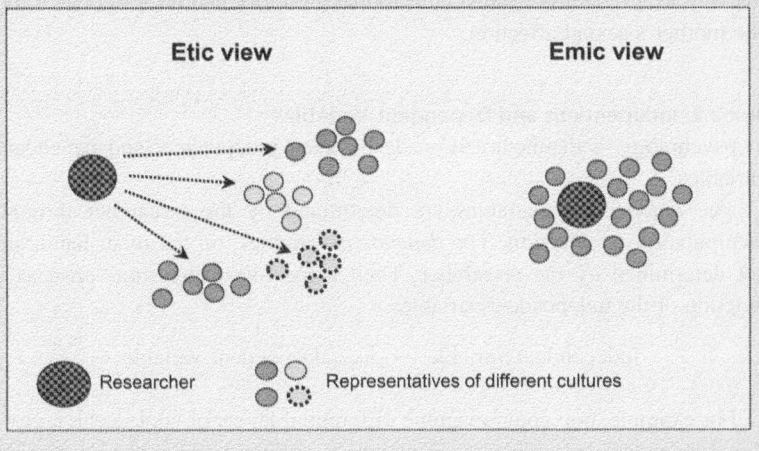

"Impact" must be understood here in a twofold sense: On the one hand, as the substantive effect of a systematic conditional factor and on the other hand as the negligible effect of a *random factor*. In the first case, in so-called *differentiation studies*, cultural factors are to be investigated as influencing factors ("antecedents"). An example here would be the extent of adolescent aggression (= dependent variable) depending on the culturally shaped upbringing style (= independent variable). In the second case, the cultural comparison in so-called *generalisation studies* strives for a validation or generalisability of psychological regularities that were originally found in a specific cultural environment. One wants to find out whether research results can be replicated in a changed cultural context or whether they have to be revised. Culture thus forms the background against which preceding research findings are illuminated. Here, cross-cultural studies should offer the possibility of "unpackaging" of supposed and actual influencing factors. An example is the altered interpretation of the so-called Oedipus complex by the cultural anthropologist Malinowski (1927) based on the consideration of the matrilineal[2] society of the Trobrianders, an island people of Papua New Guinea. Malinowski found that the Trobriander boys' aggressive dreams of annihilation were not aimed at the father as the mother's love partner, but at the mother's brother, i.e. the uncle, as the authority punishing the boy. In this case, the independent variables "love partner" and "authority figure" were disentangled through the culture comparison, with the result that the Oedipus complex was interpreted exclusively as a rebellion against educational authority and no longer as a rivalry for the mother's sexual affection.

> **Box 2.2: Independent and Dependent Variables**
> In psychology, a distinction is made between independent and dependent variables.
>
> The *independent* variables are determined by the researcher through manipulation or selection. The *dependent* variables, on the other hand, are not determined by the researcher. Their respective expressions arise as a function of the independent variables.
>
> $$\text{Independent variable} \xrightarrow{\text{Influence}} \text{Dependent variable}$$
>
> For example, one could examine differential levels of adolescent aggression (dependent variable) as a function of culturally influenced parenting style (independent variable).
>
> $$\text{Culturally influenced upbringing} \xrightarrow{\text{Influence}} \text{Level of aggression}$$

A second example involves testing the universal validity of Jean Piaget's model of cognitive development. It was found here that the sequence of stages of development postulated by Piaget occurs in its basic features in all cultures (Sect. 12.3). In this case, "culture" is regarded as an irrelevant factor that merely causes random variations.

According to the emic approach, "culture" is not an external factor outside the individual whose "effects" on the individual could be studied, but is an integral part

---

[2]Matrilinearity refers to tracing of kinship through the female line.

of human thought and action. Therefore, all psychology, without exception, is cultural psychology since psychological phenomena cannot be understood outside their cultural context and their cultural meaning. According to this view, a comparison between different cultures is not mandatory; some researchers even completely deny the possibility of a comparison and thus advocate the position of a so-called cultural relativism.

From the emic point of view, thinking and acting, which always take place in a cultural context, are not determined by *causes* that can be investigated with scientific methods, but by *reasons* that can be explicated by the people concerned themselves (Box 2.3).

> **Box 2.3: Causes and Reasons**
> In the study of human action and thought, a distinction is made between causes and reasons.
>
> *Causes* do not necessarily have to be conscious to the person concerned and can be recorded with scientific methods (etic approach), whereas the *reasons* for one's own actions and thoughts can be explicated by the person concerned (emic approach).
>
> To illustrate the difference, consider the example of a suicide attempt. Possible causes of suicide (Sect. 14.5) have included disturbed family relationships, alcohol consumption and lack of religious commitment. However, the suicide candidate himself may give as a reason, for example, his perceived loneliness.

The emic approach emphasises self-control and self-reflection of the individual (cf. Eckensberger 1992). Accordingly, qualitative research methods dominate over quantitative research methods (Box 2.4), since the individual horizon of meaning can only be uncovered qualitatively. With the help of so-called hermeneutics, the aim is to achieve a holistic understanding of meaning contexts, which is contrasted with the scientific explanation of cause-effect relationships.

> **Box 2.4: Quantitative and Qualitative Research Methods**
> There exist quantitative and qualitative research methods.
> *Quantitative* research methods are based on the approach of the natural sciences and underpin their findings with numerical data. Standardised surveys could be used as an example, in which certain answer options are fixed from the outset.
> In *qualitative* methods, the focus is on the subjective experience of the acting persons, without this having to be described numerically. Interpretations of the respective researcher are in the foreground. Qualitative methods include, for example, in-depth interviews and conversation analyses.
> Qualitative and quantitative methods are not mutually exclusive, but can complement each other.
>
> | | Quantitative methods | Qualitative methods |
> | --- | --- | --- |
> | Strength | Standardised methods
Statistical testing of hypotheses | Discovery of previously unknown phenomena |
> | Weakness | Complex preparation, as standardisation requires prior investigations | Laborious data processing
Risk of focusing on atypical cases
Subjectivity of interpretations |

According to the emic view, the cultural dependence of all psychology does not only affect the objects and methods of research, but also the underlying premises, which are often shaped by the technical and scientific worldview of Western people. In contrast, the indigenous or local psychology does not import "Western" concepts, theories and research methods unseen, but instead develops perspectives and instruments on the basis of the local cultural heritage.

2.1.2 Universality Versus Uniqueness

Closely related to the distinction between the etic and emic views is the dichotomy between "universality" and "uniqueness". It is also reflected in the controversy between the nomothetic and idiographic approaches to personality psychology. While the nomothetic approach aims at a universal descriptive system, by means of which interindividual differences can be represented as different degrees of expression of traits or trait combinations, the idiographic approach emphasises the uniqueness of each individual. At the cultural level, the idiographic approach manifests itself particularly in the form of "indigenous" personality concepts. From this point of view, the personality concepts developed in Western culture not only ignore the uniqueness of cultural phenomena such as the special need for attachment ("amae") among the Japanese or the need for protection of honor among Jordanians, but also generalise the meaning of the personality concept in an inadmissible way. However, nomothetic and idiographic approaches are not fundamentally mutually exclusive. Kluckhohn and Murray (1948) already pointed out that every person is similar in some ways to *all* other people, in other ways to *some* other people, and ultimately in certain ways to *no* other people.

2.1.3 Outside View Versus Inside View

Characteristic for the etic approach is the outside view, characteristic for the emic approach the inside view. Traditionally, the outside or external view looks for causes of human action that can be investigated using scientific methods and that the person concerned need not necessarily be aware of, whereas the inside or internal view focuses attention on the reasons for action that can be explicated best by the persons who are concerned (Sect. 2.1.1). Accordingly, when taking the outside view, behavioural observations, quasi-experimental arrangements and psychometric measurement procedures dominate, whereas when taking the inside view, qualitative methods of self-reflection and self-description are preferred (Sect. 2.3). Interestingly, however, these methodological implications are often not consistently followed through: Thus, on the one hand, questionnaires committed to the etic approach require a high degree of self-reflection; on the other hand, the emic approach also draws on outside observations by researchers – usually from outside the culture to be studied.

Both views have their limitations. The purely outside view brings with it the danger that important variables do not even come into focus at all. The purely inside view often overlooks the fact that not all actions are accessible to self-reflection. However, just as the contrast between uniqueness and universality is not irreconcilable, so is the contrast between inside and outside view. Already Morgan (1903, p. 45) suggested "double induction" as a solution. What he means is that conclusions drawn from outside observation must be backed up by conclusions drawn from self-reflection and vice versa.

The outside view and the inside view can be stages within a research process that complement each other. An initial outside view may later turn out to be "pseudo"-etics or "imposed"-etics (Berry 1969, p. 124) and then needs to be complemented by the inside view in an emic way in order to finally arrive at a cross-cultural etic view ("derived etics" (Berry 1989).

2.2 Comparability of the Objects of Investigation

2.2.1 Object of Comparison and Standard of Comparison

Cross-cultural Studies always include a comparison. Comparison presupposes an object of comparison and a standard of comparison. The former refers to what is to be compared, the latter to the common scale on which the respective differences can be mapped.

The object of comparison can be represented by a specific *hypothetical construct* such as an intellectual ability, an attitude, or a personality trait, but also by *phenomena* such as smiling or crying. A construct is never directly observable, but must be inferred from observable phenomena-such as utterances, behaviours, responses to questions, or tasks solved. The observable phenomena that must be made accessible by means of a particular measurement operation are indicators for the underlying constructs.

Both the phenomena and the constructs can vary in their degree or type of expression. In order to classify the different degrees or types of expression, a common scale is required for all cultures being compared. It forms the standard of comparison for the classification of the differences that occur.

2.2.2 Equivalence Postulates

The object of comparison and the standard of comparison must show certain similarities or equivalences across cultures (Table 2.2). Based on the classic quality criteria of psychological research, the types of equivalence can be defined as postulates and are described below.

Conceptual Equivalence
The postulate of conceptual equivalence requires that the content of the construct under study is comparable in all cultures under study. For example, if aggression is being studied, it must be ensured that it always refers to the intentional harming of another person. Expressed in terms of general psychological research, conceptual equivalence refers to the cross-cultural *validity* of a construct.

From aspect of content is to separate the value aspect. For example, terms such as "conformity" or "obedience" are certainly held in higher esteem in East Asian societies than in Western societies. However, this does not exclude the possibility of achieving agreement with regard to their content. This can be achieved even if

2.2 Comparability of the Objects of Investigation

Table 2.2 Types of equivalence

Type	Description	Example	Reference to the classical quality criteria
Conceptual equivalence	Equality of the content of the construct	Aggression as intentional harm to another person	Validity of the construct
Material equivalence	Physical or phenomenal equality of the object of investigation	Loudness or louder voice	Objectivity
Operational equivalence	Equality of the indicators for a construct	Loudness of the voice as an indicator of aggression	Validity of the indicator
Functional equivalence	Equivalence of indicators for a construct	Loud insults and silence as equivalent indicators of aggression	Validity of the indicator
Measurement or instrument equivalence	Equivalence of the relationship between the collection process and the data received	Comparability of familiarity with the examination situation (e.g. test or questionnaire)	Reliability and validity of the study instruments
Scale equivalence	Equality of the scale	Equality of the categories of a nominal scale for aggressive behaviour	Objectivity, reliability and validity of the scale

there is no suitable word for the corresponding construct in one of the cultures studied. An example would be the "amae"[3] introduced as an "indigenous" concept by the Japanese psychoanalyst Takeo Doi (1981), the content of which, after an appropriate explanation, can also be understood by members of a Western culture.

Assurance of conceptual equivalence can be accomplished in several ways. One possibility is the multiple translation and back-translation of words, phrases, and test items that denote the content of the construct in question. If the construct in question is a complex one, such as "intelligence" (Chap. 7), the overall structure of the single components, i.e., the single abilities in the example, must be comparable ("structural equivalence", cf. Van de Vijver and Leung 2000).

---

[3] According to the English title of the book by Takeo Doi, it can be translated as "dependence".

Material Equivalence

A material equivalence exists if the object of investigation contains physically or perceptually similar phenomena. Examples would be the volume of the voice or the spatial distance between mother and child. In terms of the classic quality criteria of psychological research, material equivalence corresponds to transculturally validated *objectivity* .

Operational Equivalence

Operational equivalence is given if phenomena surveyed, in addition to their material comparability, can also be used as indicators for the same constructs in each of the compared cultures. In terms of the classical quality criteria of psychological research, operational equivalence corresponds to transculturally validated *indicator validity*. In the above example of the spatial distance between mother and child, the postulate of operational equivalence would be fulfilled if the spatial distance could serve as an indicator for the attachment quality of the mother-child relationship across cultures.

Functional Equivalence

The postulate of functional equivalence refers to the significance of a particular phenomenon in terms of the psychological construct. It is met if the indicators for a construct in the compared cultures are of equal value with respect to the meaning of the construct. In terms of the classical quality criteria, functional equivalence – like operational equivalence – refers to indicator validity, in contrast to operational equivalence, however, only the equivalence, not the material sameness, of the indicators is required. Externally different (i.e., materially dissimilar) behaviours can be indicators of the same psychological construct. For example, depending on the culture, aggression could take the form of both loud insult and stubborn silence. Conversely, physically or perceptually the same phenomena do not necessarily indicate the same construct. For example, a smile could reflect both kindness and hostility toward another person. It follows that functional and material equivalence do not always have to correspond. They only have to correspond if the postulate of operational equivalence is to be fulfilled at the same time.

Measurement Equivalence

Often the phenomena to be investigated are not directly observable, but must first be evoked by a situation with a prompting character – a test situation is prototypical for this. The postulate of measurement equivalence requires that the measurement procedure for assessing the indicators must give the individual in each of the cultures under study the same opportunity. Equivalence of opportunity may be

2.2 Comparability of the Objects of Investigation

affected primarily by differences in the degree of familiarity with certain methods or instruments, such as tests, questionnaires, or interviews, or by culturally different response tendencies (e.g., the tendency to agree or the tendency to avoid extreme responses). In the sense of the classical quality criteria, measurement equivalence refers both to the *reliability* and to the *validity* of the measuring procedure.

Scale Equivalence

Assessing the differences in the phenomena or constructs under study requires a standard of comparison that allows the different degrees or types of expression in each of the cultures being compared to be represented on the same or an equivalent scale. As is generally the case in psychological research, this scale equivalence can be given at the nominal, ordinal, interval or ratio scale level. It refers to all three of the classic quality criteria, i.e. *objectivity*, *reliability* and *validity*.

An example of equivalence at the nominal scale level would be if every aggressive behaviour that occurred were assigned to a specific category such as physical injury, verbal insult or facial disrespect. In this case, the frequency of the individual categories could form the basis for a comparison.

It is particularly difficult to achieve so-called metric equivalence, i.e. equivalence at the interval or even ratio scale level, especially when a psychological construct (an example would be "intelligence") is represented by several variables that are included in the common scale with different weightings. For the cultural comparison, this results in the requirement that the weighting must be the same in all compared cultures. It would be fulfilled if the mutual correlations between the individual, quantitatively collected variables within each of the cultures examined have the same or at least a similar structure and thus the factor structure of the construct to be examined is similar.

Even then, however, numerical absolute comparisons are rarely possible, since the scale is usually an interval scale in which the zero point is arbitrary and can be located at a different point on the scale in each of the cultures being compared. In this case, a numerical comparison between different cultures is only possible with regard to intracultural differences. Only if the zero point can be fixed cross-culturally or a ratio scale is available, a direct numerical comparison of data between different cultures is justified. There are certainly few constructs that satisfy this postulate. An equivalence at the ratio scale level is only conceivable for materially equivalent objects of comparison such as spatial distance or pauses in speech, regardless of their functional equivalence, of course.

2.2.3 Consequences for Cross-Cultural Comparison

The extent to which each of the equivalence postulates listed (Table 2.2) must be fulfilled in a specific cross-cultural study depends to a not insignificant extent on the purpose of the study. In any case, it depends on the extent to which the individual postulates are fulfilled what kind of statements are possible as a result of the investigation. Thus, in special cases, functional or operational equivalence can also be the result of an investigation and need not be its precondition.

In the fulfilment of the equivalence postulates etic and emic considerations must complement each other. Whether a certain phenomenon can serve as an indicator for an underlying construct can only be decided by including the emic view. Ensuring measurement equivalence must also be done from an emic view. However, if cultural differences in the observed phenomena or the inferred constructs are to be represented on a common scale, this requires an etic view. An example can be found in Box 2.5.

> **Box 2.5: From Research: Fictitious Example**
> As an example serve a cultural comparison of the mother-child attachment (= construct).
>
> Cross-culturally, there may be agreement that the mother-infant attachment consists of sensitive behaviour on the part of the mother toward the infant (= *conceptual equivalence*).
>
> From a Western point of view, the frequency of eye contact between mother and child could be used as an indicator of the quality of the attachment. A comparison of eye contact between German and Japanese mother-child pairs (= *material equivalence*) would probably reveal that the frequency of eye contact in Japan is significantly lower than in Germany. However, if the emic view of the Japanese is included, it could turn out that direct eye contact is perceived as impolite in Japan and is thus precisely an indicator of less sensitive behaviour. Eye contact would therefore not fulfil the postulate of functional equivalence. As a consequence, functionally equivalent indicators such as a friendly voice or caresses would have to be found (= *functional equivalence*).
>
> The next step would be to determine which situations are suitable for observing or provoking the corresponding behaviour (= *measurement equivalence*).
>
> (continued)

> **Box 2.5** (continued)
> Finally, a cross-cultural ordinal scale could be formed from the totality of the indicators collected, which depicts different degrees of attachment (= *scale equivalence*).

2.3 Methods of Data Collection and Analysis

In principle, similar research methods are used in cross-cultural psychology as in other psychological disciplines. However, some modifications have to be made from time to time. This applies most strongly to the experimental procedure, which cannot be realised in its pure form in cross-cultural studies. In the following, the typical or predominant research procedures in cross-cultural or cultural psychology will be presented. Some of these are global research approaches with specific theoretical objectives (e.g. ethological approach), partly special procedures for data collection (e.g. ethnographic field research) or special procedures for data evaluation (e.g. multilevel analysis).

The approaches and procedures listed (Table 2.3) reflect the etic or emic view to varying degrees. At one extreme are the psychometric and quasi-experimental approaches, which are prototypical for the etic view. At the other extreme are the ethnographic field studies in which the emic view dominates. The individual procedures are not mutually exclusive and are often combined.

Psychometric Approach
The aim of the psychometric approach is to identify cultural differences in attitudes, personality traits, cognitive abilities or intellectual performance by means of test procedures or questionnaires. The psychometric approach is essentially differential diagnostic in nature. It was originally developed to diagnose or classify individuals within a defined population with respect to certain characteristics. The most prominent example of this is the determination of the intelligence quotient (IQ). This is a measure of the general mental ability of an individual in comparison with a standard sample (e.g. 20–25 year-olds in the Federal Republic of Germany). In cross-cultural comparisons, the psychometric procedure is used primarily in differentiation studies. The aim here is to identify differences between members of different cultures in the mean expression of individual characteristics or bundles of characteristics as "dimensions" or "factors". So the question is about cultural differences on universally valid scales. A metric equivalence of the common scales on which the

Table 2.3 Methods of data collection and analysis

Approach	Procedure	Aim	Example
Psychometric approach	Comparison of individuals of different cultural backgrounds with respect to certain characteristics by means of tests, questionnaires or behavioural measurements	Examination of the universality of structures (generalisation studies) as well as determination of cultural differences in the expression of individual characteristics (differentiation studies)	Generalisation studies: Testing the universality of the five-factor model Differentiation studies: PISA and TIMSS (Sect. 7.2)
Interrelationship analyses	Investigation of the relationship between different characteristics by means of correlation or regression analyses	Examination of the relationship between different cultural, economic, social or individual characteristics	Relationship between prosperity and individualism-collectivism
Factor analytical studies	Investigation of the relationship between different characteristics and reduction of the multitude of characteristics to a few dimensions	Identification of dimensions (factors) to characterise and distinguish cultural or individual characteristics	Hofstede's cultural dimensions; McCrae and Costa's Five factor model (Big five)
Quasi-experimental approach	Systematic study of cultural factors as "independent variables" in their impact on certain characteristics as "dependent variables"	Identification of cultural variables as influencing factors for the expression of individual characteristics	Examination of analytic vs. holistic thinking as a function of individualism-collectivism
Ex Post Facto Investigations	Analysis of the relationship between cultural variables and individual characteristics using existing data, e.g. the	Identification of cultural variables as influencing factors for the expression of	Investigation of the relationship between traffic accidents and the degree of power

(continued)

2.3 Methods of Data Collection and Analysis

Table 2.3 (continued)

Approach	Procedure	Aim	Example
	Human Relation Areas Files (HRAF) database	individual characteristics	distance of a country
Multilevel analyses	Linking cultural and individual characteristics using hierarchical statistical models	Systematic estimation of influencing variables of different levels with regard to their respective contribution to the overall variation of a characteristic	Assessment of the respective influence of cultural affiliation (cultural level) and educational level (individual level) on attitudes towards immigration
Path analyses	Multiple regression analysis to determine direct and indirect dependencies between predictors and criterion	Systematic estimation of direct and indirect influencing variables with respect to their respective contribution to the overall variation of a feature	Investigating the influence of supervisors' leadership style on employees' job performance, incorporating cultural and individual characteristics
Ethological approach	Analysis of human behaviour with the methods and axioms of evolutionary biology	Explanation of human behaviour as phylogenetic (universal) or culturally specific adaptations	Phylogenetic adaptation: Investigating the incest taboo; Culturally specific adaptation: investigating differences in infant mortality as a function of reproductive opportunities
Cross-cultural development studies	Examination of cognitive, emotional, and social ontogenesis in different cultures	Testing the universal validity of development models	Testing the universal validity of Piaget's stage model

(continued)

Table 2.3 (continued)

Approach	Procedure	Aim	Example
Ethnographic or anthropological field studies	Description of the special characteristics in thinking, feeling and acting of members of a certain culture	Identifying the culturally specific meaning of ways of thinking and behaving	Study of festivities in a cultural community
Clinical approach ("ethnopsychiatry")	Examination of individuals undergoing medical or psychological counselling, either on their own initiative or mediated by relatives	Examination of the universality or culture-specificity of diagnostic, counselling and treatment models	Examination of the incidence of schizophrenia in different countries and regions
Analysis of critical interaction situations	Evaluation of reports on conflicts between members of different cultures	Identification of central cultural standards as behaviourally effective orientation standards	Evaluation of reports from German managers in China about their situations that were perceived as alienating

constructs in question are mapped is essential. It must therefore normally be checked in a preliminary investigation. The use of psychometric methods can also serve to examine the universality of scale structures in generalisation studies.

Interrelationship Analyses

The aim of interrelationship analyses is to identify dependencies between two or more variables without, however, being able to make statements about causal links. The variables relate, for example, to cultural, socio-economic or individual circumstances. A *correlation analysis* is used to determine to what degree and in which direction a linear relationship exists between two or more variables. A measure of correlation is the so-called correlation coefficient (r), which can take on any value between -1 (maximum negative correlation) and $+1$ (maximum positive correlation). A *regression analysis* allows the conclusion to be drawn from the expression of one or more variables x ("predictor" or "predictors") to the expression of another variable y ("criterion"). While in correlation analysis the order of the individual variables is irrelevant, in regression analysis the inference from x to

y leads to a different result than the inference from y to x. Depending on the number of variables involved, a distinction is made between simple (two variables) and multiple (more than two variables) correlation or regression analyses.

Factor Analyses

Factor analysis procedures (cf. Child 2006) represent a further development of multiple correlation analysis. In a factor analysis a multitude of variables (e.g. answers in questionnaires) with similar content is reduced to a few variables of higher order ("factors"). The aim is to determine basic characteristics ("traits") of cultures (Chap. 5) or individuals (Chap. 10).

Quasi-Experimental Approach

The quasi-experimental approach focuses on the variation of the independent variables. Certain cultural factors such as countries, social value orientations, educational styles or schooling serve as independent variables. They are to be examined with regard to their effect on certain dependent variables such as thinking, perception or memory performance, attitudes or social actions.

The procedure is described as "quasi-experimental" because a cultural factor does not represent an experimental treatment factor, i.e. it does not allow any real experimental variation of conditions. Rather, it represents an *"organismic" variable* (Edwards 1971, p. 8 f.; cf. Helfrich 1999, p. 134) similar to, for example, gender, age, or social class (Box 2.6).

In contrast to an experimental conditional factor, in the case of an organismic variable, individuals cannot be arbitrarily assigned to the individual factor levels by the experimenter (e.g., by randomisation). They can only be selected according to their "natural" affiliation to a certain factor level. The experimental design therefore does not allow any differences that occur in the dependent variable to be causally attributed to the variation in the independent variable (Sect. 2.1.1). A causal interpretation can at best be justified by theoretical considerations.

Box 2.6: Organismic Variables

The quasi-experimental approach considers cultural factors as organismic variables.

Organismic variables such as gender, age or nationality cannot be arbitrarily assigned to individuals, since they are already given beforehand and determine the *natural* affiliation of an individual independently of the study.

(continued)

> **Box 2.6** (continued)
> The problem with this natural affiliation is that it usually covaries with other characteristics or characteristic values. For example, the organismic variable "gender" is almost always associated with a particular education, so that it cannot be separated from the variable "type of education". That is, the independent variable of interest cannot be isolated, but always occurs "bundled" with other variables. The experimental design therefore does not allow any differences that occur in the dependent variable to be causally attributed to the variation in the independent variable.

In addition to the cultural variables, so-called *control variables* are also frequently included. They are additionally collected in order to be able to check to what extent they change the results of the study. Examples are gender and age, which are also organismic variables.

Besides the quasi-experimental factors, real experimental condition factors such as the type of task to be processed or the type of stimulus material are usually also used. Only this variation in conditions, which can be manipulated by the investigator, allows causal interpretations.

Ex Post Facto Studies
Related to the quasi-experimental approach are ex-post-facto studies. Their aim is, on the basis of data already available, to establish correlations between certain cultural characteristics, such as educational practices or ecological conditions, on the one hand, and certain individual characteristics, such as behavioural practices or personality traits, on the other. These are therefore *secondary analyses of* of already existing ethnographic data. Often the so-called Human Relation Areas Files (HRAF), an extensive database of ethnographic material that has been maintained since 1949, are referred to. They originated from a wide variety of reports from different cultures and were systematically categorised and, in some cases, quantitatively processed. The secondary analyses can be carried out either in the form of quasi-experimental designs or in the form of correlation or regression analyses.

Multilevel Analyses
In a multi-level analysis, one attempts to separate differences at the cultural level from differences at the individual level. The aim is to quantitatively estimate the respective contribution of cultural and individual factors with regard to the overall effect on individual characteristics. The respective contribution is estimated by

means of multi-stage (hierarchical) regression analyses. An example would be assessing the respective effect of culture (cultural level) and level of education (individual level) on attitudes towards immigration (Box 2.7).

> **Box 2.7: From Research: Fictitious Example of a Multi-level Analysis**
> The aim of the multilevel analysis is to separate the effect of cultural affiliation from the effect of individual characteristics using a multilevel (hierarchical) regression analysis.
>
> An example would be the estimation of the respective effect of cultural affiliation (*cultural* level) and educational level (*individual* level) on attitudes towards immigration (dependent variable). In this case, the mean value for each culture (e.g. the degree of power distance of the culture) and the individual value of each person in relation to the level of education are used as predictors in the regression analysis.
>
> The effect of educational level on attitudes towards immigration is then derived from the effect of educational level averaged for the individuals of all cultures. The influence of culture results from the mean effect of the culture factor. For example, a high level of education (individual level) could generally be associated with a positive attitude towards immigration in all cultures, but at the same time in cultures with a high power distance there could be a rather negative attitude towards immigration. In this case, a positive effect at the individual level would be associated with a negative effect at the cultural level.

Path Analyses

Another special form of regression analysis is path analysis. With its help, not only direct relationships between predictors and criteria can be determined – as in regression analysis – but also indirect relationships – arbitrated by so-called *mediator variables* (Box 2.8, Sect. 13.3) – are revealed. Strictly speaking, no statements about causal relationships can be made from the dependencies found, nevertheless a causal model can be derived on the basis of theoretical assumptions. The model may be represented graphically as a path diagram and mathematically as a set of structural equations. The paths represent hypothetical causal relationships.

Cross-Cultural Development Studies

In cross-cultural development studies, the cognitive, social and emotional development of children (ontogenesis) is examined in different cultures. The aim is to identify general laws of human development and to search for cultural conditions that give rise to interindividual differences. For example, the question is to what extent the development of thought structures takes place according to uniform laws and to what extent it varies depending on cultural incentive conditions.

A prototypical example is the examination of the universal validity of the model of the development of children's thinking established by the Swiss psychologist Jean Piaget (Sect. 12.3).

Development studies can be designed as longitudinal studies or as cross-sectional studies. In *longitudinal studies, the* same investigation is conducted at several points in time on the same individuals with the aim of determining intraindividual changes over time. In *cross-sectional studies,* individuals of different ages are compared at a fixed point in time with the aim of determining differences between ages.

Ethological Approach

The ethological approach also known as *behavioural biology* or *comparative behavioural science* describes and analyzes human behaviour using the methods and axioms of evolutionary biology. The data can be obtained from behavioural observations as well as from existing statistics (e.g. birth or death registers). The focus is on the analysis of the organism-environment interaction typical for the human species. This includes not only, as in conventional psychology, the search for direct ("proximate") factors influencing behaviour, but also the search for phylogenetic ("ultimate") preconditions. Here, one tries to understand what adaptive functions behaviour has and how these adaptive functions have evolved. The usual *causal* view in psychology to the momentary behaviour is supplemented by a *final* view. The assumption is that "nature", i.e. the genetic basis of behaviour, and "culture", i.e. the observable behavioural patterns that have been shaped by rules and conventions, are not independent of each other, but are mutually dependent, with the consequence that all human behaviour is to be viewed from the perspective of phylogenetic adaptation. Adaptation performance is examined in both generalisation and differentiation studies.

The generalising view asks about characteristics that occur in all cultures such as the incest taboo. The differentiating view tries to explain what kind of adaptations (e.g. in the intensity of infant care, in education, in religious rituals or in expressive behaviour) specific cultures have undergone and which reasons are decisive for this.

Ethnographic or Anthropological Field Studies

The aim of ethnographic or anthropological field studies is to show the special characteristics of thinking, feeling and acting of individuals of a specific culture or subculture. The description takes place largely "from within", i.e. "through the eyes" of those concerned (Sect. 2.1.3), so that their lifeworlds are reconstructed through their own explications. Implied is the assumption that almost all human behaviour is to be understood symbolically, i.e. that all phenomena can only be understood by referring to the meaning attributed by the actors themselves.

The methods used in these studies focus on participatory observation, in-depth interviews and recordings of conversations, i.e. on methods that can be classified as so-called qualitative social research (Box 2.4). Also included herein are linguistic methods such as conversation analysis and discourse analysis.

Clinical Approach ("Ethnopsychiatry")

The clinical approach, also referred to as "ethnopsychiatry", is characterised by its focus on individuals who have become conspicuous, i.e. individuals who undergo medical or psychological counselling either on their own initiative or mediated by relatives. Diagnosis, counselling and treatment can follow different approaches, e.g. the psychoanalytical approach or the so-called *transcultural psychiatry* (cf. Cox 2018).

Analysis of Critical Interaction Situations

The analysis of critical interaction situations between members of different cultures can be regarded as a special form of the ethnographic approach. The aim is to determine so-called cultural standards. The starting point is the assumption that there are cultural rules that are not consciously accessible to the actors as "self-evident facts" in normal everyday life. However, they come to light as soon as an actor finds himself/herself in an interaction situation in which his/her own cultural rules are violated. The qualitative evaluation of reports on such interaction situations then leads to the extraction of the underlying cultural standards, which are assumed to function as culture-specific standards of orientation for action.

2.4 Selection of Suitable Study Units

As with any empirical research, the problem with cultural comparisons is that one can only examine a few excerpts from the area of interest ("samples"), but still wants to generalise the results to a larger area ("population"). The generalisability depends to a decisive extent on the representativeness of the sample. The representativeness can be determined quantitatively when the sample has been obtained by random selection from the population of interest – a condition that is almost never met in cross-cultural psychology. It is often implicitly assumed that the sample under study is a "typical" one, i.e., it is assumed that the sample under study is a good or even ideal example of the population of interest.

In cross-cultural psychology research, sample selection involves first, the selection of suitable cultures or cultural groups, second, the selection of individuals who are supposed to represent a culture or cultural group, and third, the selection of suitable situations and instruments in or with which the phenomena in question are observed, measured and, where appropriate, elicited.

2.4.1 Selection of Cultures

For the selection of suitable cultures, it is first decisive whether the study is a differentiation study or a generalisation study. In differentiation studies, cultural conditions – such as value orientation (Chap. 5), economic form, school system or educational style – are examined as factors influencing individual trait characteristics. Since the cultural variable is regarded as a systematic factor in this case, the levels included in the investigation – i.e. the cultures or cultural groups studied – must represent typical expressions of the entire factor. They must ensure at least enough variation so that a systematic relationship can be established between the expression of the cultural factor and the expression of certain psychological conditions. In extreme cases, their number may be limited to two.

The selection problem is exacerbated by the fact that cultural factors are not experimental conditional factors but "organismic" variables (Box 2.6, Sect. 2.3). Particularly in the case of bilateral cultural comparisons, it is therefore often not possible to rule out the possibility that one has not compared the cultural factor levels in question, but only countries, language communities or subcultures.

The selection problem arises in a different way in generalisation studies. Since the aim of the study in this case is to find universally valid laws, the factor "culture" is regarded as a random factor, i.e. it is assumed that although the cultural context must be taken into account, it represents a "confounding variable" in relation to the aim of the study. Applied to the problem of sample selection, this means that, ideally, the cultures studied should be selected at random from the population of all cultures.

2.4.2 Selection of Individuals

The distinction between differentiation studies and generalisation studies should also be noted when selecting individuals. In generalisation studies, the individuals included in the study must represent a sample from a universal population. In differentiation studies, they must be representative or typical of the cultures or subcultures under investigation.

The problem here is that the intracultural variation of individuals is usually different for different cultures. Especially with regard to other variables such as dialect, region, social grouping or gender, the individuals from different cultures cannot be considered homogeneous. The ideal solution would be samples selected according to the law of randomness, but this is hardly feasible in practice. Frequently, one tries to counteract the problem of inhomogeneity by parallelizing the samples, i.e. one only includes individuals with comparable characteristics of the non-interesting variables in the study. However, the parallelisation introduces new biases, when the variables for which the samples are parallelised are systematically related to the cultural variables under investigation. An extreme example is the parallelisation of two cultural groups with respect to the duration of school attendance (Fig. 2.1).

If the two populations differ significantly in their distribution of the duration of school attendance, the parallelisation results in a selection that is not only non-representative of the respective population, but also reflects different extremes of the respective population, i.e. the same duration of school attendance is atypical for one culture because it is particularly long and for the other culture because it is particularly short.

2.4.3 Selection of Situations and Instruments

Also the situations and instruments included in the study run the risk of varying representativeness for different cultures. The problem of representativeness arises in particular when selecting instruments such as test procedures. In this case, it is closely linked to the postulate of measurement equivalence. Using a test procedure, it is assumed that the result is an indicator of the underlying ability. If individuals from different cultures are to be compared with regard to the ability in question, it must be ensured that in each of the cultures compared there is a comparable relationship between the test items as indicators and the ability as the underlying construct.

Fig. 2.1 Bias due to parallelisation. (Modified after Helfrich 2003, p. 126) Note: The samples have been selected in such a way that they are comparable in terms of the duration of school attendance

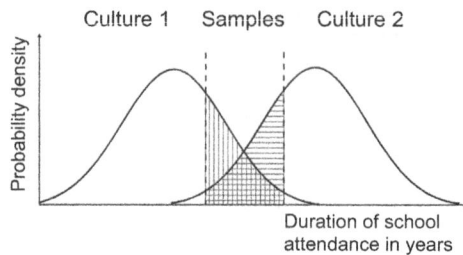

The selection of situations may also involve the use of true experimental factors such as the nature of the task or the nature of a training intervention. The selection must be guided by the aim of the study. In differentiation studies, one will use those experimental factors whose effect is assumed to be culture-specific, while generalisation studies will prefer to use factors whose effect is assumed to be cross-cultural.

2.5 Statistical Testing of Hypotheses

Often, specific statements are derived from a general question. These statements are called "hypotheses". They can refer to correlations between individual characteristics as well as to differences in the characteristics of different groups of people. An example of a *correlation hypothesis* would be the relationship between extraversion and school performance; an example of a *difference hypothesis* would be the statement that there are differences between men and women in the extent of aggressive behaviour. Difference hypotheses can often be transformed into correlation hypotheses and vice versa. The hypotheses are evaluated on the basis of data collected.

If the characteristics under investigation can be represented on a scale (Sect. 2.2.1), a hypothesis can be empirically tested using mathematical statistics. The classic procedure is to first create a statement that contradicts the hypothesis to be tested. This hypothesis is called the *"null hypothesis"* (H_0). This is to express that one is referring to a baseline condition that one is questioning. The one of interest, which is the actual hypothesis, is called the *"alternative hypothesis"* (H_1). The null hypothesis states that there is no difference in the case of the difference hypothesis, and that there is no relationship in the case of the relationship hypothesis. To test whether the alternative hypothesis is true, the sample data (Sect. 2.4) are used to

2.5 Statistical Testing of Hypotheses

reject the null hypothesis ("falsify"). The null hypothesis is rejected if it is shown to be extremely unlikely to be true using statistical methods.

What is considered "unlikely" is defined in the so-called *significance level* α. As a general convention, $\alpha = 5\%$ (or a proportion of 0.05). The significance level represents the criterion for rejecting the null hypothesis. If the probability obtained for the null hypothesis, the so-called error probability, falls below the value specified in the significance level, the result is considered "significant". Thus, a significant result means that the null hypothesis is rejected because it is compatible with the obtained findings only with extremely low probability. Referring to the above two examples, a significant result means in the first case that the statement that there is no relationship between extraversion and school performance is rejected, and in the second case that the statement that there is no difference between males and females in the level of aggressive behaviour is rejected. Conversely, the rejection of the null hypothesis is then interpreted as supporting the alternative hypothesis. In the example, this would mean that there is a relationship between extraversion and school performance or that there are differences between men and women in the extent of aggressive behaviour.

However, a non-significant result – i.e. a result in which the null hypothesis was not rejected – does not mean that the null hypothesis would be confirmed. It only means that it must be maintained until contrary findings are demonstrated. To illustrate this, a comparison can be made with criminal court proceedings. If the accused is acquitted "for lack of evidence", this does not automatically mean that he did not commit the crime with which he is charged, but only that it cannot be proved against him. Thus, the "unproven guilt" of the accused corresponds to the null hypothesis and the "guilt" to the alternative hypothesis.

In the case of alternative hypotheses, a distinction is made between undirected (two-sided) and directed (one-sided) hypotheses. In the case of an *undirected* alternative hypothesis, no direction of the difference is specified; in the case of a *directed* alternative hypothesis, it is specified whether a difference is expected in a positive or in a negative direction. In the above examples, the directed hypothesis in the first case could be that there is a positive relationship between extraversion and school performance, and in the second case that males exhibit aggressive behaviour to a greater extent than females.

Even if the null hypothesis is rejected, this is not reliable proof that the respective alternative hypothesis is true. The proof is not reliable because a significant result is highly dependent on the choice of the respective sample (Sect. 2.4). Due to errors in sample selection a result can become significant by chance ("first type error" or "α-error"), and conversely, if the sample size is small, it can happen that the significance level is not fallen short of, although the alternative hypothesis would be correct ("second type error" or "β-error").

However, even if a significant result is regarded as confirmation of the alternative hypothesis, it still does not allow any statement to be made about the strength or extent of the difference or correlation. Information on this can be obtained by calculating the so-called *effect size*. While this evidence is lacking in the majority of cross-cultural individual studies, it can be provided in summary studies on a specific research question, the so-called meta-analyses (Box 2.8).

> **Box 2.8: Meta-Analysis**
> A *meta-analysis* is a statistical procedure that quantitatively summarises and evaluates the results of different empirical studies that pursue the same research question in a research area.
>
> Unlike a meta-analysis, which is simply a quantitative summary of previous research, a *review* involves a systematic summary and critical appraisal of all previous research (both quantitative and qualitative) on a research topic.

2.6 Conclusion

The dynamics of psychological cultural research derive from the fundamental dilemma between the etic or nomothetic approach and the emic or idiographic approach. According to the etic approach, "culture" is viewed as a set of independent variables whose influence on individual competencies and behaviours is to be examined in the form of dependent variables. It is easy to overlook the fact that the definition and selection of these variables is itself culture-bound. The emic approach attempts to take this culture-boundness into account by allowing the individuals concerned to speak for themselves. The individual is seen as a self-determined being acting in culture, whose actions are amenable to self-reflection. However, the constraints that limit self-direction and self-reflection are neglected here.

Despite partially contrary positions, the etic and emic approaches – as already pointed out by Pike (1967) – are not mutually exclusive, but must complement each other within a research process. For cross-cultural psychology, the consequence is that, despite the dominance of the etic approach, it is essential to include the emic view. Ultimately, this can only be realised through increased cooperation between researchers from different cultures, i.e., through a research process that is realised cooperatively by researchers from each of the cultures concerned in all phases of investigation – from the development of the research question to the interpretation of the findings – and thereby enables a "transcultural consensual validation" (Shweder and Sullivan 1990).

2.7 Questions of Understanding

1. State the difference between a *hypothetical construct* and an *indicator*. Give an example.
2. Give an example of a mismatch of *material* and *functional* equivalence.
3. Explain the difference between *differentiation studies* and *generalisation studies*.
4. Characterise the *quasi-experimental* approach and give an example.

Further Reading

Helfrich, H. (1999). Beyond the dilemma of cross-cultural psychology: Resolving the tension between etic and emic approaches. *Culture & Psychology, 5*, 131–153.

Karasz, A. (2011). Qualitative and mixed methods research in cross-cultural psychology. In F. J. R. van de Vijver, A. Chasiotis & S. M. Breugelmans (eds.), *Fundamental questions in cross-cultural psychology* (pp. 214–234). Cambridge: Cambridge University Press.

Van de Vijver, F. J. R., & Leung, K. (2011). Equivalence and bias: A review of concepts, models, and data analytic procedures. In D. Matsumoto & F. J. R. van de Vijver (eds.), *Cross-cultural research methods in psychology* (pp. 17–45). New York: Cambridge University Press.

Culture and Phylogenetic Development 3

In Chap. 1 it was explained that "culture" is not opposed to "nature", but rather belongs to the "natural" equipment of man as a consequence of a phylogenetic tradition formation. It is assumed that man's basic psychological endowment, which also includes having a culture, arose in the course of phylogenetic development, the so-called phylogenesis. In this chapter, basic principles of phylogenetic development will be considered.

3.1 Human Universals as a Result of Natural Selection

Since "culture" is part of the natural endowment of human beings (Sect. 1.4), there must be characteristics that are common to all human beings. They are called "*universals*". Universals could have come about in various ways, such as through mutual influence of societies or through the same inventions in different places. But there is much to suggest that, analogous to the physical endowment, mental endowment of humans has evolved over millions of years in the course of phylogenetic development, or *phylogenesis*, in the service of adaptation to the external conditions of life (Box 3.1). The key to understanding this process is provided by the theory of evolution. According to this theory, originally developed by Charles Darwin (1809–1882), universals are the result of *natural selection*. It is assumed that biological species – including the human race – change over time and that natural selection is the engine of these changes.

> **Box 3.1: Ontogenesis and Phylogenesis**
> *Phylogenesis* is the phylogenetic development of all living beings. This is the subject of evolutionary biology.
> *Ontogenesis* refers to the individual development of a living being. Developmental psychology is concerned with this.

Essential for evolution is the diversity of individuals within a species. In most species, the respective parent generation produces a large number of offspring. The survival of the offspring depends largely on the interaction between the organisms and the respective environmental conditions. If for some reason a particular heritable trait increases the probability of survival and further reproduction, the frequency of that trait within a population will increase in subsequent generations. Individuals possessing the trait in question are, according to Darwin, characterised by a higher "*fitness*" compared to individuals without this trait. The increased fitness leads to a higher reproductive rate because of better chances to reproduce. Over many generations, the variation in reproductive rate as a function of fitness leads to systematic changes in the overall population. This process was termed "natural selection" by Darwin and was conceived as to be a causal factor of change under the pressure of prevailing environmental conditions.

The discovery of DNA later allowed natural selection to be formulated in terms of genetic principles (cf. Berry et al. 2011, p. 274 f.). One of these principles is the so-called Hardy-Weinberg law of genetic equilibrium. (Box 3.2).

> **Box 3.2: Hardy-Weinberg Law of Genetic Equilibrium**
> According to the Hardy-Weinberg law, genetic equilibrium occurs in a sufficiently large population with stable environmental conditions under two conditions: First, there must be no changes in hereditary features (genes and alleles) and second, the mating of individuals must occur at random.
>
> None of these conditions are normally met in human populations. Changes in the expression of hereditary features (in the alleles) can occur spontaneously as *mutations*. Furthermore, in human populations, there is normally no random mating, but rather a *targeted selection of partners*. Thus, the genetic balance is disturbed and natural selection occurs.

The starting point is the fictitious assumption of a sufficiently large population with stable environmental conditions. For this population, genetic equilibrium and thus no evolution results under two conditions: First, there must be no changes in the hereditary characteristics (genes and alleles) and, second, the mating of the individuals must be random. In reality, both of these conditions are usually not met. Changes in the expression of the hereditary characteristics, the so-called alleles, can occur spontaneously as well as due to changed environmental conditions. In the process of DNA synthesis during sexual reproduction, replication errors may occur that lead to changes in the genetic material, so-called *mutations,* in the next generation. Although mutations are relatively rare, and most mutation carriers are not survivable, they can nevertheless lead to permanent changes in the genome of affected populations. The second requirement for the Hardy-Weinberg law to apply, random mating, is also not met in human populations. Rather, targeted selection dominates. It can be based, for example, on the fact that certain characteristics of a partner are valued more than others or that social rules exist which restrict or favour the choice of partner. Disturbances of the genetic equilibrium are even more likely to occur when environmental conditions change or/and when the total population changes due to inward or outward migration. All these conditions – mutations, selective mate choice, environmental changes and migration – favour natural selection and can thus contribute to long-term phylogenetic changes called "evolution".

3.2 Adaptation and Exaptation

In evolutionary biology, when a population undergoes a major change in its genetic make-up as a result of natural selection, this is referred to as *"adaptation"*. This takes place when the environmental conditions change and the currently practiced forms of life are no longer sufficient to ensure the survival and continuation of the species or genes.

The biological purpose of adaptation was considered by Darwin to be the increase of "fitness". However, the definition of this term has undergone a transformation in the course of scientific history. While Darwin assumed that fitness is to be located at the level of the individual ("survival of the fittest"), the behavioural scientist Konrad Lorenz (1998) stated that fitness consists in the conservation of the species. However, given the self-extinction of entire tribes of monkeys (Goodall 2010), the assumption of species conservation could not be maintained. Sociobiology (cf. Dawkins 2006) therefore places fitness at the level of genes. According to this view, the motor of human behaviour is the "self-interest of genes" with the aim of maximising overall fitness ("*inclusive fitness*"), which is composed of *direct fitness*, i.e. the number of successfully reared offspring, and *indirect fitness*, i.e. the number of successfully reared offspring of relatives (Box 3.3).

> **Box 3.3: Adaptation and Exaptation**
> In evolutionary biology, *adaptation* is understood as a change in the genetic make-up of a population a that is due to natural selection as a result of changed environmental conditions.
>
> The biological purpose of adaptation is to increase "fitness". Whereas for Darwin this referred to the individual, today it is placed at the level of the genes. Human behaviour is aimed at the "self-interest of genes", with a focus on maximizing overall fitness. This is composed of *direct fitness*, i.e. the number of successfully raised own offspring, and *indirect fitness*, i.e. the number of successfully raised offspring of relatives.
>
> The principle of *exaptation* states that there are traits that, from today's view, increased fitness, but originally had a different function.

However, it is often difficult to assess what exactly the changes in the environment were that triggered the adaptation and what exactly the adaptation consists of. In any case, the nature of the adaptive pressure and the nature of the adaptation can only be identified from a retrospective, i.e. these are always post-hoc explanations that do not allow predictions about future adaptive performance.

Let us take the example of human spoken language. Changing environmental conditions could be, for example, unmanageable terrain due to extensive tree growth. This limitation of mutual visibility might have led to the use of voice as a means of communication. However, the use of voice does not yet explain why articulation emerged as an essential feature of human languages. As for the type of adaptation, it could be argued that the more protruding chin in humans compared to primates facilitated articulation. However, it is not the protruding jaw that is essential for articulation, but the structural change in the pharynx. Thus, the protruding chin is not the functional unit of the adaptive performance, but a by-product.

Almost all adaptations that manifest themselves in a change of a hereditary trait bring with them several changes in the appearance of the organism at the same time. Some of these changes are functionally necessary, others are functionally irrelevant. Yet it is difficult to distinguish between these two types of change. It is this difficulty that has prompted some researchers not to accept adaptation as the sole principle of evolution, but also to bring the principle of *exaptation* into play (Gould 1991). This means that there are features that, from today's perspective, have increased fitness, although originally they had a different function. In this vein, it is often speculated that human language did not evolve as a result of a definable pressure to adapt, but rather arose as a by-product of other adaptations. One explanatory model for this is the so-called *"tinkering"* principle (Jacob 1977). It says that some of our complex abilities did not emerge as a result of an adaptive advantage, but on the basis of random constellations of individual abilities that initially served a different purpose. These single skills form subsystems or modules that are linked to an overall performance at the organism level. A change for the better or worse happens at the level of the module, not at the level of the organism as a whole. This may certainly also lead to conflicts with other modules. The interaction of the modules is therefore often not optimal over long phases, but rather organised as a kind of suboptimal compromise along the lines of an (unprofessional) hobbyist and a do-it-yourself principle. However, if at any point in time a "threshold of complexity" (von Neumann 1958) is exceeded, then, completely new, qualitatively different system properties can emerge. In retrospect, the new potential is an accident – but the fact that it continues to be used is no longer an accident. Man exploits the newly acquired ability for certain purposes just because it is available. Thus, it is not the purposes that determine the ability, but vice versa: The ability is available and will later be instrumentalised. Applied to the human ability to speak, this means that language has no behavioural precursors that can form the basis of the subsequent evolutionary step. The comparison with the species most closely related to humans in terms of phylogenesis (the primates) therefore seems misleading, to say the least. This is because primates differ from humans in an important developmental step. This developmental step was the opportunity for the qualitative leap in the development of the central nervous system that made the use of language possible.

3.3 Conclusion

In cross-cultural psychology, "culture" is conceived as part of the natural endowment of human beings (Sect. 1.4). According to this view, no "cultureless" societies exist. Instead, it is assumed that the basic psychological endowment of modern humans, which includes having a culture, has evolved in the course of *phylogenetic* development. The common phylogenesis of all humans has led to the existence of characteristics that are common to all humans, so-called *universals*. These include, for example, that all human communities have a spoken language. The key to understanding the formation of universal features is provided by evolutionary theory. According to that theory, universals are the result of *natural selection*, which, in the service of adaptation to changing external living conditions, has led to long-term phylogenetic modifications and finally to today's "homo sapiens". Often, however, it is not possible to decide what kind of environmental conditions triggered the pressure to adapt and what exactly the adaptive effort consisted of. Often, there were by-products associated with the changes that proved beneficial only in retrospect. This has led some researchers not to accept adaptation as the sole principle of evolution, but additionally to bring the principle of exaptation into play.

3.4 Questions of Understanding

1. Explain the basic concepts of *evolution*.
2. Explain the concept of *genetic* equilibrium.
3. Explain the concept of *fitness*.

Further Reading

Chasiotis, A. (2011). An epigenetic view on culture: What evolutionary developmental psychology has to offer for cross-cultural psychology. In F. J. R. Van de Vijver, A. Chasiotis & S. M. Breugelmans (eds.), *Fundamental questions in cross-cultural psychology* (pp. 376–404). Cambridge: Cambridge University Press.

Schaller, M., Norenzayan, A., Heine, S. J., Yamagishi, T., & Kameda, T. (2010). *Evolution, culture, and the human mind*. New York: Psychology Press.

Nature-Nurture Controversy from a Cross-Cultural Perspective

4

Within scientific psychology, one of the most controversial discussions is that about "gene" and "environment" or about "nature" and "nurture", i.e. the question of what is predetermined by genetic inheritance and what is acquired through environmental learning. In cross-cultural psychology, this discussion is taken up as a debate between "nature" and "culture". In the last chapter, the concept of nature was considered in terms of the phylogenetic development common to all humans. However, this does not preclude differences in the biological make-up between individuals. This chapter examines the relative contribution of specific genetic endowment ("nature") and specific sociocultural conditions ("environment") to the emergence of different manifestations of mental structures and processes.

4.1 Universal and Differential "Nature"

The term "nature" takes on two different meanings in cross-cultural psychology, which are simultaneously associated with different questions (Box 4.1). The first meaning of "nature" refers to the *genetic endowment common* to all human beings or humanity as a species. Hence, the research aim is to discover universal laws of human behaviour that are assumed to be based on a common genetic make-up (Chap. 3).

The second meaning of "nature" focuses on the differential aspect of genetic make-up. Similar to differential psychology, one enquires into the relative contribution of *specific genetic endowment* ("disposition") and *specific sociocultural conditions* ("environment") to the emergence of differences in the expression of individual traits and abilities. While differential psychology focuses on differences between individuals *within* a culture or population, cross-cultural psychology

© The Author(s), under exclusive license to Springer-Verlag GmbH, DE, part of Springer Nature 2023
H. Helfrich, *Cross-Cultural Psychology*,
https://doi.org/10.1007/978-3-662-67558-8_4

considers differences *between* different cultures or populations as compared to each other. If, for example, consistent differences are found between individuals depending on their cultural environment, the question of "nature" and "culture" becomes more concrete as to whether these differences are more due to the different genetic equipment (disposition) or rather to the different cultural influences (environment).

> **Box 4.1: Universal and Differential Nature**
> In cross-cultural psychology, the discussion of nature and nurture is taken up as a debate between *nature* and *culture*.
> The term *"nature"* takes on two different meanings here.
>
> Nature
>
>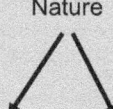
>
> **Universal nature** **Differential nature**
> Genetic make-up common Different genetic make-up
> to all humans of cultures/populations

It should be noted that "genetic make-up" does not imply "immutability". Within the framework of research in the field of so-called *epigenetics*, a special field of biology, it has been established that changes to the genetic make-up also occur in the course of individual development in the sense of an epigenetic "imprinting" (Hagemann 2009). This imprinting essentially consists in the fact that genes are "switched on" or "switched off" depending on environmental conditions as well as one's own lifestyle and can thus modify the genetic make-up.

4.2 Genetic Make-Up and Cultural Influence

Within differential psychology, the so-called twin method (Box 4.2) is often applied to estimate the relative contribution of genetic and environmental influences to the development of a trait, especially intelligence. This method attempts to estimate the relative contribution of the *environment* by comparing genetically identical individuals (monozygotic twins) who grow up together (i.e. in the same environment) to those who grow up separately (i.e. in different environments). The relative

4.2 Genetic Make-Up and Cultural Influence

proportion of *genetics* is assessed by comparing genetically identical individuals (monozygotic twins) growing up together to genetically only half identical individuals (dizygotic twins) growing up together. The measure of comparison is the correlation between the test score of one twin and the other.

> **Box 4.2: Twin Method**
> In the twin method the relative contribution of the *environment* is estimated by comparing monozygotic twins (MZ) grown up in the same environment with monozygotic twins grown up in different environments. The relative proportion of *genetics* is determined by comparing monozygotic twins grown up together with dizygotic twins (DZ) grown up together.
>
> The measure of comparison here is the correlation between the test score of one twin and that of the other.
>
> | Comparison | Result |
> |---|---|
> | MZ grown up together versus MZ grown up separately | Difference in correlation coefficients provides information about *environmental* contribution |
> | MZ grown up together versus DZ grown up together | Difference in correlation coefficients gives information about contribution of *genetics* |

If one transfers the logic of such a procedure to the comparison of cultures, one could compare genetically similar individuals growing up in the same culture to those growing up in different cultures in order to estimate the contribution of culture (environment). To estimate the contribution of nature (genetic disposition), genetically similar individuals could be compared to genetically dissimilar individuals within one and the same culture.

Since it is hardly possible to use twin pairs because of their rare occurrence, the correlation analyses based on pair formation would have to be replaced by difference analyses. Such difference analyses could be realised in the form of quasi-experimental designs (Sect. 2.3). A schematic study design is given below as an example (Box 4.3).

> **Box 4.3: Extrapolation of the Twin Method to the Cultural Comparison**
> The contribution of *culture* is estimated by comparing genetically similar individuals (e.g. Japanese) grown up in one culture (e.g. Japan) with those grown up in a different culture (e.g. USA).
>
> The contribution of *genetics* is determined by comparing genetically similar individuals (e.g. Japanese) with genetically dissimilar individuals (e.g. US Americans) grown up within the same culture (e.g. Japan). Mean differences are used as a measure of comparison.
>
> With regard to the notation, the following simplification is made:
>
> - Individuals with genetic make-up 1 (e.g. Japanese)
> - Individuals with genetic make-up 2 (e.g. US-Americans)
> - Culture 1 (e.g. Japan)
> - Culture 2 (e.g. USA)
>
> | Comparison | Result |
> |---|---|
> | Individuals with genetic make-up 1, grown up in culture 1, versus Individuals with genetic make-up 1, grown up in culture 2 | Magnitude of the difference in mean values provides information about the contribution of *culture* |
> | Individuals with genetic make-up 1, grown up in culture 1, versus Individuals with genetic make-up 2, grown up in culture 1 | Magnitude of the difference in mean values provides information about the contribution of *genetics* |

However, since both cultural affiliation and genetic makeup are "organismic variables" (Sect. 2.3), which always occur "bundled" with other variables (Sect. 2.3), this procedure – even more so than in twin studies – is subject to strong natural limitations. This restriction does not fundamentally argue against the realisation of such quasi-experimental designs, but it does impose considerable limits on the interpretation of the results obtained. Studies of this kind – such as that of Herrnstein and Murray (2010), who believed to have proved the intellectual inferiority of black Americans compared to white Americans (i.e. genetically dissimilar individuals in the same cultural environment) – have therefore been rightly criticised (cf. e.g. Ogbu 2002; Reifman 2000).

Moreover, estimating the relative contributions of nature and culture or environment tends to obscure the causal interplay of the two factors, since such an approach assumes an additive model of the contribution of nature and environment, i.e. internal and external forces are assumed to have independent causal effects in shaping the individual. In fact, however, at both the individual and the cultural level, genetic disposition and environment are always interrelated. At the individual level, the well-known example of Kaspar Hauser shows that the learning necessary for the ontogenetic development of the human being can only take place within the social context. But also at the cultural level, the genetic basis and the cultural rules are not independent of each other, but are mutually dependent. Already Darwin (1859) pointed out that cultures are not created irregardless of genetic inheritance. Culture is also subject to evolution, in a double sense. On the one hand, all human cultural systems are linked through descent to a common culture of our ancestors (cf. Durham 1990; Richerson and Boyd, 2005); on the other hand, specific cultural traditions can also emerge in each case from the interaction of socially mediated information structures and genetic selection. A driving force of this specific cultural development could be the symbolically valued self-worth or prestige (cf. Barkow 1989). According to this, people strive for what is considered successful in their own living environment. They internalise the prestige criteria conveyed by their own culture, and these lead them to prefer and develop certain characteristics and courses of action over others. At the same time, when choosing a mate, preference is given to individuals who display to a high degree the characteristics that are highly valued in a culture, so that the expression of the highly valued characteristics is also increased by genetic selection (Chap. 3).

4.3 Conclusion

The common phylogenetic history of all human beings does not rule out that there are genetic differences between individuals. The extent to which these differences are significant is discussed within psychology as a problem of "gene and environment". In cross-cultural psychology, this discussion is taken up as a debate between "nature" and "culture". In contrast to phylogenetic "nature"- as understood in the previous chapter - one focuses here on the differential aspect of genetic equipment. One asks about the relative contribution of specific genetic endowment ("genetic disposition") and specific sociocultural conditions ("culture") to the emergence of differences in the expression of individual characteristics and abilities.

One way to estimate the contribution of culture could be to compare genetically similar individuals raised in different cultures. To estimate the contribution of the genetic endowment, genetically similar individuals would have to be compared with genetically dissimilar individuals within the same culture. However, since both culture affiliation and genetic endowment are "organismic variables" (Chap. 2) that cannot be manipulated or isolated, this approach is subject to strong natural limitations.

4.4 Questions of Understanding

1. Characterise the ambiguity of the term *"nature"*.
2. Apply the logic of the *twin method to* the comparison of cultures. Point out weaknesses of this approach.
3. Explain why *genetic make-up* and *culture* are not independent entities.

Further Reading

Chasiotis, A. (2011). An epigenetic view on culture: what evolutionary developmental psychology has to offer for cross-cultural psychology. In F. J. R. Van de Vijver, A. Chasiotis & S. M. Breugelmans (Eds.), *Fundamental questions in cross-cultural psychology* (pp. 376–404). Cambridge: Cambridge University Press.

Helfrich, H. (2007). Parsimony or reductionism? – Against the g-factor of nations. Invited commentary on: H. Rindermann, The g-factor of international cognitive ability comparisons: The homogeneity of results in PISA, TIMSS, PIRLS and IQ-tests across nations. *European Journal of Personality, 21*, 724–727.

Keller, H. (2011). Biology, culture and development: conceptual and methodological considerations. In F. J. R. van de Vijver, A. Chasiotis & S. M. Breugelmans (Eds.), *Fundamental questions in cross-cultural psychology* (pp. 312–340). Cambridge: Cambridge University Press.

Description and Classification of Cultures

5

If "culture" is examined as a possible factor influencing individual thinking, feeling and acting, it is not viewed as a global whole. Rather, one would like to know which cultural characteristics or features are responsible for the influence in detail. This requires a specification of cultural conditions.

5.1 Cultural Factors

If one were to compare the behaviour of inhabitants of a remote mountain region in Central Asia with that of inhabitants of a small European town and find differences, it would not be possible to decide whether the differences were due to geographical location, to certain religious beliefs, to certain educational practices or to other circumstances. Since there are a large number of different cultures, it would be difficult to arrive at generalisable conclusions even with a great amount of comparisons.

One way of escaping this dilemma is to combine cultures that are similar to one another into so-called culture areas. This approach was taken by Huntington (1996) in his book "Clash of Civilizations".

Another possibility is to specify cultural factors that are suitable for both characterizing and distinguishing individual cultures. This approach dominates in cross- cultural psychology. An example of such a factor is "hierarchy orientation". Differences in hierarchy or power exist in all cultures, but they are particularly emphasised in some cultures (e.g., China), while in others they tend to be leveled out (e.g., Norway). Such factors are also called *"culture-differentiating factors"* (cf. Eckensberger and Plath 2002).

Ideally, one tries to conceptualise them as dimensions along which cultures can vary. Accordingly, each culture can be represented as a specific combination of locations on the single dimensions. Various such dimensional approaches have been proposed; the following sections present the most important ones.

In contrast to these culture-differentiating factors which refer to the content characteristics of a culture, factors can also be identified which serve to characterise the general circumstances of life, such as wealth or poverty, schooling and minority status. They are referred to as *"context"* or *"demarcation" factors* (Box 5.1).

> **Box 5.1: Culture Differentiating Factors and Context Factors**
> When describing and classifying cultures, cultural factors can appear either as culture-differentiating factors or as context or demarcation factors.
>
> *Culture differentiating factors* are used to describe the tradition of a culture or subculture. They are content characteristics ("traits") of the culture, which can also be used to characterise other cultures. Ideally, one tries to conceptualise them as dimensions along which cultures can vary. Accordingly, each culture can be represented as a specific combination of locations on the dimensions.
>
> *Context* or *demarcation factors* are suitable for describing imposed patterns and certain life circumstances such as wealth, poverty or schooling. Thus, in contrast to the culture-differentiating factors, they are not defined by a culture-related content.

5.2 Cultural Dimensions According to Hofstede

The starting point of the Dutch researcher Geert Hofstede (cf. Hofstede et al., 2010; Hofstede, 2011) was the assumption that all societies are confronted with similar basic problems, but to which they have found different answers. Four such basic problems[1] were specified (Hofstede 1980):

- the relationship between the individual and society
- social inequality and the relationship to authority
- the concepts of masculinity and femininity
- dealing with conflicts and uncertainty

---

[1] The order has been slightly changed by me.

5.2 Cultural Dimensions According to Hofstede

Hofstede conducted extensive surveys on attitudes and values of subjects from initially over 50 (later over 90) different countries – all employees in a multinational corporation (IBM). The data obtained were checked for similarities by means of correlations and reduced to four dimensions ("factors") by means of factor analyses. The dimensions identified corresponded to the four postulated basic problems (Hofstede 1980) and were described as "individualism-collectivism", "power distance", "masculinity-femininity" and "uncertainty avoidance".

The four dimensions were later supplemented by two more (cf. Hofstede et al. 2010). One of these relates to the use of time and can be described as "long-term versus short-term orientation" (cf. Hofstede 2011). It is also referred to as "Confucian Dynamics" (Hofstede and Bond 1988) because its characterizing features are based on the teachings of Confucius. The values of one of the two poles (saving face and respect for tradition) are more concerned with the present and the past, while the values of the other pole (perseverance, persistence and thrift) are more concerned with the future. The sixth dimension, named "indulgence", refers to the treatment of moral norms and extends between the poles of permissiveness ("indulgence") and strictness ("restraint").

The dimensions and factors identified (Table 5.1) are to be understood as *bipolar scales* the two poles of which represent the respective extremes. Hofstede assigned

Table 5.1 Culture dimensions according to Hofstede

Dimension	Description	Extreme characteristics (poles)
Individualism – collectivism	Extent of integration into the social environment	individualist– collectivist
Power distance	Extent to which unequal distribution of power is accepted	low power distance – high power distance
Masculinity – femininity	Extent of gender role differentiation as well as importance of "male" values such as achievement and assertiveness versus importance of "female" values such as caring and modesty	masculine – feminine
Uncertainty avoidance	Extent to which unsafe situations are safeguarded by the establishment of rules	low uncertainty avoidance – high uncertainty avoidance
Long Term – short term orientation or Confucian dynamics	Extent of future orientation	long time horizon – short time horizon
Indulgence	Extent of regulation of moral norms	permissive – strict

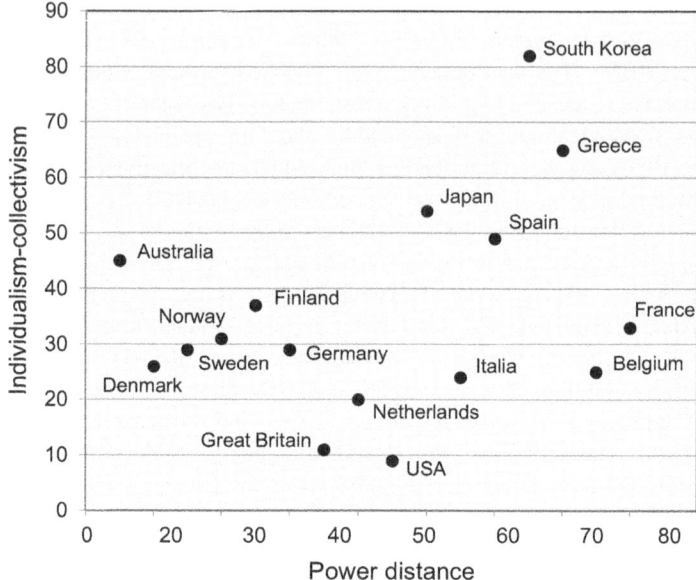

Fig. 5.1 Relationship between power distance and individualism-collectivism
Note: The higher the individualism-collectivism value, the stronger the collectivist expression. Correspondingly, the lower the individualism-collectivism value, the stronger the individualist expression

measurement numbers to the individual countries, which indicate the degree of expression of the factor.

The *individualism-collectivism* factor is not completely independent of the *power distance* factor: Collectivist cultures tend to have higher power distance and individualist cultures tend to have lower power distance (Fig. 5.1). In cultures with high power distance, *vertical*, i.e. hierarchically structured relationships are more important than horizontal, i.e. relationships among equal-ranking partners, whereas in cultures with low power distance *horizontal* relationships dominate and differences in hierarchy play a minor role (cf. Triandis 1995).

With the same high power distance, however, differences in hierarchy are justified differently in collectivist cultures than in individualist ones: The former emphasise above all mutual cooperation and obligation, the latter above all competition and achievement. Thus, in vertical-collectivist cultures, hierarchical relations are characterised by the fact that a lower-ranking person must show a high degree of respect to a higher-ranking person, but at the same time may expect strong support. This reciprocity is less prevalent in vertical-individualist cultures.

Table 5.2 Sample questions from Triandis' cultural orientation questionnaire (1995, pp. 205–206)

HI	Horizontal individualism i.e. tendency to low power distance and to individualism: "I am a unique individual"
VI	Vertical individualism, i.e. tendency to high power distance and to individualism: "It is important that I do my job better than others"
HC	Horizontal collectivism, i.e. tendency to low power distance and collectivism: "The well-being of my co-workers is important to me"
VC	Vertical collectivism, i.e. tendency to high power distance and collectivism: "I would do what would please my family, even if I detested that activity"

Countries with a vertical-collectivist orientation are mainly the East Asian, most Latin American and Arab countries. The group of horizontal-individualist countries is formed primarily by the "Germanic" countries of Northern and Central Europe as well as the Anglo-American countries (USA and Canada) and Australia, while the "Romanic" countries of Europe, i.e. France, Italy and Spain, are classified as vertical-individualist cultures (cf. Hofstede 2011).

The measures for the individual countries are to be understood as mean values for the respective country. At the same time, however, one must assume that there are large individual differences within each country. In order to take this into account, Triandis (1995) has developed a questionnaire that measures the degree of individualism-collectivism and power distance at the individual level. Sample questions are listed in Table 5.2.

5.3 Cultural Dimensions According to Schwartz

The Israeli researcher Shalom Schwartz (1994, 2006) identified three key social problems:

- Autonomy versus embeddedness
- Hierarchy versus equality
- Mastery versus harmony

The first two are similar to the basic problems identified by Hofstede, the third concerns the management of human and natural environmental resources. Based on questionnaire data from students and teachers in 73 countries, factor analytic and related techniques (cluster analyses), attitudes towards the three key issues were represented as three bipolar dimensions. According to the combinations of values on the three dimensions, Schwartz assigns the countries studied to different culture areas.

5.4 Cultural Dimensions According to the GLOBE Research Group

In a research programme named GLOBE (= Global Leadership and Organizational Behaviour Effectiveness Research Program), which is still running today, cultural dimensions are to be determined that have a significant influence on corporate management and its effectiveness (House et al. 2004). The project builds on Hofstede's research, but by involving scientists from different cultural backgrounds (from a total of 62 countries) the aim is, first, to overcome the one-sided Western perspective and, second, to update Hofstede's findings. The dimensions identified are based on surveys of middle managers from three industrial sectors (financial services, food industry and telecommunications). Seven of the nine dimensions (Table 5.3) are very similar to Hofstede's dimensions.

Table 5.3 Culture dimensions according to the GLOBE research group

Dimension	Description
Uncertainty avoidance	Extent to which unsafe situations are avoided by the establishment of rules
Power distance	Extent to which unequal distribution of power is accepted
Institutional collectivism	Extent of community orientation in relation to society as a whole
In-group collectivism	Extend of loyalty to own groups (e.g. family, company)
Gender egalitarianism	Extend of equality between men and women
Assertiveness	Extent of tendency to be overbearing and aggressive in interpersonal relationships
Future orientation	Extent of future-oriented thinking and acting
Performance orientation	Extent to which achievements and improvements in performance are valued and encouraged by society
Human orientation	Extent to which fairness and consideration are valued and encouraged by society

5.5 Cultural Dimensions According to the World Values Survey

The focus of the "World Values Survey" research project, which is also still running today, is the investigation of changes in cultural values ("value change"), but it also aims to identify current similarities and differences between the various cultures (Welzel and Inglehart 2010). The data basis consists of extensive questionnaire surveys in 100 countries. Using factor analytic techniques, the answers to the questions were reduced to two bipolar dimensions, that are described as "survival vs. self-expression" and "traditional vs. secular values" (Table 5.4). According to the expression combinations on the two dimensions, the countries studied are currently classified into eight culture areas (Fig. 5.2).

What is striking here is that the Confucian countries are assigned to the secular values in the *traditionality* dimension, although respect for authority – which is an indicator of traditionality – is highly pronounced in these countries. This assignment is thus somewhat at odds with the findings of Hofstede, Schwartz and the GLOBE study. The presumably best explanation for this is that in the World Values Survey the lack of religious values is weighted more heavily than respect for authority. Moreover, this may also violate the postulate of structural equivalence (Sect. 2.2.2), since the (negative) correlation between the lack of religious values and respect for authority is probably higher in Protestant Europe than in Confucian countries.

5.6 Cultural Dimensions According to Trompenaars

The studies by Dutch researcher Fons Trompenaars are based on surveys in 50 countries, with 75% of the total respondents consisting of managers and 25% of administrative staff (cf. Trompenaars 2012). Seven dimensions are identified from the questionnaire responses (Table 5.5).

Table 5.4 Culture dimensions according to the World Values Survey

Dimension	Extreme characteristics (poles)
Survival – self-expression	Striving for material security – striving for self-realisation
Traditional – secular values	Emphasis on religious values and respect for authority – emphasis on secularised rationality and autonomy

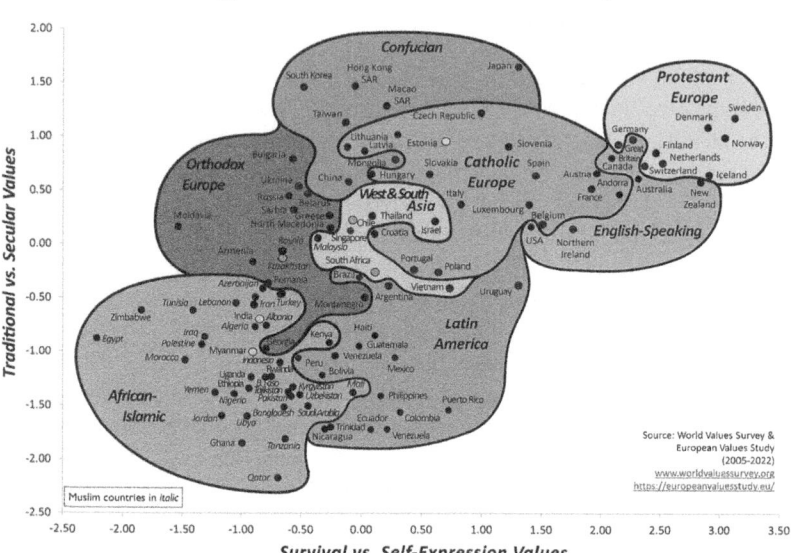

Fig. 5.2 Culture groups according to the World Values Survey. (Source: The Inglehart-Welzel World Cultural Map – World Values Survey 2023. http://www.worldvaluessurvey.org)

5.7 Cultural Dimensions According to Hall

While the classification systems discussed so far mainly refer to work-related attitudes and behaviour, the American anthropologist Edward T. Hall (cf. Hall and Hall 1990) focuses on communication behaviour. On the basis of observations and interviews with people from different occupational groups, he postulates four dimensions, each with dichotomous expression (Table 5.6): *contextual reference, time orientation, spatial orientation* and *speed of information*.

5.7 Cultural Dimensions According to Hall

Table 5.5 Cultural dimensions according to Trompenaars

Dimension	Description
Universalism-particularism	In *universalistic* cultures, rules are considered generally binding; in *particularistic* cultures, rules are situation-dependent
Individualism-collectivism	*Individualist* cultures emphasise the independence of the individual, *collectivist* cultures emphasise social integration
Neutrality-affectivity	In *neutral* cultures, feelings tend to be suppressed; in *affective* cultures, feelings tend to be displayed openly
Specificity-diffusion	In *specific* societies professional and private life are strictly separated, in *diffuse* cultures the spheres of life overlap
Achievement – ascription	In *achievement-oriented* cultures, a person's status is based on his or her own achievements; in *ascription-oriented* cultures, status is based on personal characteristics such as age, gender or ancestry
Time orientation	Past, present and future experience culturally different meanings. In *monochronic* cultures (Chap. 13), there is a clear demarcation of successive events; in *polychronic* cultures, past, present, and future overlap, and many activities occur simultaneously
Relationship to the environment	In cultures with *high environmental control,* humans are considered self-determined; in cultures with *low environmental control,* humans are considered subject to nature and fate

Table 5.6 Culture dimensions according to Hall

Dimension	Description
Contextual reference	In *high context* cultures, communication tends to be implicit due to the long-term social relationships, i.e. not everything has to be said, whereas in *low context* cultures, all information is conveyed explicitly due to the low level of social integration
Time orientation	In cultures with a *monochronic* time setting there is a preference for successive processing of individual activities according to a strict schedule, whereas in cultures with *polychronic* time setting, work is done on several tasks at the same time and schedules are handled flexibly
Spatial orientation	In *high distance* cultures, strict adherence to privacy is emphasised, whereas in *low distance* cultures, greater proximity to others is tolerated
Information speed	In cultures with *high information speed,* keyword-type messages are preferred, while in cultures with *low information speed,* information is presented in more detail

5.8 Comparison of the Dimensional Approaches to Culture Description

Depending on the type of approach, on the areas of life involved, on the samples studied and on the period of data collection, different culture-differentiating factors were defined, but the similarities cannot be overlooked. Table 5.7 illustrates the similarities and differences.

Since most classification systems are based on surveys, major differences arise already from the type and number of questions included as well as from the type of data reduction method used in each case (especially different types of factor analysis). In addition, it is often not possible to decide whether the answers to the questions reflect the actual state of affairs or whether they are rather characterised by "social desirability". This may also explain why, even when a dimension is labeled in a similar way, the degree of expression varies considerably between countries (cf. Hofstede 2010). Figure 5.3 illustrates this fact using the example of the dimension "uncertainty avoidance".

Differences also arise from the sample selection – both with regard to the countries included and to the individuals included. Let us look at Hofstede's investigations. With regard to the countries, due to the fact that they belong to the multinational corporation examined by Hofstede, only countries with a relatively high degree of industrialisation were involved, i.e. members of so-called primitive peoples hardly appear at all. With regard to the persons studied, the parallelisation of the samples (in each case employees of the same multinational group), is accompanied by a different representativeness of the individual country samples. Being an employee of the group under study (IBM) implies a different class affiliation in emerging countries than in highly developed countries (Sect. 2.3).

5.9 Context Factors: The Human Development Index (HDI)

If culture refers to a lifeworld that is associated with certain patterns of thinking, feeling and acting, then a distinction must be made as to whether it is a question of normative patterns that reflect certain value orientations or whether they are patterns that concern life circumstances (so-called context factors) and which are often perceived as imposed. The phenomenon of *poverty* can be regarded as such an imposed pattern. It is essentially characterised by low household income, low social status, cramped housing conditions and malnutrition. If one tries to measure poverty against a universal yardstick, it is certainly not independent of culture - as indicated

5.9 Context Factors: The Human Development Index (HDI)

Table 5.7 Comparison of the dimensional approaches to culture writing

Hofstede	Schwartz	GLOBE	World Values Survey	Trompenaars	Hall
Individualism – collectivism	Autonomy – embeddedness	Institutional collectivism, in-group collectivism, human orientation	Survival – self-expression	Individualism – collectivism	Context reference
Power distance	Hierarchy – equality	Power distance	Traditional – secular values	Achievement – ascription	
Uncertainty avoidance		Uncertainty avoidance		Universalism – particularism	
Masculinity – femininity	Mastery – harmony	Gender egalitarianism, self-assertion	Traditional – secular values	Neutrality – emotionality	
Long term – short term orientation		Future orientation, performance orientation		Time orientation	Time orientation
Indulgence			(Traditional – secular values)		
	Mastery – harmony	Human orientation		Relationship to the environment	
					Spatial orientation
					Information speed

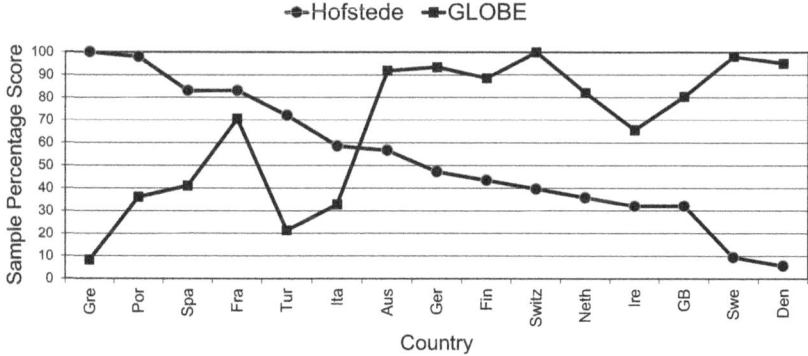

Fig. 5.3 Uncertainty avoidance indices of some countries according to Hofstede and GLOBE. (Modified after Magala 2007; Data from Hofstede 2001 and House et al. 2004)

by its uneven distribution across countries. Nevertheless, the lifeworld associated with it must be seen as an imposed pattern rather than a normative value system.

The *Human Development Index (HDI)* represents an attempt to represent different context characteristics on a common dimension with different degrees of expression (Box 5.2). In a sense, it could also be understood as an index of the degree of civilisation (Sect. 1.4).

> **Box 5.2: Human Development Index (HDI)**
> The *Human Development Index (HDI)* is an indicator of human development in the countries of the world. It has been published since 1990 in the annual Human Development Report of the UNDP (United Nations Development Programme).
>
> The HDI takes into account the gross domestic product (GDP) per inhabitant of a country as PPP (purchasing power parity or income) in US dollars, life expectancy and the level of education (literacy rate and school enrolment rate of the population).
>
> *Life expectancy* is considered to be an indicator of health care, while level of *education* and *income* are intended to reflect acquired knowledge and participation in public and political life. Sub-indices are formed for each of the three indicators, which are then combined on a weighted basis to form an overall index.

Table 5.8 Country examples for the development levels of the Human Development Index (HDI) (data from 2021)

Development level	Country	Index	Rank
Very high	Switzerland	0.962	1
	Norway	0.961	2
	Australia	0.951	5
	Germany	0.942	9
High	Albania	0.796	67
	Iran	0.774	76
	Mainland China	0.768	79
	Cuba	0.764	83
Medium	Philippines	0.699	116
	Iraq	0.686	121
	India	0.633	132
	Nepal	0.602	143
Low	Senegal	0.511	170
	Ethiopia	0.498	175
	Afghanistan	0.478	180
	Central African Republic	0.404	188

On the basis of this index, which can vary between 0 and 1, very highly developed countries (HDI $\geq$ 0.8), highly developed countries (0.7 $\leq$ HDI $<$ 0.8), moderately developed countries (0.55 $\leq$ HDI $<$ 0.7) and low developed countries (HDI $<$ 0.55) are distinguished (Table 5.8). Very highly developed countries include Norway, Australia and Germany, while low-developed countries include Senegal, Afghanistan and Ethiopia (United Nations 2022).

5.10 Conclusion

In order to be able to empirically test the potential influence of cultural conditions on individual experience and behaviour, a specification of cultural conditions is required. Not every cultural community or every country are considered as independent influencing factors themselves. In spite of this, attempts are made to define factors or dimensions on which each cultural community can be represented as a specific combination of characteristics. The determination of the factors is based on general considerations about living together in human societies as well as on surveys and observations.

Depending on the type of approach, the areas of life included, the samples studied and the period of data collection, different factors were identified, but similarities cannot be denied. The highest level of agreement is found in the factor "individualism-collectivism", which has also inspired most of the cross-cultural research. Nevertheless, none of the established classification systems can be considered exhaustive. This is mainly due to the fact that the factors essentially reflect the Western working world and, for example, religious ideas are almost exclusively found in the form of secularised work attitudes.

In addition to the factors defined in terms of content, as listed in the classification systems, contextual or demarcation factors must also be taken into account. Although these are often not completely independent of the actual cultural factors, they relate less to the values prevailing in a cultural community than to accompanying life circumstances such as poverty or wealth and level of education.

5.11 Questions of Understanding

1. Define the terms *"culture area"* and *"cultural dimension"*.
2. Describe Geert Hofstede's approach to identifying *cultural dimensions*.
3. Explain the objective and content of the *Human Development Index (HDI)*.

Further Reading

Browaeys, M.-J., & Price, R. (2018). Understanding cross-cultural management (3rd ed.). Edinburgh Gate: Pearson Education Limited.

Hofstede, G., Hofstede, G. J., & Minkov, M. (2010). *Cultures and organizations: Software of the mind* (3rd ed.). New York: McGraw-Hill.

Lonner, W. (2008). Searching for meaningful psychological categories, dimensions, and patterns of culture. In H. Helfrich, A. V. Dakhin, E. Hölter & I. V. Arzhenowskiy (eds.), *Impact of culture on human interaction: Clash or challenge?* (pp. 203–217). Cambridge, MA: Hogrefe & Huber.

Yeganeh, H. (2013). A compound index of cultural dimensions: Implications and applications. *International Journal of Organizational Analysis, 21*, 53–65.

Perception 6

One of the most elementary mental processes is certainly the perception of the environment around us. One can now ask whether this environment is perceived in the same way by all people or whether experience determines which objects we see and how we see them. Here, cultural comparison offers the possibility of separating biological factors from factors gained through experience, since cultures differ in their members' background of experience. The background of experience here can refer to geographical conditions, to the social and technical environment, and to the type of linguistic designations that are common for the objects perceived.

6.1 Perception and Experience

The question whether human perception depends solely on the biological-physiological endowment (*nativist* position) or whether it is the result of an active interaction with the environment (*empiricist* or *interactionist* position) represents one of the oldest controversies in experimental psychology. According to the nativist position, for example, the two-dimensional image on the retina of the eye contains all the necessary information to allow an accurate, three-dimensional image of the world to emerge in the brain immediately and without any active intervention on the part of the perceiving person. According to this view, the higher brain areas responsible for visual perception have developed structures that enable a three-dimensional view of the world. In contrast, according to the empiricist or interactionist position, it is only the experiences gained in constant interaction with the environment that enable the construction of a three-dimensional world of perception. Human beings must therefore learn through experience in the course of their ontogenesis how to interpret the external stimuli received with their sense organs.

© The Author(s), under exclusive license to Springer-Verlag GmbH, DE, part of Springer Nature 2023
H. Helfrich, *Cross-Cultural Psychology*,
https://doi.org/10.1007/978-3-662-67558-8_6

6.2 Brunswik's Theory of Transactional Functionalism

Egon Brunswik, a representative of the empiricist position, developed in his theory of transactional functionalism (Brunswik 1956) the idea that the organism structures and transmits the sensory incoming stimuli on the basis of previous experiences (*transactional*) in such a way that they can serve the concrete coping with life (*functional*). Following this theory, identical stimulus patterns would have to elicit different perceptual performances depending on the respective environment, since the individual environments require different types of adaptive performances. "Environment" in this context means the "eco-cultural" lifeworld which includes both the geographic conditions and their cultural over-formations. Cross-cultural comparison is one way of testing Brunswik's theory.

In this case, the phenomena known from the psychology of perception as "optical illusions" can be used as an object of comparison. According to Brunswik's theory, the "illusions" are ecologically meaningful perceptual "corrections" in an atypical task structure. This structure is atypical in that a two-dimensional stimulus template (consisting of single lines), which in everyday life is normally perceived as a perspective representation of a (three-dimensional) spatial configuration, must be interpreted in two dimensions in order to cope with the experimentally specified task (estimating the length of the lines). However, the extent of illusion should vary depending on the experience with the three-dimensional entities in question. Based on these considerations, Segall et al. (1966) tested, in a quasi-experimental study, the hypothesis that an individual, depending on his or her ecological-cultural environment, should be particularly susceptible to certain types of optical illusions and hardly susceptible to others (Box 6.1).

> **Box 6.1: From Research: Study on Perceptual Illusions Depending on the Ecological Environment**
> Segall et al. (1966) used a quasi-experimental approach to investigate perceptual illusions, so-called optical illusions, as a function of ecological environment.

(continued)

Box 6.1 (continued)
Study
It was hypothesised that an individual is particularly susceptible to certain types of optical illusions and hardly susceptible to others, depending on his or her ecological-cultural environment.

Thus, subjects in whose environment many right angles occur ("carpentered world"), should be particularly susceptible to angle illusions such as the *Müller-Lyer illusion*. Subjects whose environment allows a lot of experience with spatial depth should be particularly susceptible to the *horizontal-vertical illusion*.

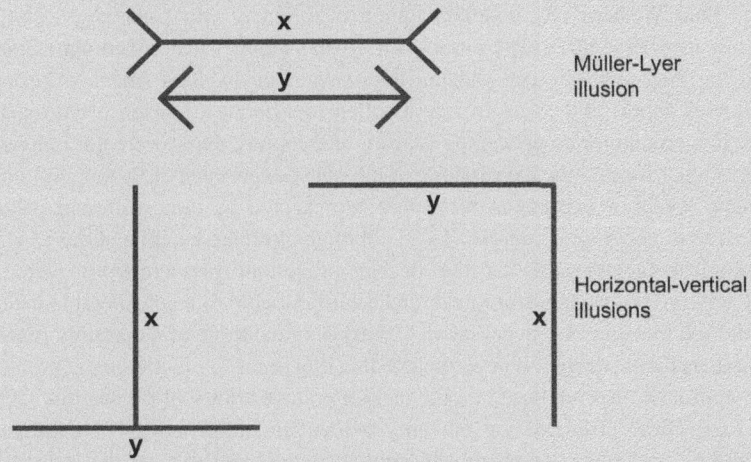

Müller-Lyer illusion

Horizontal-vertical illusions

The degree of experience with right angles was varied in two levels: Criterion was the type of predominant house types (right-angled versus round). The degree of experience with spatial depth was varied in three levels: Inhabitants of tropical rainforests were expected to have little spatial depth experience, inhabitants of cities with street alignments were expected to have moderate spatial depth experience, and inhabitants of

(continued)

> **Box 6.1** (continued)
> deserts or savannas were expected to have a great deal of spatial depth experience.
>
> **Results**
> Overall, the research hypothesis of differential susceptibility to deception was supported.

The hypothesis was supported (Fig. 6.1): Savannah and rainforest dwellers (little experience with right angles) succumbed significantly less to the Müller-Lyer illusion than Western city dwellers (much experience with right angles), while rainforest dwellers (little experience with spatial depth) succumbed significantly less to the horizontal-vertical illusion than savannah dwellers (much experience with spatial depth) and Western city dwellers (moderate experience with spatial depth). It is crucial for assessing the validity of the study that it were not individual "cultures" that formed the expressions of the quasi-experimental factors, but rather that equal levels of expression were each represented by quite different cultures from different geographic regions. Thus, although alternative explanations (e.g., by physiological factors such as the degree of retinal pigmentation) were not completely ruled out, they were nevertheless improbable to a considerable extent.

Although the study by Segall et al. (1966) is an example of a carefully planned quasi-experimental design, it nevertheless also illustrates the fundamental problems of this approach, that are based on the lack of controllability of organismic factors (Box 2.6). These problems are not only evident in the difficulty of eliminating confounding variables, but also in the mutual interdependence of the influencing variables under investigation. This led to the fact that a complete variation of the two quasi-experimental factors was not possible: The natural covariation of the variables did not allow to form an experimental group that simultaneously had both little experience with spatial depth and a lot of experience with right angles, or an experimental group that simultaneously had both a high degree of spatial depth experience and a high degree of experience with right angles (Fig. 6.2).

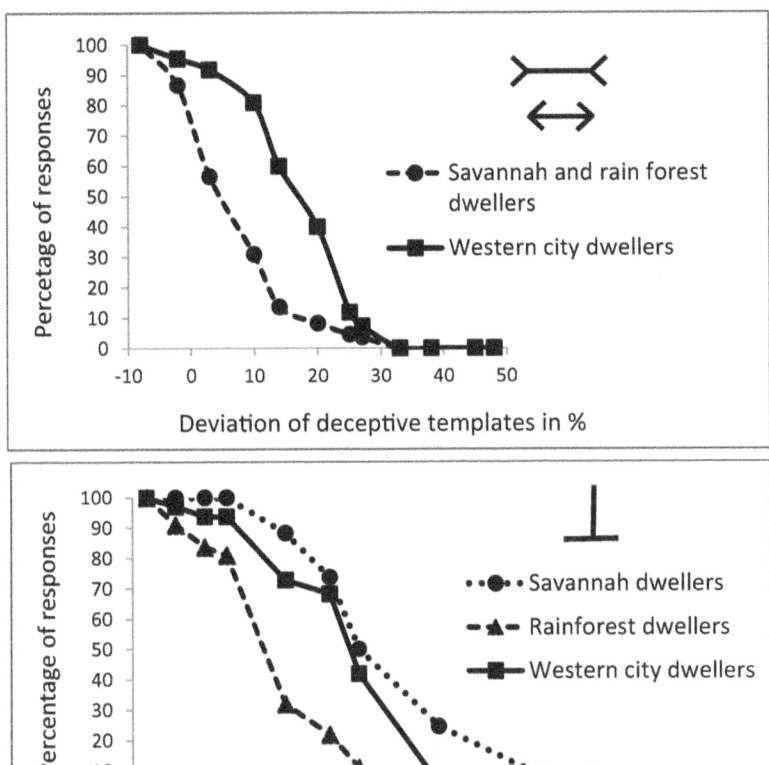

Fig. 6.1 Susceptibility to deception of subjects from cultures with different angular and spatial depth experience in the study of Segall et al. (1966). (Modified after Vogel and Eckensberger 1988, p. 600)

6.3 Whorf's Principle of Linguistic Relativity

A special form of the empiricist position is the thesis that perception depends on language. The starting point is the observation that different languages differ in the way they structure the sensory world with the help of the available words and

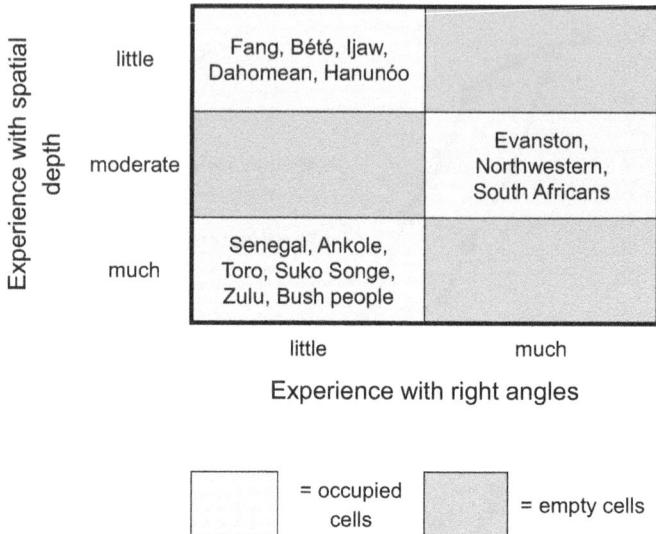

Fig. 6.2 Insufficient realisation of the factor levels: Groups of subjects as representatives of the different levels of the factors "experience with right angles" and "experience with depth of space" . (Modified after Helfrich 2003, p. 124)

sentence constructions. According to von Humboldt (1906), Sapir (1933) and Whorf (1956, 2008), this categorisation imposed by the respective language not only concerns the expression of ideas and thoughts, but already, how the object world is perceived. This thesis has entered the research literature as the *"principle of linguistic relativity"* or as the *"Sapir-Whorf hypothesis"* (Chap. 9).

In contrast to the linguistic relativist or empiricist position there is a linguistic universalist or nativist view developed in cognitive psychology (Mervis and Rosch 1981), according to which all cultures have common, experience-independent basic categories, so-called *prototypes*. According to this view, superficial linguistic differences have no effect on perception and memory.

For an empirical test of the controversy, the colour perception lends itself. Colours exist in all cultures and always refer to physically measurable external qualities, the so-called colour spectrum. At the same time, the number of colour terms varies considerably among cultures. For example, in many cultures there is only one word for the two colours "blue" and "green", and some cultures even have only two names for the entire colour spectrum. Thus, it makes sense to examine whether a larger number of available colour names is associated with a more differentiated colour perception.

While early studies (e.g. Brown and Lenneberg 1954) seemed to support the linguistic relativist position, it was later argued that the linguistic-historical development of colour terms is not unsystematic, but has a universally valid sequence of stages (Berlin and Kay 1969; Kay et al. 1997). Differences arise only with regard to the level at which the colour vocabulary is located – a point of view that has already been advocated by Magnus (1877) towards the end of the nineteenth century in the course of Darwinian thought.

Thus, the Sapir-Whorf hypothesis can be made more precise as to whether differences in the linguistic-historical stage of colour vocabulary correspond to differences in perceptual and memory performance. A compromise answer is proposed by MacLaury (1997) with his *"vantage" theory* ("line of sight" theory): He distinguishes between a universal "perception" of the six basic hues (white, black, red, yellow, green, and blue) and a "cognition" downstream of perception, which involves a culture-dependent selective emphasis on similarities and differences in the individual hues and is also reflected in linguistic designation.

The basic idea of the Vantage Theory is supported in an exemplary investigation by Kay and Kempton (1984) (Box 6.2).

> **Box 6.2: From Research: Study on the Vantage Theory**
> On the Vantage theory, Kay and Kempton (1984) conducted research.
>
> **Study I**
> In the investigation participated on the one hand US-Americans and on the other hand members of the Tarahumara. In the language of this Mexican Indian tribe, there is only one name for the blue-green range. With the help of several colour plates from the blue-green range of the colour spectrum, the perception of the two groups of test subjects was examined. It was hypothesised that two similar hues would be better distinguished from each other if different names were available for the two hues. Conversely, it should be more difficult for the test subjects to distinguish between the two hues if they are given the same name.

(continued)

Box 6.2 (continued)
Results of study I
The hypothesis was supported. For the Tarahumara, all perceived differences between any two adjacent hues on the colour spectrum were essentially the same. In contrast, for the US-Americans, the perceived difference turned out to be greater when one hue could be named as "blue" and the other as "green".

Kay and Kempton attribute the different perceptions of the subject groups to a *naming strategy*. Thus, naming serves as an additional discrimination criterion when two stimuli (here: green and blue) are very difficult to distinguish sensorially.

Study II
To challenge the results of the first investigation, Kay and Kempton conducted a second experiment. In this one, they changed the task and thus tried to circumvent the naming strategy. The subjects now had to distinguish between the stimuli in terms of their "greenness" and "blueness". If there was no difference in the perception of the hues between the two groups of subjects, i.e. if the Sapir-Whorf hypothesis did not come into play, this would support the naming strategy.

Results of study II
The Sapir-Whorf hypothesis could not be supported. Similar results were obtained for both groups of subjects. The previously larger perceptual differences between blue and green hues in the US Americans narrowed now, and the results thus corresponded to those of the Tarahumara in the first experiment.

Summary
In summary, a radical view of the Sapir-Whorf hypothesis has been refuted, for it has become clear that language does not entirely determine colour perception. However, as Kay and Kempton have shown, a radical opposite position, i.e. that language does not influence colour perception at all, cannot be maintained either.

The study by Kay and Kempton suggests that language does not influence the basal ability to discriminate, but is able either to accentuate or to level out differences perceived by the senses. Thus, sensory impressions themselves are not influenced by language, but their evaluation and cognitive organisation are (Sect. 9.7).

6.4 Conclusion

The function of perception is to process the changing sensory impressions in order to build from them a stable representation of the environment that enables the individual to act in that environment. One of the oldest controversies in experimental psychology is the question whether the perception of the environment depends solely on the biological-physiological endowment (nativist position) or whether it is the result of experience gained through active interaction with the environment (empiricist or interactionist position). Here, the cultural comparison offers the possibility to separate biological factors from those gained through experience, since cultures differ in their background of experience. From the studies presented, it can be deduced that a strictly nativist theory cannot be maintained, i.e. that perception is always also influenced by experience.

6.5 Questions of Understanding

1. Characterise the difference between the *nativist* and *empiricist* positions regarding human perception.
2. Justify why so-called *optical illusions* have been studied in cross-cultural comparisons.
3. Explain the so-called *Sapir-Whorf hypothesis*.

Further Reading
Berry, J. W., Poortinga, Y. H., Breugelmans, S. M., Chasiotis, A., Sam, D. M., & Seger, M. (2011). *Cross-cultural psychology* (3rd ed.). Cambridge: Cambridge University Press.
Thomas, A., & Helfrich, H. (2003). Wahrnehmungspsychologische Aspekte im Kulturvergleich. In A. Thomas (ed.), *Kulturvergleichende Psychologie* (2nd ed, pp. 207–243). Göttingen: Hogrefe.

Cognitive Abilities and Performance

All humans try to take in information from their environment, process it, draw conclusions from it and use it to solve problems in an effective way. Such activities, which include perceiving (Chap. 6), recognising, remembering, thinking, and problem solving, can be summarised under the term "cognition". This chapter looks at recognising, remembering, thinking, and problem solving. People differ in how and how well they perform these activities. Thus, one can ask whether the differences reflect differences in underlying capabilities required to carry out these activities.

7.1 Deficit Versus Difference Model

Cross-cultural studies in the field of cognition are often based on one of two premises, which can be characterised as the "deficit" model and the "difference" model (Box 7.1). The *deficit model* implicitly assumes different stages of development of cognitive abilities, with the respective "stages" frequently understood in terms of social evolutionism (Spencer 1876; Tylor 1865). The *difference model*, on the other hand, emphasises the "otherness" of foreign thought, without thereby wanting to make a value judgement. In a way, the two models of thought correspond to the distinction between the etic and emic views. The former seeks to identify differences in characteristics on universally valid dimensions of cognitive ability and performance, the latter emphasises the need for a context-bound or "native" approach. The supposition here is that cognitive performance always involves coping with problems at hand and that these problems are of a very different nature depending on the cultural context (see, e.g., Diamond 2012). Of course, the difference model and the deficit model are not mutually exclusive, nor are the emic and etic views. Thus, an emic approach can uncover previously unknown cognitive phenomena ("differences") that can be made accessible to quantitative comparisons (with the possibility of identifying "deficits") in a later step. An example of investigating differences would be the studies on collectivist and individualist modes of thinking (Sect. 7.3.1).

> **Box 7.1: Deficit and Difference Model**
> In cultural studies on cognitive abilities, deficit models can be distinguished from difference models.
>
> The *deficit* model implicitly assumes different levels of development of cognitive abilities. The *difference* model on the other hand, emphasises the otherness of foreign thinking without making a value judgement. The two models are not mutually exclusive, but can complement each other.

7.2 General Intelligence Versus Specific Abilities and Performances

Various attempts have been made to identify cultural differences in the level of general intelligence, of the so-called *g-factor*, using the psychometric approach (cf. Lynn and Vanhanen 2002). General intelligence can be conceived either in the sense of Spearman's *general factor model* (1904) as a common basis of many different test items or as a context-free *basic ability to process information* (Jensen 1998).

In the sense of the general factor concept, various test items operationalise the construct "intelligence" in its entirety and map it on a common scale. The decisive factor is not the content of the individual items, but their overall structure and representativeness for the construct "intelligence". For cultural comparisons, this results in the requirement that both the structure and the selection of test items must be comparable. However, both postulates can hardly be fulfilled simultaneously, since structural equality (i.e. comparable correlations between the individual tasks) can only be achieved by accepting a different representativeness of the individual tasks for the construct as a whole. Thus, a comparable competence structure can no longer be inferred from the same observed performance.

Theoretically, however, it is not at all to be expected that a concrete task selection represents a random sample from a task universe that is common to all cultures, because the definition of what counts as "intelligent" behaviour overall is always culturally mediated, namely as the mastery of the cognitive tasks that are

7.2 General Intelligence Versus Specific Abilities and Performances

significant in the respective culture. Since some accomplishments are highly valued within one culture but given little consideration within another, the definition of general intelligence must be per se culture-specific. Even within the Western world, the definition of what all counts as intelligence has expanded over recent decades to include abilities such as "creativity" (Sternberg 2012), "emotional Intelligence" (Goleman 1995) and even "kinesthetic-motor intelligence" (Gardner 1993). The result is that it is virtually impossible to make a quantitative comparison in the level of this overall cognitive system between different cultures.

A comparison seems more feasible if general intelligence is conceived as an experience-independent basic aptitude that governs both the formation of specific abilities and the acquisition of knowledge. This so-called "fluid" intelligence is distinguished from a "crystallized" intelligence (Cattell 1987). *Fluid intelligence* is conceptualised as independent of experience and thus culture-independent, whereas *crystallized intelligence* is considered the result of individual engagement with the sociocultural environment.

For a long time, the prototypical procedure for measuring fluid intelligence was considered to be the *"Progressive Matrices"* test (Raven's Progressive Matrices, RPM, Raven 1987; SPM, Horn 2009). Here, the task consists in recognising elementary principles of pattern formation (Fig. 7.1).

Task: Tick which of the lower six parts fits into the above figure.

However, a generational comparison in several industrial nations showed that the test is by no means "culture fair": The average overall level of intelligence measured has risen massively over the 30-year period under investigation (Flynn 1987, 1994). Genetic factors can hardly be held responsible for this finding, which is referred to as the "Flynn effect". The most plausible explanation for the "rise" in intelligence is the increasing familiarity with abstract visual patterns that accompanies industrialisation and mechanisation (Clark et al. 2016; Dickens and Flynn 2001). This explanation is not contradicted by the fact that recently, in some countries, an "Anti-Flynn effect", i.e., a decline in IQ scores can be observed (Woodley of Menie et al. 2017): These countries show, in their recent history, a high proportion of immigrants from less technologically developed countries. A currently interesting question in this context would be whether individuals belonging to countries that are far advanced in the digitisation of everyday life (e.g. Estonia) display significantly higher test scores than individuals in countries with low levels of digitisation. In any case, both the Flynn effect and the Anti-Flynn effect indicate that a culture-free measurement of general intelligence is still beyond realisation.

While the definition of general intelligence in terms of a general factor has proved to be highly culture-dependent, cross-cultural conceptual equivalence is

Fig. 7.1 Example item from the "Progressive Matrices" test (test for measuring "general intelligence")

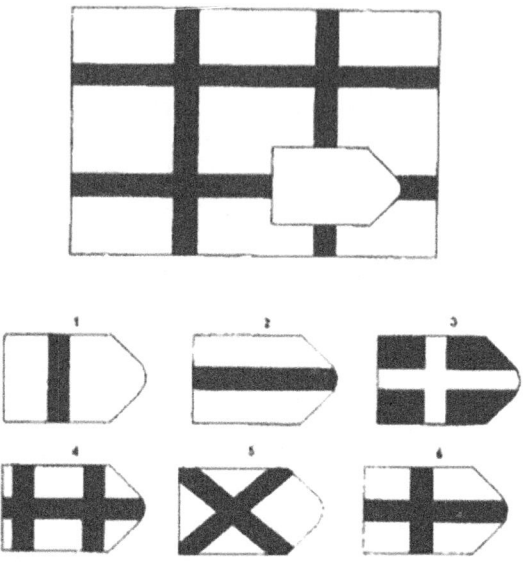

more readily established in the definition of specific abilities. Cultural comparisons have been made primarily on spatial perception, memory capacity, mathematical comprehension, deductive reasoning, and object categorisation. Two study series can be considered prototypical: the so-called *TIMSS study* (Trends in International Mathematics and Science Study; cf. Wendt et al. 2016) and the *PISA studies* (Programme for International Student Assessment; cf. Hammer et al. 2016; Reinhold et al. 2019). They compare the mathematical and scientific competencies acquired at school in different countries (mostly OECD countries) (Box 7.2). The test items were selected in such a way as to produce a factor structure that is comparable for all participating countries and that allows the expression of abilities to be mapped on a common scale (cf. Baumert et al. 2000a, p. 60).

> **Box 7.2: PISA and TIMSS Studies**
> The PISA (Programme for International Student Assessment) studies involve the international comparison of the abilities in mathematics, science and reading of students aged 15. They have been conducted by the Organisation

(continued)

> **Box 7.2** (continued)
> for Economic Co-operation and Development (OECD) every 3 years since 2000.
>
> The TIMSS studies (Trends in International Mathematics and Science Study) involve the international comparison of students' mathematical and scientific abilities at the end of primary school. They have been conducted every 4 years since 1995 in more than 40 countries, 27 of which belong to the OECD.

According to the results of recent studies, the mathematical performance of German students in the TIMSS studies – like the performance of US students – was located in the middle range (cf. Wendt et al. 2016), and in the PISA studies – in contrast to the below-average performance of US students – in the top third (cf. Hammer et al. 2016; Reinhold et al. 2019). The top group always included the East Asian countries of Singapore, Taiwan, Hong Kong, Korea, and Japan. The differences in performance found can possibly be explained by a culturally different appreciation of practice and learning (Sects. 7.3.2 and 12.4).

7.3 Antecedents of Cognitive Differences

7.3.1 Individualist Versus Collectivist Mode of Thinking

From the "indigenous" point of view of collectivist-oriented cultures, the Western distortion ("bias") of cognition research was pointed out. This primarily focuses on analytical, deductive thinking, which finds its prototypical expression in the Western understanding of science. Other forms of cognition are almost completely ignored. Nisbett and his colleagues (cf. Nisbett 2003; Nisbett et al. 2001, 2008) distinguish between two modes of thinking: one that separates *analytically* and one that connects *holistically* (Box 7.3). The analytical mode of thinking is considered typical of individualist oriented cultures, whereas the holistic mode of thinking rather corresponds to collectivist oriented cultures.

> **Box 7.3: Analytical and Holistic Thinking**
> Nisbett and his colleagues (cf. et al. 2001) distinguish two modes of thinking: the analytically separating and the holistically connecting mode. The *analytical* mode of thinking is considered typical of individualist oriented cultures, while the *holistic* mode of thinking rather corresponds to collectivist oriented cultures.
>
> In *individualist* cultures, the individual separates himself or herself from the environment and therefore prefers a way of thinking that constructs opposites.
>
> In *collectivist* cultures, the individual sees himself or herself as part of the environment and therefore tends to embed facts in a context and harmonise opposites.

To test this assumption, Nisbett and his colleagues carried out several quasi-experimental comparisons between East Asian (collectivist) and American (individualist) subjects. The following overview (Box 7.4) shows the study as an example.

Nisbett and his colleagues point out that both ways of thinking are possibly universal, but that they vary in their intensity and frequency according to their appreciation in the respective culture (cf. Nisbett et al. 2001, p. 306). This view is supported by the fact that the repective opposite way of thinking can be adopted if attention is appropriately directed (cf. Kühnen et al. 2000) or if appropriate training is provided (cf. Dasen and de Ribaupierre 1988).

> **Box 7.4: From Research: Study on the Holistic Versus Analytical Mode of Thinking**
> Nisbett et al. (2001) conducted several quasi-experimental studies on the two modes of thinking, the *analytical* mode and the *holistic* mode.
>
> **Study**
> First, the East Asian (collectivist) and US American (individualist) subjects were presented with various pictures showing fishes in an aquarium. The following figure shows an example.

(continued)

Box 7.4 (continued)

In the subsequent test phase, the subjects were shown test images and asked whether they had seen the respective image before. On the one hand, pictures were used on which any fish was depicted against a background presented previously to the subjects (test example 1), and on the other hand, pictures were used which depicted a fish already shown in the presentation phase against a different background (test example 2). It was hypothesised that the East Asian subjects would remember the background better (test image example 1) and the American subjects would remember the fish better (test image example 2).

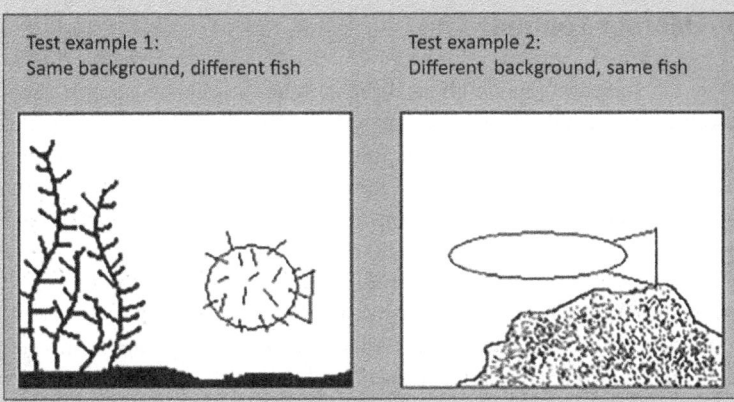

Test example 1:
Same background, different fish

Test example 2:
Different background, same fish

Results

The hypothesis was supported. The East Asian subjects as representatives of the holistic thinking mode remembered better the background of the pictures shown (test e example 1). The US-Americans as representatives of the analytical mode of thinking remembered better the fish depicted in the original picture (test example 2).

7.3.2 Confucian Dynamics

The superiority of the East Asian countries of Singapore, Taiwan, Hong Kong, Korea and Japan over the USA in mathematics performance, as demonstrated by the TIMSS and PISA studies (Sect. 7.2), makes the characterisation of the East Asian way of thinking as "holistic" – in contrast to a Western-style "analytical" way of thinking – appear at least questionable, since the solution of mathematical tasks is generally associated with an analytical way of thinking. However, the performance superiority of the East Asian countries could also be linked to the factor of *Confucian dynamics* identified by Hofstede as the fifth cultural dimension. Among the 23 countries studied by Hofstede, Japan, Korea and Singapore are located significantly closer than the USA to the pole of the dimension which can be characterised by perseverance and persistence (Sect. 5.2). The associated appreciation of learning and practice could provide an explanation for the better performance of the East Asian countries in the achievement tests (Sect. 12.4).

7.3.3 Mother Tongue

Although all societies known to us have a fully developed spoken language (cf. Cavalli-Sforza 2000), the specific language a person speaks is to a large extent culture-dependent (Chap. 9). Based on this difference between languages, it is of interest from a psychological point of view to what extent the respective mother tongue promotes or inhibits cognitive operations. Above, this question has already been discussed related to perception as the so-called *Sapir-Whorf hypothesis* (Chap. 6). This states that linguistic specifications "calibrate" (Whorf 1956, 2008) or even "determine" (Sapir 1933, p. 7) perception and thinking. For example, Whorf wrote that the language of the Hopi Indians[1] does not have any words and no grammatical forms that refer to past, present, and future. He concluded that the Hopi Indians have no concept of time and perceive temporal processes in a completely different way than we do.

However, looking at language alone is not sufficient to describe cognition. To test the Sapir-Whorf hypothesis, non-linguistic indicators must also be taken into account. As was shown in Chap. 6, with respect to perception, the Sapir-Whorf hypothesis in its strict form has not withstood empirical testing.

---

[1] The Hopi live in the west of the USA.

7.3 Antecedents of Cognitive Differences

The dependence of cognitive processes on language structure has been revisited in more recent studies (Hedden et al. 2002; Lass et al. 2000). Therein, memory performance was examined as a function of language structure (Box 7.5).

> **Box 7.5: From research: Studies on Memory Span as a Function of Mother Tongue**
>
> Some studies (Hedden et al. 2002; Lass et al. 2000; Lüer et al. 1998) revisited the Sapir-Whorf hypothesis and examined cultural differences in elementary cognitive performance.
>
> **Study I**
>
> Subjects with Chinese as their native language and subjects with an Indo-European native language (English or German) were compared with regard to their memory span. *Memory span* is defined as the maximum number of items that a subject can reproduce in correct order immediately after presentation. It was determined by forward and backward reproduction of numbers. That is, subjects had to reproduce the numbers in the original order and in the reverse order. In addition to numbers, other stimulus materials such as common geometric shapes were used.
>
> **Results of study I**
>
> The Chinese subjects showed a higher memory span in all stimulus categories compared to both the German and the US subjects.
>
> According to the memory model by Baddeley (1997), the higher memory span of Chinese should be due to a shorter articulation time. That is, Chinese words can be articulated faster than German or English words, increasing the capacity of the phonological loop.
>
> **Study II**
>
> To test whether language really is crucial for the high Chinese memory span, the study was repeated with irregular geometric figures as stimulus materials.
>
> (continued)

Box 7.5 (continued)

The factor "language" could thus be excluded as a critical influencing factor, since the irregular geometric shapes did not allow for articulation.

Results of study II
The cultural differences disappeared: Germans, Americans, and Chinese showed a similar memory span. Consequently, the short articulation time of Chinese words seems to be responsible for the higher memory span of the Chinese.

The starting point is Baddeley's (2007) memory model, according to which short-term memory – referred to by Baddeley as "working memory" due to its active nature – has a "sketchpad" for visuo-spatial information and a "phonological loop" for verbal information. Constitutive of the phonological loop is a kind of internal articulation that supports the transfer of verbal content into long-term memory. Based on this model, it was examined to what extent the phonological structure of the mother tongue modifies the capacity of the phonological loop and thus the memory span. In quasi-experimental experimental designs, students with Chinese as their mother tongue and students with an Indo-European mother tongue (English or German) were compared in their memory performance. The two language types (Chinese versus English or German) differ in their phonological structure: Chinese words can individually be articulated faster and sequentially concatenated faster than their English or German counterparts. The stimulus material used consisted of geometric figures, names of geometric figures, numbers, and number words (Box 7.5).

It was postulated that shorter articulation durations increase the total capacity of the – time-limited – working memory, since more individual items can then be recorded within the same time. The results show that the Chinese subjects were able to remember significantly more items than the German or the American subjects. This was not only the case when the items had to be reproduced verbally, but even when an answer was required by pointing to the corresponding geometric figure.

It is surprising, however, that the performance advantage of the Chinese subjects disappears if meaningless random figures have to be remembered and thus there is no possibility of verbalisation (Box 7.5). This suggests that it is actually due to the phonological structure of the language and not to the difference in familiarity with visual patterns – caused for example, by the pictographic writing system of Chinese as opposed to the phonetic writing system of Indo-European languages. The phonological structure of the language as a decisive factor is also supported by the fact that the superiority of the subjects with Chinese as their mother tongue is already apparent at kindergarten age (Hedden et al. 2002), i.e. at an age when oral language has already been largely acquired but cannot yet be written.

7.3.4 School Education

Regular schooling may also be considered a cultural influence factor with a potentially beneficial effect. The relationship between formal schooling and deductive reasoning has frequently been studied. Reasoning is considered the basis for scientific thinking and is particularly valued as an intellectual skill in Western cultures. Nevertheless, one can pose the question to what extent the underlying basic aptitude is universally expressed and can also be observed independently of regular schooling.

According to Piaget (1966) at least, all people tend to develop formal-logical abilities. However, it is not easy to find test items whose requirement structure is comparable for all individuals, i.e., test items that are "new" to all individuals to a similar extent. Even highly "artificial" problem-solving situations, which are not known to any of the test subjects, give test persons with formal schooling a solution advantage insofar as these persons are more accustomed to meaningless tasks and therefore recognise the type of task more easily.

The frequent observation that in traditional cultures without formal schooling reasoning tasks need to be embedded in a meaningful context in order to be solvable, led some researchers – including the Russian neuropsychologist Luria and the Russian sociohistorian Vygotsky – believe that abstract thinking originated in ancient Greece and from there, through the spread of regular schooling, has penetrated different cultures and changed people's consciousness. This view is supported by the observation that in areas where school attendance is not a matter of course, subjects with school education perform significantly better in solving logical problems than those without schooling.

However, the transfer of knowledge acquired at school to the solution of real problems is not always successful. One might assume that it is particularly unsuccessful if the Western school system is imposed on a non-Western culture without regard to living conditions, learning styles and life requirements. In fact, this often seems to be the case (cf. Trommsdorff 2003, p. 155). In the light of the research on so-called cognitive illusions (cf. Pohl 2022) – these are errors that occur similar to the "optical illusions" in perception (Sect. 6.2) as "errors of reasoning" – it seems, however, that also Western subjects frequently fail to transfer their knowledge to novel problems. Although the rules of reasoning (e.g., deductions from if-then relationships) are correctly applied in abstract tasks, systematic errors occur as soon as the task is embedded in a context that contradicts action schemata used in everyday life (cf. Cosmides and Tooby 2002).

Even if the competence-promoting influence of school education is not to be questioned, it must rather be seen as a mediating one: Through the acquisition of new symbol systems and increased mastery of language, as well as the detachment of learning content from the situational context, access to new knowledge is facilitated to a considerable degree.

7.3.5 Minority Status

Minority status is an important cultural context factor. A minority is characterised by the fact that its members are socially effectively demarcated from the majority population and occupy a special position in society. It is not the minority status per se that is to be regarded as inhibiting performance, but rather the attitude towards the dominant culture repectively associated with it. Ogbu (2002) distinguishes two types of minorities: "voluntary" and "involuntary". In relation to the USA, the former are immigrants (Afro-Caribbeans, Asians, Jews and Latinos), the latter are non-immigrants (Black Americans, Native Americans and Hawaiians).

Involuntary minorities differ from voluntary minorities in several variables that have a decisive influence both on competence in terms of crystallized intelligence and on its manifestation in performance measured by means of an intelligence test. The most important influencing variable is the extent of integration into the dominant culture. This manifests, among other things, in an adequate mastery of the respective lingua franca, the frequency of contact with members of the majority culture and the attitude towards the performance expected by the majority culture. Greater integration entails, on the one hand, on the part of the individual, greater motivation to acquire the competencies highly appreciated in the dominant culture and, on the other hand, on the part of society, a greater opening of avenues for the acquisition of the corresponding competencies. In the case of involuntary minorities, the degree of integration is often low, with the consequence of both reduced competencies and test performance below the level of competence. In this way, the "Black-White test score gap" (Ryan 2001) in the USA is explained.

As the PISA studies (Box 7.2) show, in Gemany, children or young people with a migration background score significantly worse in their school-related performance (reading literacy, mathematical thinking) than their native peers. The main reason for this is the lack of language proficiency (cf. Baumert et al. 2002), which not only has a direct effect on language-related performance, but also indirectly on task comprehension and access to new knowledge. There is also a clear difference to the native population with regard to the school-leaving qualifications achieved. What is striking, however, is the significant variability within the various migrant groups.

To explain the immense variability, the distinction between "voluntary" and "involuntary" minorities cannot be used here without further ado. In the above sense, these are usually "voluntary" minorities, although voluntariness does not necessarily refer to the individuals themselves, but rather to their parents. In Germany, therefore, the level of education and the social class of the parents' generation should be taken into account to explain the differences (Baumert et al. 2002; Sarrazin 2012).

7.3.6 Poverty

The phenomenon of poverty in the sense of an imposed pattern of the living environment (Chap. 5) can also be regarded as an antecedent for culturally observable cognitive differences. As studies from India, Latin America, and other parts of the world show, malnutrition associated with poverty appears to impair not only physical growth but also the development of cognitive and linguistic skills (cf. Crane and Heaton 2008). The deficits appear to be caused primarily by learning difficulties that arise from social exclusionassociated with poverty. If the deficiency conditions are not eliminated, over the years the *"cumulative deficit syndrome"* can develop (cf. Sinha 1990, p. 83). With appropriate countermeasures, however, the deficits can be reversed. Thus, Korean orphans who, after malnutrition in early childhood, came into more favourable environments through adoption, showed significantly better intelligence and school performance in later years than comparable children who remained in their old environment (Lien et al. 1977).

It would be premature to assume that material poverty alone is the causal factor for the cognitive deficits. The attitudes and behaviour of the mothers seem to play a mediating role. For example, several studies have shown that children from poor backgrounds whose mothers underwent training in child rearing and health behaviour achieved significant improvements in performance after this intervention compared to children of untrained mothers (cf. Sinha 1990, p. 82).

The PISA studies (Klieme et al. 2010) also suggest that the relationship between poverty and cognitive abilities is not deterministic. Although a clear gap between the lowest social class on the one hand and middle and higher social classes on the other is evident in all countries studied, there is considerable cultural variability with regard to the extent of this gap. While in Germany a very close correlation between the social situation of the family and the competence level of the children can be observed, other countries with very different geographical locations and cultural traditions seem to succeed in limiting the negative effects of weak socio-economic conditions. The authors attribute this to more successful support for the children and young people concerned.

7.4 A Model for the Interaction of Culture and Cognition

As a framework model for the classification and evaluation of studies and findings on the development of cognitive abilities as a function of cultural factors, the "principle of triarchic resonance" is presented below (cf. Helfrich 1999).

The principle is called "triarchic" because every observable cognitive performance is regarded as the result of the interaction of three (Greek: tria[2]) components that can be distinguished from each other: the *task*, the *individual* and the *culture*.

The metaphor "resonance" is used to describe the specific type of interaction between the three components. The term is borrowed from acoustics, where it describes the interaction and resulting changes in state due to the vibrations of a stimulating system (the "exciter") and an excited system (the "resonator"). The resonator has a natural tendency to vibrate in certain frequency ranges. These "natural vibrations" can be amplified by the exciter.

---

[2] τρία.

7.4 A Model for the Interaction of Culture and Cognition

The closer the resonator's frequencies to the frequencies of the stimulating system, the greater the amplitude of the excited vibrations. In other words, the resonator has a certain range of "natural frequencies", some of which are amplified by external excitation, while others are not.

Depending on the resonator's natural frequencies and the strength and type of excitation by external forces, the resulting resonance can vary with regard to the frequency range and amplitude of the individual frequencies. Generally speaking, the idea of resonance means that existing tendencies may be strengthened by external stimulation.

Applied metaphorically to human beings, resonance suggests that every individual has a basic biological equipment, the characteristics of which can be strengthened by external forces (see Eccles, 1989). These external forces can be described as the totality of experience the individual has been exposed to. Delineated in a simplified way, the exponents of these experiences are the situational demands, or *tasks*, and the traditional (or historically derived and selected) patterns (i.e., the *culture*).

Although it is mainly the individual who acts as a resonator, resonance is not restricted to unidirectional effects of the task or the culture on the individual. Instead, each of the three components – individual, task, and culture – affects the others, albeit to differing degrees.

Selective amplification unfolds as a temporal process with three implications. First, the effect of a single event weakens over time if the event is not repeated. Subsequent events then overlay the earlier ones. Second, once a certain state has been reached after repeated stimulation, it will affect other regions through internal feedback processes in the sense of selective excitation or inhibition, thus leading to new activity patterns. Third, the impact of an external force depends on the current state of the resonating system and the position on its developmental path. That is, the impacts of situational demands and cultural influence on a human individual vary with his or her developmental phases.

Based on the three components, the time dimension needs to be viewed in terms of three aspects: First, the *microgenetic* aspect of the task, second, the *ontogenetic* aspect of the individual, and, third, the *culture-genetic* aspect of the tradition of a society.

The *microgenetic* aspect refers to the development from the task as an external demand to its completion as a principally observable performance. The "task" here is not to be understood in the narrower sense of a test item, but in the broader sense as a situational demand of cognitive, social and emotional nature, i. e., more generally speaking, as a problem-solving situation. Although the tasks with which an individual is confronted are strongly influenced by the respective culture, in principle the possibility always exists to encounter unkwown new tasks not previously having been acquainted with.

The task, as an external force, stimulates the individual's competence and motivation, and the resulting mental processes may then lead to observable performance. The strength and nature of the stimulation depend on the individual's previous experience with that particular task. Completing a relatively novel task may require full attention. By contrast, when a task is carried out repeatedly, it becomes more familiar, and eventually its completion becomes automated.

Following Rasmussen (1986; see Helfrich, 1999), three hierarchically different levels of competence can be distinguished: skill-based, rule-based, and knowledge-based levels. The *skill-based* level refers to automated actions, and the *knowledge-based* level refers to actions for which no existing solution patterns are available yet. The *strategy-based* level occupies an intermediate position.

Which level is addressed by a task depends on the task type as well as on the individual and cultural previous experience. Thus, the same task can be performed at different levels depending on the individual and cultural prior experience. For example, for tasks that were originally novel and solved at the knowledge-based level, solution patterns can be automatically retrieved with increasing expertise.

The *ontogenetic* aspect refers to the individual's biological development and previous experience through learning. Here, the timing, quality and quantity of prior experience are important, and the strength (i.e. amplitude) and quality (i.e. range) of the resonance depends on the individual's biological developmental stage, with probably the strength of influence being highest in childhood. Depending on the individual developmental stage at which one comes into contact with cultural traditions, the acquisition of associated skills falls into different levels of action. Much of what is learned in childhood is acquired implicitly, i.e. without explicit pedagogical instruction.

The *culture-genetic* aspect refers to the tradition of a society, i.e. the cultural tradition. On the one hand, it can be seen as a result, i.e. as an entity that is already found by the individual. At the same time, however, it also represents a process which is itself subject to development. Due to cultural genesis, the requirement structure of a task may have undergone a culture-specific transformation, as the level of competence stimulated may change. What is a skill-level action for members of one culture may be a rule- or knowledge-level action for another. Modern industrialised societies have, for example, transformed simple arithmetic tasks such as taking a square root into using a calculator to obtain the solution – presumably without being able to understand the solution process themselves.

As a product, cultural tradition modifies individual competencies and actions insofar as individual characteristics are strengthened or weakened depending on

7.4 A Model for the Interaction of Culture and Cognition

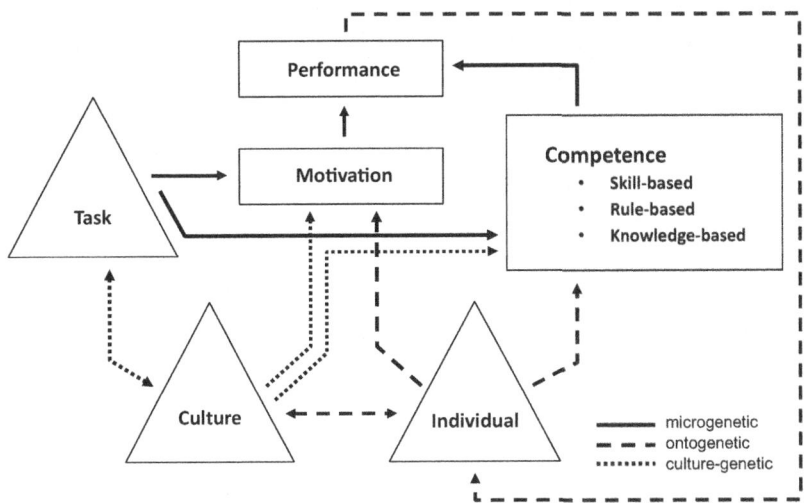

Fig. 7.2 Interaction of task, individual and culture according to the principle of triarchic resonance

their cultural evaluation. Thus, an individual's motivation and interest are influenced in a culturally specific way, because certain achievements are highly valued within a culture, while others receive rather low esteem (cf. Richerson and Boyd, 2005). Parents, teachers and peers play an important role here by paying special attention – positively or negatively – to certain achievements and ways of acting and ignoring others.

Figure 7.2 summarises the reciprocal relationships in terms of the principle of triarchich resonance. The arrows represent the mutual influences between task, individual, and culture. Based on the situational demand structure of the task, a specific achievement or performance can be observed in the individual. The microgenetic process leading to this performance is influenced (indicated by solid arrows) by the respective activated motivation and competence, which in turn are influenced by both ontogenetic (indicated by dashed arrows) and culture-genetic processes (indicated by dotted arrows). The way in which tasks are mastered then has repercussions on the individual and, via the individual, also on culture (indicated by dashed arrows leading from performance to the individual and to culture).

The principle of triarchic resonance also attempts to resolve the tension between "etic" and "emic" approaches (Sect. 2.1). If the interaction between individual, culture and task is to be taken into account in its temporal unfolding, this requires both an external and an internal view, i.e. etic and emic approaches must complement each other. A one-sided etic approach runs the risk of drawing inadmissible conclusions from differences in observed performance with regard to culture-related differences in competence, since it disregards the culture-specific genesis and meaning of a task, that can only be explicated by including the emic perspective. However, even an exclusively emic perspective does not take all processes involved into account. Thus, the self-interpretation of behaviour must be corrected by an external view, as it is in danger of overemphasising normatively desirable behaviour and ignoring undesirable behaviour.

The triarchic resonance principle bears strong similarities to two other models: to Sternberg's "triarchic" view of intelligence (Sternberg 1985, 2012) and to Vygotsky's theory of the "sociohistorical formation of higher mental processes" (Vygotsky 1978, 1981).

Sternberg (1985, 2012) has proposed a "triarchic" view of intelligence. The term "triarchic" which he uses in a different way than here, points to three constituents of intelligence: components, contexts, and experience. The components of intelligence are universal, although their contexts, i. e. the environments of life that are significant to the individual, differ across cultures. Since general intelligence is defined as adaptation to contexts, this leads to different weighting regarding the involvement of basic components in general intelligence. Although the nature of experience varies across cultures, its role is universal: The criterion of novelty and automation applies to all cultures. The basic ideas of Sternberg's model are consistent with the principle of triarchic resonance. The difference between the two models is primarily that Sternberg's model is a taxonomy, whereas the triarchic resonance principle, moreover, attempts to account for the interrelationships of effects between individual, culture, and task.

Important constituents of the principle of triarchic resonance can already be found in Vygotsky's theory of the "sociohistorical formation of higher mental processes" (Vygotsky 1978, 1981). Vygotsky also specifies different levels of developmental processes. An extension to Vygotsky is the metaphor of resonance to characterise the interplay between individual, culture, and task. In a way, this metaphor specifies Vygotsky's "zone of proximal development": It illustrates that there must be a certain "fit" between the individual, task, and culture in order to allow external stimulation to lead to a higher level of development, and at the same time makes clear that stimulation is not a unidirectional process.

7.5 Conclusion

In cross-cultural research on cognition, the question is asked, on the one hand, whether there are cultural differences in cognitive abilities and, on the other hand, whether there are certain cultural factors that can be held responsible as influencing factors (antecedents) for different manifestations of cognitive abilities. Empirical studies are often based on one of two premises, which can be simplistically characterised as the deficit model and the difference model. The deficit model mainly follows the etic approach, the difference model mainly the emic approach.

The findings reported and the related considerations should have shown that it is almost impossible to investigate cultural differences in general intelligence, since the necessary conceptual equivalence and measurement equivalence as prerequisites for comparison can hardly be established. They should also have shown that it is not easy to identify biological "basic components" of thinking, since even these – as, for example, the research on the connection between language and memory and the generation comparisons have demonstrated – may already be superimposed in a culturally specific way.

In order to take into account cultural overlap, the static view of influencing variables and their effects must be supplemented by a dynamic view. A framework model for such an approach is the "principle of triarchic resonance". It emphasises the temporal dynamics in the development of individual cognitive performance. The dynamics unfold on three temporal levels: on the microgenetic level of a concrete performance requirement, on the ontogenetic level of individual development over the life span, and on the historical level of cultural change.

7.6 Questions of Understanding

1. Describe approaches to the study of *general intelligence* in cultural comparison. List the weaknesses of these approaches.
2. Explain the objectives and procedures of the *PISA* and *TIMSS* studies.
3. Define the terms *"analytical thinking"* and *"holistic thinking"*.

Further Reading

Berry, J. W., Poortinga, Y. H., Breugelmans, S. M., Chasiotis, A., Sam, D. M., & Seger, M. (2011). *Cross-cultural psychology* (3rd ed.). Cambridge: Cambridge University Press.

Diamond, J. (2004). The wealth of nations. *Nature*, 10, June 2004.

Flynn, J. R. (2007). *What is intelligence? Beyond the Flynn-Effect*. Cambridge: Cambridge University Press.

Matsumoto, D., & Juang, L. (2008). *Culture and psychology* (4th ed.). Thomson Wadsworth (Chapter 5).

Miyamoto, Y., & Wilken, B. (2013). Cultural differences and their mechanisms. In D. Reisberg & D. Reisberg (Eds.),*The Oxford handbook of cognitive psychology* (pp. 970–985). New York: Oxford University Press.

Trahan, L. H., Stuebing, K. K., Fletcher, J. M., & Hiscock, M. (2014). The Flynn effect: A meta-analysis. *Psychological Bulletin*, 140 (5), 1332–1360.

Emotion

8

Some emotional expressions seem to be universal – for example, fear of snakes is found everywhere. On the other hand, everyday observations suggest that there is considerable variation in the extent and nature of expressions of emotion. Think of the earthquake in Japan in March 2011, when Western observers marveled at the composure of the Japanese. Can we conclude that the Japanese are less emotional compared to Westerners, or are they just more in control of their emotions? So we can ask whether people from different cultures experience and express feelings in a similar way, or whether feelings are experienced or at least expressed differently, depending on cultural affiliation. Answering this question has practical consequences for intercultural encounters in both business and everyday life. There, for example, it is often important to know how to interpret an emotional expression of a communication partner and whether one should show or rather suppress one's own feelings.

8.1 Feeling and Emotion

In psychology, a distinction is made between feeling as a temporary condition ("state") on the one hand and emotionality as a permanent behavioural disposition or personality characteristic ("trait") on the other hand. In cross-cultural comparison, the emphasis is on the study of feelings as states.

Feeling as a state is usually subsumed under *"emotion"* in psychology (Box 8.1). This is a more or less involuntary reaction to an internal or external stimulus state. The reaction is reflected in changes at three levels: at the level of experience and thought ("feeling"), at the level of physiological states (e.g., increase in blood pressure or sweating), and at the level of behaviour (e.g., facial expression or crying). Emotions can be qualitatively very diverse, they can include pleasure or displeasure, and they can vary in intensity.

> **Box 8.1: Emotions**
> *Emotions* are (involuntary) reactions to an internal or external stimulus state.
> They can be differentiated according to *quality* and *intensity* and can be expressed in experience ("feeling"), in physiological changes (e.g. sweating), and in behaviour (e.g. crying).

8.2 Categorisation of Emotions

Based on Darwin's theory of evolution, it is often assumed that there are basic emotions that are rooted in phylogenetic development and therefore occur universally. Such basic emotions are considered to be joy, sadness, anger, fear, disgust and surprise (Ekman 1993). One can now ask whether the content-related meaning of these basic emotions is similar across cultures, i.e., whether there is conceptual equivalence (Chap. 2). One way of checking this is to form an overall structure of terms out of a large set of individual emotion concepts and synonyms in a culture for the sake of finding out similarities to other cultures. The technique used here resembles the so-called *semantic differential* developed by Osgood et al. (1957) where different words have to be assessed in terms of bipolar pairs of adjectives (e.g. beautiful – ugly, good – bad). In fact, it has been found in such studies that the responses of people from quite different cultures can be arranged on two dimensions which are represented by comparable terms or paraphrases. One dimension, *valence*, refers to the evaluation of the feeling (pleasant versus unpleasant or positive versus negative). The other dimension, *intensity*, refers to the degree of arousal (low versus high). For example, sadness can be characterised in this scheme as negatively valued and associated with low arousal (Fig. 8.1).

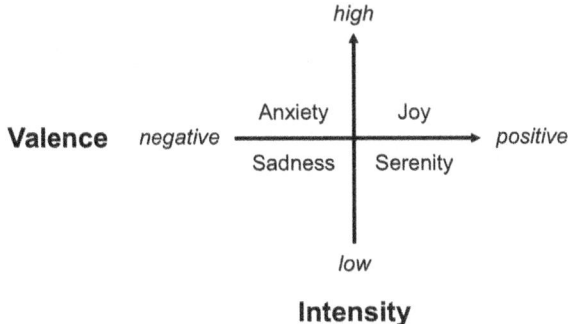

Fig. 8.1 Valence and intensity as universal emotion dimensions (with examples). (Modified after Myers 2004, p. 504)

8.3 Emergence and Expression of Emotions

8.3.1 Emotion Theories

There are many theories about the origin of emotions. These can be roughly divided into biological and cognitive theories. In cross-cultural psychology, the majority of theories assume a universal biological basis, which is, however, superimposed by a culturally specific cognitive component.

Exponents of biological theories are the so-called James- Lange theory (1894; cf. Myers 2004, p. 500f.) and the theory of Cannon (1927; cf. Myers 2004, p. 500f.). According to the former, emotions are consequences of bodily reactions that occur reflexively in certain situations. For example, one does not cry because one is sad, but one is sad because one cries. According to Cannon, on the other hand, it is certain stimuli that trigger both a physical and an emotional reaction at the same time.

The exponent of cognitive theories is the two-factor theory developed by Schachter and Singer (1962), according to which emotions are the result of the interaction of physical reactions to certain stimulus situations and their subsequent cognitive evaluation. It is assumed that the cognitive evaluation depends to a large extent on the social environment.

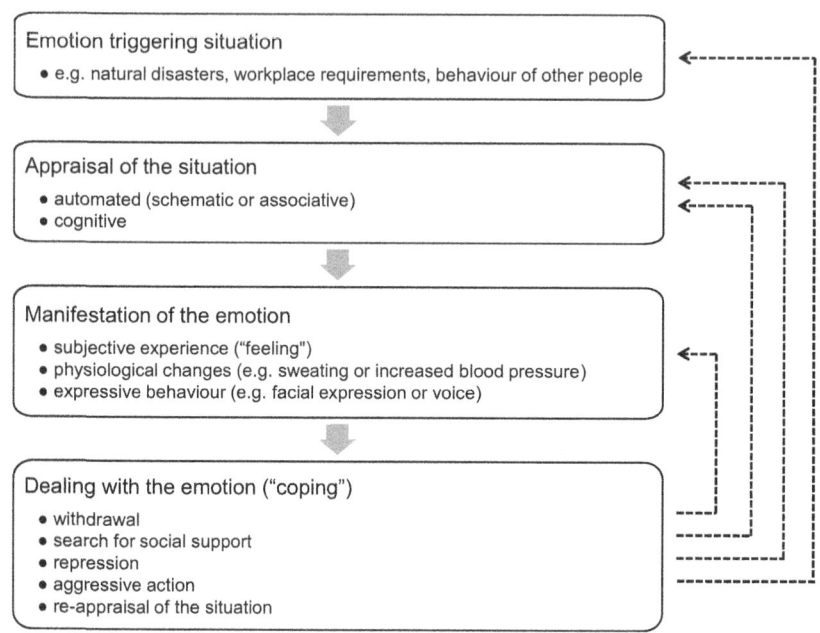

Fig. 8.2 Process model of emotion development and coping

8.3.2 Process Model of Emotion

In order to systematically classify the empirical findings of cross-cultural studies, a process model as proposed by Scherer (2009) is useful. Figure 8.2 shows a modified version. The model describes the process from the triggering of an emotion to its action-effective consequences.

The starting point is an emotion-triggering stimulus or situation. This can be external environmental circumstances, such as requirements at the workplace, as well as internal states, such as ideas or thoughts.

So that an objectively definable stimulus can be able to trigger an emotional process at all, it has to be perceived by the person, even if it cannot yet be interpreted in the form of a specific emotion. Then the emotion-triggering stimulus undergoes an evaluation ("appraisal"), which can take place consciously on the cognitive level as well as automatically or unconsciously on the level of schemata or associations. The appraisal is followed by the manifestation of the emotion. It can express itself in subjective experience ("feeling"), in physiological changes (e.g. sweating or increased blood pressure) and in expressive behaviour (e.g. facial expression or voice). The final step is dealing with the emotion in terms of action, often referred to as "coping" (Lazarus and Folkman 1984). The coping mechanisms used can, for example, consist of repression, withdrawal, acts of aggression or re-appraisal of the situation.

The chronological sequence of the single phases is not strictly fixed, but must rather be understood, following the stress model of Lazarus and Folkman (1984), as a complex regulatory process. For example, perception and appraisal influence each other, and the way in which emotions are coped with in turn has repercussions on perception and appraisal and often even on the triggering stimuli. The reciprocal influence must be seen in the short term in relation to the current process and in the long term in relation to subsequent emotional processes.

It is assumed that the basic structure of the model is universal, but that the way in which the single components are expressed varies along with culture. In particular, the long-term interactions between the individual components are likely to be strongly culturally shaped.

8.3.3 Situations that Trigger Emotions

Cross-cultural studies on situations that trigger emotions are usually based on interviews. In an examplary study, subjects from Korea, Samoa, and the United States were asked to describe events that triggered joy, sadness, anger, fear, surprise, and disgust in them. A selection of the stories collected was presented to other subjects from the three countries with the task of indicating which of the six emotions would occur together with each story. Surprisingly, high levels of agreement were found here both within and between cultures (cf. Berry et al. 2011, p. 169).

It can be concluded from the research that there are prototypical events that are perceived across cultures as triggering a certain emotion. However, it is not possible to conclude from this the frequency and importance of such events in everyday life. It is also impossible to derive which circumstances are suitable as triggers at all. To give an example, one can easily imagine that danger signals in cultures with high uncertainty avoidance (Chap. 5) are perceived more readily than in cultures with low uncertainty avoidance. Regarding the type of triggering situations, differences between individualist and collectivist cultures (Chap. 5) are to be expected. Thus, externally caused disruptions in the planned workflow often evoke anger in individualist cultures, whereas they tend to be ignored in collectivist cultures (Strohschneider 2001, p. 51).

In this context, Markus and Kitayama (1991) distinguish between "self-related" and "other-related" emotions (Box 8.2). The former occur in situations concerning a person's personal needs and abilities, the latter in situations concerning the social surroundings. Even in similar situations, self-related emotions are more likely to be elicited in individualist oriented individuals, while collectivist oriented people tend to repond with other-related emotions. For example, a particularly good work performance may trigger pride in an individualist oriented person, whereas it presumably rather evokes embarrassment in a collectivist oriented person, as such a person is uncomfortable with standing out through performance from the group of colleagues.

> **Box 8.2: Self-Related and Other-Related Emotions**
> Markus and Kitayama (1991) distinguish between self-related ("independent") and other-related ("interdependent") emotions.
> *Self-related* emotions concern a person's personal needs and abilities; *other-related* emotions are directed at the social environment.
> The former are more prevalent in individualist cultures and the latter more prevalent in collectivist cultures.

8.3.4 Appraisal of Emotion Triggering Situations

According to the process model of emotion, emotion triggering situations undergo an *evaluation* ("appraisal") which happens more or less consciously. Cognitive appraisal processes in particular have been studied in cross-cultural comparisons. In such studies, subjects are usually asked to think of past events that have triggered a particular emotion and to evaluate those events on different dimensions (e.g., pleasant versus unpleasant, expected versus unexpected, and fair versus unfair). In a study with subjects from 37 different countries (Scherer 1997), it was found that the rating profiles showed a surprisingly high degree of agreement across countries. The highest agreement was found for events that elicited joy, the lowest for events that elicited disgust.

It is typical for studies using interviews or questionnaires that only conscious cognitive evaluations can be recorded, which may in addition be distorted by a *response bias* such as social desirability. As the emotion researcher LeDoux (1996, 2000) has shown, however, most appraisal processes take place as associative reactions below the level of consciousness and are therefore difficult to access by self-reflection. One way of recording such reactions is offered by the so-called

Implicit Association Test (IAT) (Greenwald et al. 1998). The type and extent of automated associations are recorded with the help of choice reactions that have to be very quickly executed and thus can hardly be influenced voluntarily. Essentially, it is tested whether an object or certain groups of people evoke rather pleasant or rather unpleasant associations in comparison to other objects or groups of people. For example, self and other evaluations of hostile ethnic groups, e.g., American students with a Korean background.and those with a Japanese background, were compared (Greenwald et al. 1998). As expected, the results showed a positive evaluation of one's own descent group and a negative evaluation of the foreign descent group. More recently, attempts have also been made to use neurophysiological measures to capture unconscious or preconscious evaluations, e.g. as activity changes in the amygdala[1] (cf. Ames and Fiske 2010). However, cross-cultural studies on this are still pending.

8.3.5 Manifestation of Emotions

Of the various forms of manifestation of emotion, expressive behaviour has been studied the most. Sometimes quasi-experimental arrangements have been used. In such studies, individuals of different cultural affiliations are experimentally placed in situations that can be expected to elicit a particular emotion. Such a situation may be, for example, a movie with cruel content, whereby it is assumed that the movie will evoke fear. One then looks at whether and under what conditions the fear is visibly expressed to the outside. A relevant investigation is given in Box 8.3.

> **Box 8.3: From Research: Study by Ekman and Friesen (1971)**
> Ekman and Friesen conducted a study on culturally specific manifestations of emotions.
>
> **Study**
> In this quasi-experimental design, American and Japanese subjects were shown a horror movie. In addition, the social situation was varied: Each

(continued)

---

[1] The amygdala (almond nucleus) is a part of the limbic system and is responsible for the fast and automatic processing of emotions.

Box 8.3 (continued)
subject viewed the movie either alone (i.e., unobserved) or with other subjects (i.e., observed). The facial expression of the subjects served as the dependent variable.

Results
The Americans always showed a facial expression that indicated their fear regardless of the social situation. In contrast, the Japanese showed the fear-indicating facial expression only when they were unobserved. When they were with other people, their faces did not show fear, the majority of them displayed a smile.

Ekman and Friesen (cf. Ekman 1984) conclude from their study that – as already assumed by Darwin (1872) – there are universal "deep structures" in the expression of emotions, which are, however, superimposed by culturally shaped patterns, so-called display rules (Box 8.4). In Western cultures, for example, it is considered appropriate to show negative emotions such as fear, sadness or anger openly, whereas in East Asia restraint is expected (cf. Sims et al. 2017).

Box 8.4: Display Rules
"Display rules" (presentation rules) are culturally shaped patterns that determine in which situations and in which way emotions may or even must be expressed, and in which situations they should rather be suppressed or even masked (e.g. by smiling).

The cultural rules of presentation can affect all emotions that occur. Using the example of shame, it is assumed that its expression in Western cultures is associated with loss of control and is therefore suppressed, whereas in Eastern cultures it serves as a means of conflict resolution and may therefore be shown openly.

Since in early infancy the expression of basic emotions still shows universally great similarities and can even be observed in children born deaf-blind in a similar way as in physically healthy children (Grammer and Eibl-Eibesfeldt 1993), it can be concluded that the cultural display rules are gradually acquired in the course of ontogenetic development.

8.3.6 Coping with Emotions

There are hardly any systematic cross-cultural studies on how people deal with their own emotions in terms of action, often referred to as "coping". This is not least due to the fact that actions in response to emotions can hardly ever be clearly distinguished from the manifestations of the emotion. For example, the verbal expression of anger or an apology as an expression of shame can already be interpreted as an action. Differences between individualist and collectivist cultures can be expected in that individualist cultures tend to favor actions that involve behavioural impacts on the environment such as aggressively toned acts, whereas collectivist cultures tend to prefer actions that maintain social harmony, such as those of seeking social support (Kim et al. 2008). A particular form of coping with negative emotions involves re-evaluation ("cognitive reappraisal"), which casts the emotion-triggering situation in a more favorable light. In a quasi-experimental design, it was shown that Chinese subjects used this strategy significantly more often than American subjects (Qu and Telzer 2017).

8.4 Recognition of Emotions

Just as one wonders whether emotions arise and are expressed in similar ways universally, one can also wonder if emotions can be recognised equally well across cultures. In the tradition of Darwin (1859, 1872) it is assumed that both the expression and recognition of emotions follow a biological schedule and are therefore universal. A weakening of this assumption states that perceived emotional responses can be appraised according to the dimensions of valence and intensity of arousal listed above, but that attribution to a particular emotion varies culturally. The most widely accepted position is probably the "interactionist" position (Elfenbein and Ambady 2002). According to this, emotions have a universal biological basis, but both their expression and their recognition are shaped by culture-specific learning processes. Accordingly, members of another culture often find it difficult to adequately assess the emotions of the other person in everyday situations – whether because they interpret the situational context differently or because they cannot adequately recognise masking.

The recognition of emotions, however, becomes much easier when it is not a matter of spontaneous expression, but rather of the intentional display of emotions. Research on this question also goes back to Darwin, who presented photographs of mimed emotions to members of highly different cultures with the request to name

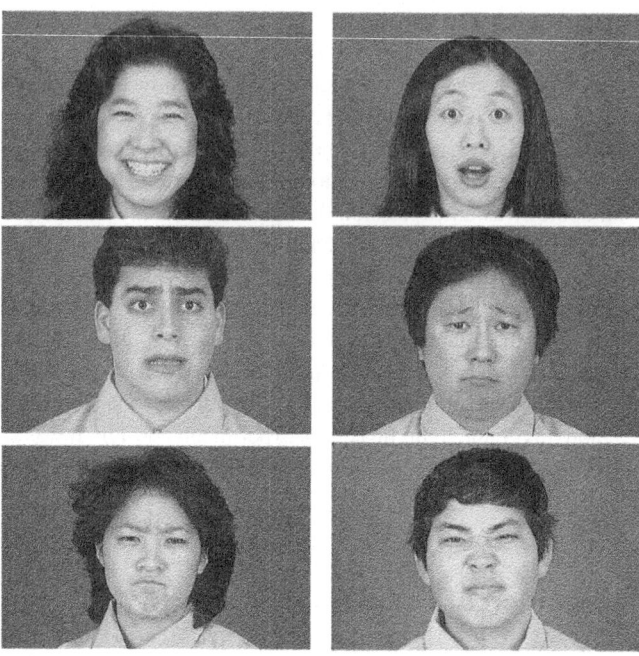

Fig. 8.3 Examples of representations of the six basic emotions: (1) joy, (2) surprise, (3) fear, (4) sadness, (5) anger, (6) disgust. (Source: cf. Myers 2004, p. 515)

the emotion depicted. Numerous studies make use of this technique, employing not only photographs but also voice samples and video recordings. Usually the material presented consists of acting performances of the six basic emotions (joy, surprise, fear, sadness, anger, and disgust). An example of photographic stimulus material is given in Fig. 8.3, where the task for the subjects is to assign each of the photos to one of the given response alternatives (names of the six basic emotions). The accuracy of the assignment serves as the dependent variable.

In a meta-analysis (Box 2.8, Sect. 2.5) of such studies, Elfenbein and Ambady (2002) concluded that in almost all studies the obtained accuracy of attribution is significantly above chance. This is even independent of whether the performers belonged to the same culture or to a foreign culture. Joy was generally best identified, fear and disgust worst. Although the studies presented here prove that emotions can be recognised universally, their transferability to everyday life, the so-called ecological validity, must nevertheless be viewed critically. On the one hand, we are dealing with acted emotions produced for communication purposes, whereas in everyday life one must assume that felt emotions are not always intended to be shown to other people and are therefore more difficult to recognise. On the other hand, the accuracy achieved in choice reactions between fixed response alternatives cannot be transferred to everyday situations, simply because in everyday situations there are no clues for possible assignments.

8.5 Conclusion

In this chapter, emotions have been considered both in terms of their universal biological basis and in terms of their culture-specific superimpositions. From comparative cultural studies it can be stated that, on the one hand, there is obviously agreement on the nature of the basic emotions, but that, on the other hand, there are considerable differences between cultures as to which emotions are evoked in which situations and to what extent the respective emotions may or even must be expressed. In this context, one speaks of culture-specific "display rules". These rules control the appropriate expression of emotions according to the social background.

If emotions are portrayed intentionally, they can even be recognised by people who come from a culture different from that of the performers. Joy was recognised best, fear and disgust worst. However, doubts are raised as to the transferability of the findings to everyday life, since the recognition consisted of choice reactions between fixed response alternatives, whereas in everyday life one has no clues for possible assignments.

8.6 Questions of Understanding

1. Describe a study on culture onculture-specific *manifestation of emotions*. Draw conclusions from the results.
2. Explain what is meant by *"display rules"*. Give an example.
3. Describe the procedure of studies on the *recognition of emotions*. Draw conclusions from such studies.

Further Reading

Elfenbein, H. A., Beaupre, M., Levesque, M., & Hess, U. (2007). Toward a dialect theory: Cultural differences in the expression and recognition of posed facial expressions. *Emotion, 7*, 131–146.

Matsumoto, D., & Juang, L. (2008). *Culture and psychology* (4th ed.). Belmont (CA): Thomson Wadsworth (Chapter 8).

Scherer, K. R., Clark-Polner, E., & Mortillaro, M. (2011). In the eye of the beholder? Universality and cultural specificity in the expression and perception of emotion. *International Journal of Psychology, 46*, 401–435.

Wylie, M. S., Colasante, T., De France, K., Lin, L., & Hollenstein, T. (2023). Momentary emotion regulation strategy use and success: Testing the influences of emotion intensity and habitual strategy use. Emotion, *23* (2), 375–386.

Yan, X., Andrews, T. J., & Young, A. W. (2016). Cultural similarities and differences in perceiving and recognizing facial expressions of basic emotions. *Journal of Experimental Psychology: Human Perception and Performance, 42*, 423–440.

Language and Communication

Cultures differ in many ways. One of the most obvious differences is certainly the language predominantly used by the members of a culture. As compared to one's own language, a foreign language is characterised by other sounds and other combinations of sounds, other words are used, and the concatenation of words to form utterances seems to follow different organisational rules. At the same time, however, it cannot be overlooked that in every culture individuals can communicate with each other and that no culture can do without the use of language. Thus, it must be asked whether, despite the manifest diversity, similar principles of linguistic communication can be discovered in all cultures, or whether the respective culture creates conditions that modify the use of language or even the structure of thought in a decisive way.

9.1 Language as a Means of Exchanging Information

It is certainly indisputable that humans – like other living beings – are in constant exchange with their physical and social environment. During this exchange, information is received, processed and converted into actions that serve to satisfy one's own needs and achieve one's own goals. A large part of the information absorbed by humans comes from their fellow human beings. In this process, each person can take on the role of both sender and receiver, i.e. an exchange of information takes place. This exchange is called "communication".

The human exchange of information usually takes place with the help of an encryption system, a so-called code. The *code* consists of symbols that have a certain meaning and that can be combined with each other to set up a certain system.

The most important symbol system is language. However, not all information transmitted is encrypted. Consider, for example, an interlocutor who blushes while talking. This probably conveys to the listener the information that the interlocutor is excited. Thus, one distinguishes the "linguistic" or "verbal" communication from the "non-linguistic" or "non-verbal" communication. The latter is sometimes popularly referred to as "body language". In natural communication situations, linguistic communication is usually already interspersed with non-verbal elements. For example, the voice has a certain pitch and tone, and the flow of speech is interrupted by pauses or even periods of silence. Such non-verbal aspects of verbal communication are discussed in the following insofar as they directly affect speech, i.e. insofar as they are conveyed by vocal features in the broadest sense.

9.2 Language as a Species-Specific and Culture-Specific Characteristic

The ability to speak can be regarded as a species-specific characteristic of humans. Although animals also use a code when communicating with each other, their codes differ from human language. Non-human codes are based on one of three patterns or a mixture of them (cf. Pinker 1994): They consist either of a limited repertoire of calls with a fixed meaning (decoy call, warning call, territorial defense call, etc.), or of a signal that can be varied in a continuous-analogous manner (e.g., the vivacity of the bee's dance indicates the abundance of the food source the bee is reporting), or of variations on one and the same theme (e.g., the song of a bird that is modified somehow with each repetition). Compared to animal language, human language is distinguished primarily by the fact that the relationship between the phonetic form and the meaning is conventionally defined. A phonetic form is therefore not a self-explanatory ("iconic") image of the meaning. The single elements of language are combined according to conventionally determined rules at different hierarchical levels (phonological, morphological, lexical, syntactic and semantic). Through this system of structuring, an infinite number of meanings can be formed compositionally by rearranging the single elements.

The uniqueness of human language, however, does not exclude evolutionary continuities (Chap. 3) between animal and human communication. It can be assumed that these manifest themselves primarily in the non-verbal features – for example, in the voice or in body movements.

While the capacity for language is to be seen as a species-specific characteristic, the concrete language a person speaks is to a large extent *culture-specific*. Since culture is transmitted to a large extent through symbols, language is a "vehicle of

9.2 Language as a Species-Specific and Culture-Specific Characteristic

culture" (Hofstede 1986, p. 314, Hofstede 2001, p. 5). In a sense, language itself is even part of culture, having emerged simultaneously with cultural tradition (cf. von Humboldt 1988, pp. 416–419). Similar to other cultural patterns, the respective language has to be acquired by the individual in the course of his or her ontogenesis (Box 3.1), while the language in turn already exists as a given framework before the birth of the individual.

In every society, therefore, specific rules of language use must be acquired by the individual. A distinction can be made here between linguistic rules in the narrower sense, which depend to a large extent on the respective individual language, and rules of language use or social "norms of communication" (Herrmann and Grabowski 1994, p. 445), which are predetermined to a much lesser extent by the respective language. The linguistic rules in the narrower sense include above all the *phonological* rules of sound formation, the *morphological* rules of word formation, the *syntactic* rules of sentence construction and the *semantic* rules of word and sentence meaning.

The rules of language use or social norms of communication are referred to in linguistics as *"pragmatic"* rules (Wierzbicka 1991). They refer to the fact that an utterance can only be adequately understood if the cultural, social and situational context as well as the individual knowledge base of the interlocutors involved are taken into account. These rules may vary from culture to culture; for example, in some cultures age, gender and hierarchical differences between interlocutors must be taken into account to a greater extent than in others. The degree to which social communication norms are binding can also vary, i.e. cultures differ in the extent to which the rules may be violated without social sanctions being imposed.

In spite of being bound by rules, language allows its users a wide scope of freedom. On the one hand, an infinite number of different utterances can be formed by observing the rules. On the other hand, a certain utterance content can be expressed using different rules. For example, different sentence constructions can be used to characterise one and the same fact. This also applies to social norms of communication: The same social norm is redeemable by different linguistic rules; for example, an utterance perceived as "polite" can be realised by quite different words and sentences. Language is also creative in that it can be used to represent previously unknown facts or concepts as soon as they become important to its users. In terms of the history of language, this can be seen, for example, in shifts in meaning (e.g. "surfing"), in the creation of new words (e.g. "lying press", " shoot-'em-up ", "google" or "twitter") and in the adoption of words from other languages (e.g. "Waldsterben").

From a psychological point of view, when considering linguistic communication across cultures, one would like to regard the linguistic rules in the narrower sense as confounding variables whose influence should be abstracted from, if possible, in the cross-cultural view of linguistic communication. Unlike in linguistics, one is not interested in the structure of different languages, but in the culture-specific use of language. For this reason, the social communication norms that are usually only implicitly taken for granted, are of particular interest. They influence not only what information is passed on, but also which information from the physical and social environment is paid particular attention to and which tends to be ignored.

9.3 Comparability of Verbal Utterances

In order for verbal utterances in different cultures to be examined for similarities or differences at all, they must be fundamentally comparable and thus exhibit certain equivalences in the cultures being compared (Chap. 2).

Material equivalence occurs when the features are physically or linguistically similar. In the material analysis of verbal communication one can distinguish between linguistic and paralinguistic features. Table 9.1 gives an overview of the features relevant for cultural comparison.

Linguistic features include both global aspects ("macro-level") such as the choice of language (e.g. mother tongue or lingua franca) as well as specific aspects ("micro-level") such as word choice and syntax. *Paralinguistic* features are phonetic features which have no immediate function according to the rules of language (Graumann 1972, p. 1216), but which always accompany speaking. These are, on the one hand, features of the voice such as pitch, tone of voice, pitch modulation and volume, and, on the other hand, features of the manner of speaking such as periods of silence, pauses and embarrassment sounds (e.g. "uh"), often referred to as "hesitation phenomena", and disturbances of the flow of speech (e.g. stuttering). They are often physically measurable and can therefore be considered *materially equivalent* across different cultures. In addition to voice and manner of speaking, which always refer to the person speaking, paralinguistic features also include features of reciprocal conversation control. Here, above all, the opening and ending of conversations, interruptions as well as feedback signals such as "hm", "yes" or "so" are to be mentioned.

Functional equivalence exists when the linguistic utterance is used for similar purposes and thus the object of comparison is based on a comparable psychological construct. Examples of such equivalence would be "asking" or "requesting" as well as business negotiations or doctor-patient conversations.

9.3 Comparability of Verbal Utterances

Table 9.1 Linguistic and paralinguistic features of communication

Linguistic features		
	Choice of language	
	Choice of topics	
	Speech style ("register")	
	Argument structure	
	Choice of words "wording")	
	Syntax	
Paralinguistic features		
	Voice	
		Pitch, Pitch modulation
		Voice sound, Tone
		Volume
	Manner of speaking	
		Speech rate, Periods of silence
		Pauses, Embarrassment sounds (e. g. "uh")
		Stuttering
	Conversation control	
		Conversation opening end ending, Turn taking (speaker change)
		Interruptions, Feedback signals

Functional and material equivalence do not have to correspond under any circumstances. Thus, physically identical features can be used for different purposes. For example, silence can mean both politeness and disinterest, depending on the situational or cultural context. This would give material equivalence, but not functional equivalence. Conversely, the same purpose can be achieved by different features. For example, the materially different utterances "Please turn down the music" and "Your music is much too loud" can both be understood as requests.

9.4 Linguistic Universals

It seems undisputed that all societies known to us have a fully developed spoken language (cf. Cavalli-Sforza 2000). There are no "primitive" languages that can be qualitatively distinguished from "high-level" languages. The basic translatability of utterances from one language into another also speaks in favour of equivalence. All languages have rules of sound formation, i.e. phonological rules, rules of word formation, i.e. morphological rules, and rules of sentence construction, i.e. syntactic rules. Also, in all languages, modifications of meaning of the utterance can be realised by varying the sentence melody. On the pragmatic level, "speech acts" (Searle 1969) such as negations, requests, invitations and questions can be expressed in all languages. At the same time, this does not imply that the rules of linguistic construction are the same in all languages. For example, in Indo-European languages the plural has to be marked specifically, whereas in Altaic languages there is usually no distinction made between singular and plural. Despite this manifest diversity, attempts have been made to find universal regularities that might be anchored in the biological make-up of humans. Here, the American linguist Noam Chomsky (1998) speaks of a "deep structure", which is common to all languages, and a "surface structure", which is specific to each language. Comparative language development studies can be used to explore this deep structure. No matter how difficult the grammar of a foreign language may seem to a non-native speaker, a child growing up in that language acquires it with relative ease. Although some single language rules appear to be easier and others more difficult to learn, the studies suggest certain invariances in the sequence of language acquisition independent of the specific language that a child learns. Most surprisingly, children make similar errors during speech development regardless of the specific grammar of their native language (cf. Pinker 1994). This is taken by some researchers as evidence for a biologically based deep structure in the sense of a universal grammar (Chomsky 1998, 1999). So-called "creole languages" serve as further evidence for the existence of a universal grammar (Box 9.1). Although they originated independently of each other in distant regions of the world far apart from each other, they share similar structural principles (cf. Bickerton 1999).

> **Box 9.1: Creole Languages**
> A *creole language* is a language developed by children who have grown up speaking what is known as a pidgin language.

(continued)

> **Box 9.1** (continued)
> The parents of these children use the *pidgin language,* which is made up of set pieces, as an auxiliary language to conduct business with speakers of another language. If the children of these parents learn only the – simply structured – pidgin language and no longer the parental mother tongue, they are not content with the language they have acquired, but develop its structure to such an extent that even complex matters can be represented linguistically (cf. Pinker 1994).

In addition to relatively fixed regularities, there are also certain linguistic variations that are universally met. Thus, in all cultures there are differences in the way of speaking, so-called *"registers"* (cf. Gallois and Callan 1997), depending on the relationship of the interlocutors. Even children change their style of speech in terms of speech rate, word choice and syntax depending on whether they are talking to younger children, to peers or to adults. The universality of the so-called *"baby language"*, i.e. the phenomenon that infants or toddlers are addressed in a more easy special language, is not entirely undisputed. At least this baby language is very widespread. Some of its characteristics are even universal: high-pitched voice, distinctive sentence melody, doubling, using of diminutives (= belittling forms) as well as substitution of personal pronouns by names. The function of baby talk seems to be, on the one hand, to signal a special affective attention to the child and, on the other hand, to adapt the utterance to the child's attention and memory span and thus to facilitate the language acquisition process (cf. Kitamura et al. 2002).

9.5 Linguistic and Communicative Relativity

Starting from the specific surface structure, from a psychological point of view it is above all interesting to what extent the individual language given as the mother tongue imposes restrictions on the individual in the realisation of linguistic acts respectively limits his or her options. An important question in this context is to what extent the respective individual language influences the respective thought structures in a culture-specific way. In Chaps. 6 and 7, this question was referred to as the "principle of linguistic relativity" or as the "Sapir-Whorf hypothesis".

One topic that comes into focus beyond linguistic relativity is the question of a "communicative relativity" (cf. Semin and Zwier 1997). Just as Sapir and Whorf posed the question of a perception of the object world predetermined by language, nowadays the question arises with regard to the influence which the respective language specifications have on the shaping of concrete linguistic acts of communication. For example, one can ask whether the fact that the Japanese language has a more differentiated system of forms of politeness than the German language leads to the conclusion that real communication between Japanese conversation partners is more polite than that between Germans. If one wants to answer the question in a cultural comparison, one would have to presuppose an equivalence of the standard of comparison (Sect. 2.2). However, this may at best be possible at the material level – for example, the frequency of the use of different polite verbs – but hardly at the functional level of a scale that measures the characteristic "politeness". The creation of the latter encounters difficulties primarily because in every language there are ritualised forms of speaking, so-called *"language routines"* (cf. Liang 2003, p. 249), which have long since lost their literal meaning. Hardly any Bavarian interprets the greeting "Grüß Gott" as a profession of faith, just as little as a Chinese derives an invitation to eat from the greeting "Have you already eaten?" A comparison on the functional level is nearly always only possible as a relative comparison between different communication situations. Different communication situations can be constituted, for example, by different addressees or different occasions for conversation. A prerequisite for such a relative comparison is that in each language there can be gradations in the politeness of variants of utterances to designate the same factual content, which are unanimously accepted as such by the speakers of the respective languages. The importance of a specific linguistic feature within a culture as compared to other cultures can only be deduced from the situational variation of the different utterance variants.

9.6 Communication Model According to Schulz von Thun

Speaking is not an end in itself. Usually one speaks in order to achieve some other purpose. Just as with other actions, the purpose does not necessarily need to be conscious to the speaking individual. Many different purposes have been identified; they are usually referred to as *"functions"* (cf. von Helversen and Scherer 1988). Examples include marking one's identity, expressing inner states, regulating social actions, and influencing the addressee. Here, language is seen as a tool or "organon" (Bühler 1990) for achieving certain purposes or goals. Bühler assigns in his "organon model" a threefold function to every linguistic sign: First, it is an "expression" for states of the sender, second, an "appeal" to the receiver, and, third a "representation" of objects and facts (Bühler 1990). The communication

9.6 Communication Model According to Schulz von Thun

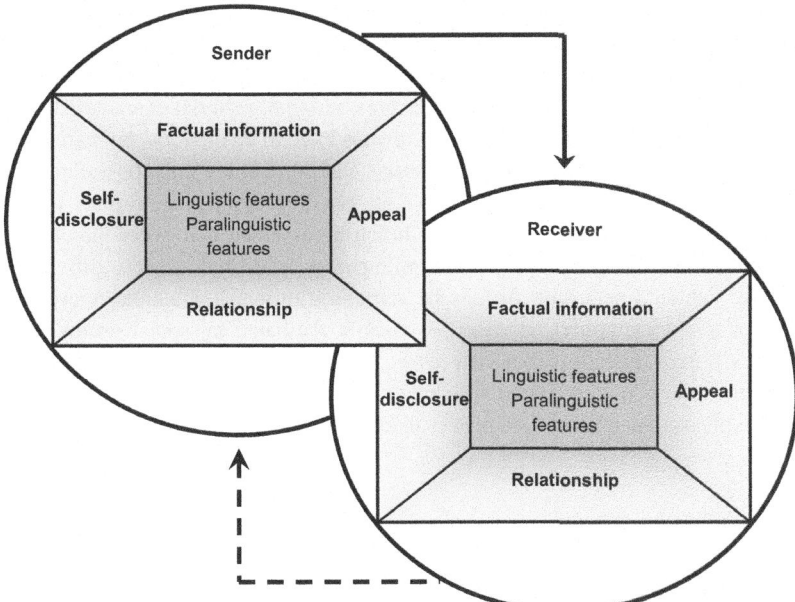

Fig. 9.1 Functional and material aspects of communication. (Modified after Schulz von Thun 1999) Note: The solid arrow refers to processes directed from the sender to the receiver, the dashed arrow to feedback processes directed from the receiver to the sender

model of Schulz von Thun (1999) represents a further development (Fig. 9.1). It builds on the speech act theory (Searle 1969) as well as on Watzlawick's communication theory (cf. Watzlawick et al. 2015), according to which every message has a content and a relationship aspect. The content aspect refers to what *is* being communicated, while the relationship aspect indicates *how* the content is to be understood, whether it is to be taken as praise, criticism, request, or simply an explanation of a fact. Whereas the content aspect ("factual information") largely corresponds to the representation function in Bühler's model, the relation aspect includes, in addition to the expressive function ("self-disclosure") and the appeal function ("appeal"), a relationship aspect in the narrower sense, which defines the mutual bond between the communication partners. Thus, every message contains four sides: The *factual content* indicates what is being talked about, the *self-disclosure* provides information about the speaker's state of mind, the *appeal* indicates what the interlocutor is being prompted to do, and the *relationship* refers to the bond between the interaction partners.

The four sides of the message according to Schulz von Thun are to be understood as functional characteristics and can be expressed by all material characteristics, as shown in Fig. 9.1. The four sides do not always have to be obvious, but can just as well be implicitly included in the message and sometimes only be inferred by recourse to the situational context. Above all, not all four sides are usually present in the same way or to the same extent. It can be assumed that every language in principle offers the possibility of weighting the individual aspects differently. However, which aspect must or may be verbalised in which situation in any case, or is better not explicitly expressed, is mainly regulated by social norms. Such norms exist in every culture, but their respective manifestation can vary greatly from culture to culture. With recourse to Schulz von Thun's model, the cultural variation of the expression can be systematically examined.

9.7 Cultural Factors as Antecedents of Language Use

9.7.1 Individualism-Collectivism and Power Distance

Many studies compare the communication behaviour of members of individualist cultures with that of members of collectivist cultures. Since individualist cultures are usually cultures with a low power distance and collectivist cultures are those with a high power distance (Chap. 5), the studies almost always involve comparisons between horizontal-individualist and vertical-collectivist cultures. The findings suggest that in collectivist cultures, compared to individualist ones, the factual content takes a back seat in favor of a relationship orientation and that the perspective adopted by the speaker is partner-centered rather than self-centered. In collectivist cultures, one's own opinion tends to be withheld, and a more indirect rather than a direct style of speech is preferred. This is expressed in the choice of topics and words, in syntax and in the flow of speech. In addition, since situational and contextual information is given more attention, silence is not considered an embarrassing interruption but a necessary part of communication. In individualist cultures, on the other hand, verbal explanations or reasons for one's own behaviour are given more frequently, since situational and contextual information is perceived to a lesser extent.

Additionally, in collectivist cultures, people are more sensitive to paralinguistic signals, which are generally considered less direct compared to verbal messages.

Kitayama and Ishii (2002) demonstrated this using information where the voice contradicted the content of what was said (Box 9.2).

> **Box 9.2: From Research: Study on Sensitivity to Paralinguistic Signals**
> Kitayama and Ishii (2002) conducted a quasi-experimental study on sensitivity to paralinguistic signals.
>
> **Study**
> The subjects in this study were Japanese, representing a collectivist culture, and English, representing an individualist culture. The task resembled a "Stroop" test i.e., a recognition task in which the printed colour of a word conflicts with the lexical meaning of the printed word. In the given task, the lexical meaning of a word heard conflicted with the voice in which the word was uttered, so, for example, the word "joy" was presented in a sad-sounding voice. After each word, a judgment had to be made either about the word meaning or about the voice sound.
> The hypothesis was that the Japanese subjects would make more errors in judgments about word meaning and the English subjects would make more errors in judgments about voice. That is, the Japanese subjects' judgments of word meaning should be more affected by the competing voice sound, whereas the English subjects' judgments of voice sound should be more irritated by word meaning.
>
> **Results**
> The hypothesis was supported: The Japanese subjects were more irritated by the sound of the voice and the English subjects were more irritated by the word meaning.

From the results, it can be concluded that the attention of the Japanese subjects, representing a collectivist culture, was more focused on the voice, while the English subjects, representing an individualist culture, paid more attention to the word content.

The striving for harmony, which is prevalent in collectivist cultures, was investigated by Li (2001) in simulated doctor-patient dialogues among Chinese (representing a collectivist culture) and Canadians (representing an individualist culture). Dependent variables were speech interruptions on the part of the "doctor". The comparison revealed that interruptions in the Chinese doctor-patient dyads were more likely to be cooperative feedback signals (e.g., nodding in agreement), whereas in the Canadian dyads they were more likely to be conflict-inducing objections (e.g., saying "I can't imagine that"). Thus, the Chinese "doctor" sought harmony rather than conflict with the "patient". Surprisingly, the cultural difference disappeared when the dyads were interculturally composed, i.e., one Chinese and one Canadian each. Here, the conflict-inducing objections always dominated. This might suggest that within collectivist cultures the maintenance of social harmony is only important when members of one's own group are involved.

9.7.2 Masculinity-Femininity

In virtually all cultures, women typically seem to use a different way of speaking than men. Often characterised as "women's language" (Langenmayr 1997), female speech is said to be characterised primarily by those linguistic attributes that reflect the lower status and power of women compared to men (Günthner 1996, p. 448). What these attributes are in detail, is not clear. They may be characteristics that directly express the feeling of inferiority, such as the frequent use of apology and polite phrases (Lin-Huber 1998, p. 125). However, they may also be features that can be interpreted more as compensation for inferiority, such as an upscale choice of words, use of socially prestigious forms (Gordon and Heath 1998; Labov 1972) or a particularly "direct" mode of expression (Keenan 1993).

How and, above all, to what extent the female way of speaking differs from the male way of speaking is likely to depend, on the one hand, of course, on universally demonstrable gender differences (Chap. 11), and, on the other hand, to a large extent on the ideas of masculinity and femininity prevailing in a culture.

As explained in Chap. 5, cultures differ with regard to their ideas about masculinity and femininity. It would be expected that in more masculine cultures the differences between typically feminine and typically masculine ways of speaking would be greater than in more feminine cultures, since in masculine cultures a stronger role differentiation predominates. However, such a hypothesis is difficult to test on the basis of the available studies for two reasons. One reason is that most comparisons have been made either within or between more masculine cultures, so comparisons to more feminine cultures are mostly missing.

But perhaps it is also not a coincidence that precisely those cultures where differences are expected, i.e. the more masculine cultures such as Japan, Austria or Mexico, have been studied, whereas there is a lack of research where differences are hardly expected, i.e. in the more feminine cultures such as the Scandinavian countries. The second reason is that in the cultures studied, the degree of masculinity usually covariates with the degree of power distance, so that the gender differences that do occur are overlaid by the status and power differences.

9.8 Conclusion

The cross-cultural consideration of linguistic communication raises the question to what extent similar principles of language use can be found in all cultures and to what extent specific basic communicative structures on the part of the speaking individuals go hand in hand with the respective culture. The answer to this question is made more difficult by the fact that language itself is part of culture and, like culture, must be acquired by the individual during ontogenesis. Thus, it must first be asked to what extent the respective individual language imposes restrictions on the individual with regard to certain patterns of thought and forms of communication. To investigate these topics, neither a systematic comparison of language systems nor an absolute comparison of language use is sufficient. It is only possible to separate linguistic restrictions and conventions from cultural differences in the narrower sense if, in addition to the cultural and linguistic variation in language behaviour, the intracultural variation of different situations is also taken into account.

Relatively consistent statements can be made about the possible impact of the factor "individualism-collectivism" on language behaviour. Here it can be stated that in collectivist compared to individualist cultures, speech is characterised by a stronger restraint.

With regard to other cultural factors as antecedents of language behaviour, only few clear statements can be derived. This is mainly due to the fact that many studies represent bilateral comparisons at best, whereby it cannot be decided whether the differences shown are only country- resp. language-specific or whether they reflect real cultural differences.

9.9 Questions of Understanding

1. State what circumstances might argue for the existence of a *universal grammar*.
2. Define the terms *"linguistic relativity"* and *"communicative relativity"*.
3. Point out differences in communication behaviour between *individualist* and *collectivist* cultures.

Further Reading

Helfrich, H. (2007). Sprachliche Kommunikation im Kulturvergleich. In G. Trommsdorff, & H.-J. Kornadt (Eds.), *Erleben und Handeln im kulturellen Kontext. Enzyklopädie der Psychologie (C VII 2,* pp. 109–155). Göttingen: Hogrefe.

Kumbier, D., & Schulz von Thun, F. (2009). *Interkulturelle Kommunikation: Methoden, Modelle, Beispiele* (3rd ed.). Reinbek near Hamburg: Rowohlt TB.

Matsumoto, D., & Juang, L. (2008). *Culture and psychology* (4th ed.). Thomson Wadsworth (Chapter 9).

Mejía-Arauz, R., Roberts, A. D., & Rogo, B. (2012). Cultural variation in balance of nonverbal conversation and talk. *International Perspectives in Psychology: Research, Practice, Consultation, 1* (4), 207–220.

Perlman, M., Paul, J., & Lupyan, G. (2022). Vocal communication of magnitude across language, age, and auditory experience. *Journal of Experimental Psychology: General, 151* (4), 885–896.

Personality   10

"Personality" in psychology is viewed from two perspectives. From the first perspective, it is considered to be what distinguishes a particular person from other people and thus constitutes their respective individuality. From the second perspective, one tries to describe the "nature" of the human being common to all people. The first perspective corresponds to that of "differential psychology" (e.g. Eysenck and Eysenck 1985), the second perspective to that of "personality psychology" (Freud 1940; Jung 2011). The two views are not mutually exclusive, but complement each other. The representatives of differential psychology try to establish a common framework within which individual differences can be classified, and the personality theorists refer to individual differentiations of the general composition. The focus of attention in the first case is on the differences, in the second case on the similarities between people. In cultural comparison, both approaches experience a new challenge. Differential psychology wants to examine the extent to which the dimensions of personality – primarily identified in Western cultures – are universally valid and cultural differences can thus be described as differences in the respective parameter values of the individual dimensions. Personality psychology has to ask whether the composition of the person is functionally and structurally universal or whether the essence of the human being cannot be determined at all independently of the cultural environment.

10.1 Culture and Personality from a Psychoanalytical Point of View

In the tradition of the culture and personality school (Sect. 1.5), the relation between culture and personality was to be interpreted psychoanalytically, thus underpinning the universal claim to validity of psychoanalytic theory. However, there are also attempts to question this claim to validity and to prove that Freud's theorising is culture-dependent. An altered interpretation of the Oedipus complex by the cultural anthropologist Malinowski (Sect. 2.1) has become a historical milestone.

From a Japanese perspective, not only the interpretation of the Oedipus complex, but also its universal existence in general has been questioned. The starting point is the need for dependence ("amae"), which is often considered "typical" for Japanese people (*"amae"*, Sect. 2.2) and described in detail by the Japanese psychoanalyst Doi (1981). The "ajase *complex"* is held responsible for the existence of the "amae" and is opposed to the Freudian Oedipus complex (Box 10.1).

> **Box 10.1: Ajase Complex**
> From the Japanese point of view, the Freudian Oedipus complex is contrasted with the so-called Ajase complex. The starting point is the need for emotional dependence (*"amae"*; cf. Doi 1981), which is often considered "typical" for the Japanese, and which has its origin in the Ajase complex.
>
> Like Oedipus, Ajase (an Indian prince from a royal house) is a mythical figure who symbolises hate and love towards the parents. But whereas in the Oedipus complex hate and love are divided between father and mother and find expression in the desire to enter into sexual relations with the mother and to kill the father, in the Ajase complex both hate and love are directed at the mother.
>
> Both complexes are said to have their origin in the longing for the mother, which is assumed to be universal. In Ajase, however, unlike Oedipus, this longing is blocked not by the father but by the mother, who destroys the illusion of oneness. The result is a resentment against the mother, which, however, is resolved through the complicated interplay between feelings of guilt, remorse and mutual forgiveness.
>
> The paternal (i.e. fatherly) principle embodied in the Oedipus complex, according to which the father represents the unchallenged authority, leads to an internalisation of strict moral norms. In contrast, the maternal (i.e. motherly) principle, embodied in the Ajase complex promotes the feeling of reciprocity, in which norms are flexibly adapted to time, place, and atmosphere.

However, the description of the Ajase complex should not be interpreted in the direction of an extreme cultural relativism. On the one hand there are strong points of contact to the archetype theory of C. G. Jung (1875–1961), on the other hand Doi himself points out that without the method of psychoanalysis imported from the West the cultural specificity of the Ajase complex could not have been recognised at all.

10.2 Dimensional Description of Personality

10.2.1 Cross-Cultural Validity of Personality Factor Models

Using the psychometric approach (Sect. 2.3), a large part of the cross-cultural research oriented towards differential psychology attempts to prove that the characteristics required to describe the overall personality are universally, i.e. applicable in all cultures.. Implicit in this is the assumption that there are personality characteristics ("traits"), which persist over time and hence can be regarded as dispositions, i.e. predominant tendencies that control behaviour. Such basic personality traits are hypothetical constructs (Sect. 2.2) and can be represented as dimensions (= factors) on which individual differences are depicted as different expressions.

Factor-analytical procedures (cf. Child 2006), which are applied to the self-description data usually collected in questionnaires, serve to obtain higher-level units. They allow a large number of similar data to be combined into a few bundles ("dimensions" or "factors") (Chap. 5). In the cross-cultural comparison, the factor analyses are used to check whether the same dimensions of personality can be found in all cultures and whether their overall structure shows a similar pattern.

In particular, the so-called five-factor model ("Big Five") by McCrae and Costa (1997, 2008) with the factors "extraversion", "agreeableness", "conscientiousness", "emotional stability" and "openness to experience" has been studied (Box 10.2).

In fact, the structure of the five factors identified in the Western cultural sphere could be reproduced in very many non-Western countries (cf. Poortinga and Van Hemert 2001), i.e. from the questionnaire data of non-Western countries, the same five factors could be derived.

A Western "bias" nevertheless cannot be ruled out. On the one hand, it refers to the selection of the items originally included in the questionnaire, and on the other hand, to the assumption of stable personality traits.

> **Box 10.2: The Five-Factor Model (Big Five) by McCrae and Costa (1997, 2008)**[1]
>
> **I. Extraversion**
>
> - retiring – sociable
> - reserved – outgoing
> - subordinating – self-asserting
>
> **II. Agreeableness**
>
> - unkind – kind
> - uncooperative – cooperative
> - hard-hearted – soft-hearted
>
> **III. Conscientiousness**
>
> - careless – organised
> - irresponsible – responsible
> - hedonistic – dutiful
>
> **IV. Emotional stability** *("neuroticism")*[2]
>
> - worrying – calm
> - impatient – patient
> - tense – relaxed
>
> **V. Openness to experience** *("intellect")*
>
> - narrow interests – broad interests
> - cautious – curious
> - uncreative – creative

---

[1] The names of the five factors and the respective extreme values (low – high) of single facets are listed.

[2] In the case of neuroticism the poles are reversed, e. g. calm (low neuroticism) – worrying (high neuroticism).

With regard to item selection it was argued that a raw selection from an "indigenous" Chinese perspective resulted in a factor that deviated from the five-factor model. It was first referred to as "Chinese tradition", later on as "interpersonal relatedness" (Cheung and Leung 1998; Cheung et al. 2001) and found its way into questionnaires such as "Chinese Personality Assessment Inventory" (CPAI) and "Cross-Cultural (Chinese) Personality Assessment Inventory" (CPAI-2). These questionnaires have also found access to Western cultures (Cheung 2004, 2006; Lin 2003).

A more fundamental critique questions the existence of stable personality traits in general. According to this view, the search for personality traits reflects a typically "individualist" view with the effort to distinguish between individuals. This is contrasted, from a "collectivist" point of view, with the social embeddedness of the individual as a "self" (Markus and Kitayama 1998). Accordingly, personality traits can only serve to a limited extent to predict behaviour in collectivist cultures, since behaviour is determined more by social roles and norms than by internal dispositions.

This intensifies the criticism of the dispositional concept already voiced in Western culture in the context of the *situationism* debate (Mischel and Shoda 1995), according to which the observable behaviour of a person is determined less by personality traits than by the pressure of the situation (cf. Laux 2003, p. 17). It is argued that in collectivist cultures, due to the higher normative pressure, behaviour is even more situation-dependent than in individualist cultures, where a higher consistency across different situations can be observed (cf. Church and Lonner 1998).

The integration of the self into the social context also means that the individual's own identity is less salient or "accessible" and that self-descriptions such as those required in questionnaires cannot be made at all, because they require a reflection on one's own person that is unusual in collectivist cultures (cf. Church 2000). The self-descriptions in questionnaires are thus in danger of reflecting more cultural normative ideas than abstractions with regard to one's own behaviour. In addition to the conceptual equivalence of the trait construct, the measurement equivalence (Sect. 2.2) of the questionnaire method must be called into doubt. It could certainly be increased by tailoring the individual statements in a questionnaire more closely to concrete situations and possibly supplementing them with behavioural observations. Approaches in this direction are provided by the *Twenty Statements Test* (TST; cf. Lam et al. 2014; Matsumoto 1999, p. 293), the *Behavioral differential* (cf. Marsella et al. 2000, p. 57), and the *Ambulatory measurement* (Fahrenberg et al. 2007). Only with the postulate of measurement equivalence being fulfilled, a subsequent analysis is able to clarify whether a more complex factor structure conceptualised as interaction between person and situation is compelling. Alternatively, behavioural consistency against situational flexibility could possibly itself be conceptualised as a personality trait.

10.2.2 Cultural Differences in Single Personality Factors

If one assumes a universally similar factor structure of personality, the question of cultural differences in the expression of the single dimensions arises. Cultural differences are to be expected above all when the description of a personality factor shows similarities to the description of a cultural factor. As can be seen from Table 10.1, there are obvious similarities between the characteristics of the individualism-collectivism factor and the characteristics of four of the five factors of the Big Five model.

Consistent with these conceptual overlaps, collectivist orientation was indeed found empirically to be positively correlated with *agreeableness* and negatively correlated with *openness to experience* and with *extraversion* (cf. Church and Lonner 1998).

However, the reciprocal assignment is not always clear: Thus, pronounced extraversion may manifest itself in sharing the concerns of family members and would thus represent the collectivist pole of the *individualism-collectivism* factor, but at the same time as well in an extreme self-disclosure and would thus be indicative of the individualist pole.

Table 10.1 Comparison of typical characteristics of the individualism-collectivism dimension with the personality factors of the Big Five model

Features of the individualism-collectivism dimension[a]	Big five dimension
Self-assertiveness vs. subordination	Extraversion
Going out vs. reserved	Extraversion
Hedonism[b] vs. emphasis on social obligations	Conscientiousness
Self-centeredness vs. group-centeredness	Agreeableness
Competitive orientation vs. cooperation	Agreeableness
Utilitarianism[c] vs. person orientation	Agreeableness
Independence vs. conformity	Openness to experience

[a]The listing of the characteristics of the individualism-collectivism dimension is based on a summary of the characteristics compiled from various studies in Kagitçibasi (1997)
[b]Lustfulness
[c]Benefit-oriented

Cultural differences in the expression of a factor may also be due to different response tendencies ("response sets"). There is concrete evidence for the existence of two specifically East Asian response tendencies. First, there is a tendency to avoid extreme response categories when using multi-level response options (e.g. of the Likert scale type), i.e. there is a *"tendency towards the middle"*. Second, compared to American subjects, East Asian subjects have a stronger tendency towards *"modesty"*, i.e., they are more likely to portray themselves in a less favourable light. In these cases, a comparison of the mean values of cultures is only possible if the values are "corrected" by adjusting the scale range.Furthermore, the tendency to answer questions in terms of "social desirability" seems to be more pronounced in collectivist than in individualistic societies (Kemmelmeier 2016), since conformity with social norms is of greater importance there.

All in all, the obvious presence of different response tendencies in questionnaires must lead to a rather sceptical interpretation of occurring position differences. It would be absolutely necessary to supplement this with other methods, such as behavioural observations in different situations, in order to achieve a higher validity in the recording of the personality traits in question.

Finally, the question can be asked whether – as assumed in the "culture and personality school" (Sect. 1.5)–something like a *"national character"* exists. Undoubtedly, there are stereotypes about the characteristics of the members of individual countries – for example, the Germans are attributed characteristics such as punctuality and orderliness – but it is by no means certain to what extent the stereotypes correspond to reality (cf. McCrae et al. 2010). The lack of agreement is certainly not least due to the fact that the personality measurements are based on questionnaire data, while the stereotypes are based on generalisations from everyday observations of conspicuous behaviour.

10.3 Conclusion

Various disciplines and research directions have dealt with the comparative study of personality; in addition to cross-cultural psychology and cultural psychology, cultural anthropology and psychoanalysis should be mentioned here. The relationship between culture and personality is judged differently and sometimes controversially. The basic question is to what extent universal psychological structures can be found and to what extent culture-specific constructs may be expected. Representatives of a radically "emic" or "indigenous" view claim that the construct of personality already reflects a typically Western scientific understanding that overvalues interindividual differences, and contrast this construct with a "self" embedded in the social context, where stable personality dispositions recede into the background. Conversely, proponents of a radically "etic" view argue that the factor structures identified in Western cultures to describe personality as well as to characterise individual differences can also be reproduced in non-Western countries.

10.4 Questions of Understanding

1. State the objectives of studying the relationship between *culture and personality*.
2. Give an example of an *indigenous* approach to personality psychology.
3. Explain what is meant by a *"response set"* and what consequences this has for cultural comparison.

Further Reading

Berry, J. W., Poortinga, Y. H., Breugelmans, S. M., Chasiotis, A., Sam, D. M., & Seger, M. (2011). *Cross-cultural psychology* (3rd ed.). Cambridge: Cambridge University Press.

Bock, P. K. (2000). Culture and personality revisited. *American Behavioral Scientist, 44*, 32–41.

Helfrich, H. (2007). Persönlichkeit im Kulturvergleich. In H.-J. Kornadt & G. Trommsdorff (Eds.), *Erleben und Handeln im kulturellen Kontext* (pp. 377–433). Enzyklopädie der Psychologie. Göttingen: Hogrefe.

Neyer, F. J., & Asendorpf, J. B. (2018). *Psychologie der Persönlichkeit*. Berlin: Springer.

Matsumoto, D., & Juang, L. (2008). *Culture and psychology* (4th ed.). Thomson Wadsworth (Chapter 10).

Trommsdorff, G. & Mayer, B. (2004). Kulturvergleichende Ansätze (Cross-Cultural Approaches). In H. Weber & T. Rammseyer (Eds.), *Handbuch der Persönlichkeitspsychologie und Differentiellen Psychologie*. Göttingen: Hogrefe.

Yamagata, S., Suzuki, A., Ando, J., Ono, Y., Kijima, N., Yoshimura, K., Ostendorf, F., Angleitner, A., Riemann, R., Spinath, F. M., Livesley, W. J., & Lang, K. L. (2006). Is the genetic structure of human personality universal? A cross-cultural twin study from North America, Europe, and Asia. *Journal of Personality and Social Psychology, 90* (6), 987–998.

Sex and Gender

Within differential psychology, it has been found that men are, on average, more aggressive, less anxious, more assertive and more independent than women. In contrast, women are more cooperative, emotionally empathetic, and expressive. In the cognitive domain, male subjects, on average, outperform female subjects in figurative-spatial tasks, while conversely women perform better in verbal tasks (cf. Amelang and Bartussek 2006). Most of the studies were carried out in Western cultures. Thus, it is reasonable to argue that many of the differences found reflect the gender roles assigned to men and women in Western culture and that these roles are continually reaffirmed by appropriate educational measures. One way to support or weaken such an argument is to compare different cultures with the inclusion of non-Western cultures.

11.1 Universality and Culture-Specificity of Gender Differences

Two conclusions can be drawn from cross-cultural studies on gender differences: First, the gender differences found consistently point in the same direction. Second, there is considerable cross-cultural variation in the magnitude of the differences found (Costa et al. 2001). The first finding argues for a universal basis of sex differences that is biologically justifiable. The second finding suggests that biological differences can also undergo cultural modifications.

It should not be ignored that all the gender differences found are mean differences, which should not be overestimated in terms of their magnitude (the so-called effect size, Sect. 2.5): In studies in which the values were standardised, the magnitude of the difference is relatively small compared to the inter-individual differences within the sexes (cf. Costa et al. 2001). Nevertheless, the fact that the magnitude of the differences varies considerably across cultures requires explanation.

The question of causes still boils down to the controversy between biological factors on the one hand and socio-cultural factors on the other. Hence, a distinction is often made between biological sex ("sex") and social sex ("gender"). As with the debates in other fields on the contribution of genetic endowment and environmental factors, biological and social explanations are not mutually exclusive. For example, because of the relatively larger body height and strength found in all cultures, men may be more likely to be assigned leadership roles and thus more power and status, which would encourage the emergence of corresponding gender-differentiating childrearing practices (Costa et al. 2001).

11.2 Biological Basis of Gender Differences

The universally equal direction of gender differences argues in favour of a biological basis. From the point of view of *evolutionary theory*, the selection pressure typical for women results from the limited possibilities to bear a large number of offspring and from the high contribution to the care of a child. Partner choice and partner commitment are therefore disproportionately more important for women than for men (Hej 2001). Attractive partners for women are those who, in addition to a good genetic endowment, can also guarantee the long-term provision of children. In the course of evolution, both partner-relatedness and the provision of the offspring made those traits more prominent in women that relate to empathy, adaptation and the search for support in the interpersonal sphere, while in men traits emerged that enable them to beat rivals out of the field and to make maximum use of resources. The results of studies based on the five-factor model (Chap. 10) are compatible with such considerations: According to them, women across cultures achieve higher average scores in anxiety (emotional lability or neuroticism) and agreeableness as well as in those facets of extraversion that include the need for affection, warmth, and emotional expressiveness. In men, on the other hand, those facets of extraversion that refer to self-assertion and hunger for experience are more pronounced (Costa et al. 2001, p. 327).

In explanations that emphasise *hormonal* factors the higher testosterone level in men is held responsible for the increased propensity to aggression and the higher concentration of the hormone prolactin in women for the greater tendency to depression. The findings with regard to gender differences in the cognitive domain, however, are not quite so clear. Evolutionary selection pressure could have favoured the stronger development of spatial abilities in men and the stronger development of communicative-verbal abilities in women, but concrete evidence for this is difficult to provide. The more pronounced asymmetry of certain functional brain regions, especially the asymmetry between the left and right hemispheres of the brain (lateralisation), which develops in early childhood, is considered to be the biological basis for the stronger development of spatial thinking in men. The less pronounced asymmetry, however, only provides an insufficient explanation for the higher verbal abilities in women.

11.3 Gender Differences and Economic Development

Already in the tradition of the culture and personality school (Sect. 1.5), attempts were made, within the framework of the ecological approach, to connect sex differences with the economic form preferred in traditional societies. For example, Barry et al. (1959) distinguished between societies with low stockholding (hunters and gatherers) and those with higher stockholding (rural farmers and cattle breeders). The former emphasise more initiative, creativity, and independence in education; the latter place greater emphasis on obedience and responsibility. Parallel to this, the different educational ideals are associated with different degrees of gender role differentiation. Although the education to become independent is more strongly enforced in boys, the fact that girls are left "unmolested" means that less coercion is imposed on them at the same time. On the other hand, it is mainly the girls who are affected by the upbringing to cooperate and accept responsibility: Conformity and obedience are particularly required of them, since sedentary life means that freer activities outside the home are reserved almost exclusively for men, while women have to devote more time to preparing food and raising children at home. Accordingly, gender differences should be less pronounced in hunter-gatherer cultures than in agrarian cultures. This assumption was confirmed insofar as nomadic societies such as the Inuit, the Australian Aborigines and some Canadian Indian tribes were actually found to have fewer sex differences than some agrarian societies such as the Temne, the Ibo and Zulus in Africa and the Maori in New Zealand (cf. Segall et al. 1999, p. 232). However, as soon as other traditional societies were included, the findings could not be generalised.

According to the socio-cultural explanatory approach, it should be assumed that gender differences are less pronounced in the industrialised, more prosperous countries, since both the relief provided by mechanisation and egalitarian legislation should bring about a softening of traditional roles. Thus, one might assume that in highly industrialised countries, women tend to be more likely to have skills that are traditionally considered "masculine", and women in these countries are also more likely to occupy corresponding occupations and positions. The natural sciences, especially physics, are certainly considered a traditionally male domain. However, as statistics (cf. Baringa 1994) show, it is not true that the "most advanced" countries offer women the best opportunities in the natural sciences. On the contrary, precisely in some of the highly industrialised and wealthier countries the share of women employed in physics institutes is lowest. It even seems to be the case that the proportion of women among scientists in the natural sciences decreases with increasing wealth (measured in terms of gross national product).

So, are women in the less affluent countries better suited to physical tasks than women in the more affluent countries? Another explanation is more probable: In the less affluent countries, scientific positions – compared to positions in business and administration – are lowly respected and poorly paid, and are therefore not particularly attractive to men seeking a career. In the more affluent countries, on the other hand, positions in science are associated with comparatively higher prestige. Thus, it is not so much specific skills that give access to certain professions, but rather the status associated with a profession. In almost all societies, men tend to be expected to occupy a higher status and are put under pressure to do so in the course of their upbringing.

11.4 Gender Differences and Cultural Values

As Hofstede (2011) has pointed out, the prevailing notions of masculinity and femininity differ considerably between cultures – even in industrialised countries (Chap. 5). The differences relate, on the one hand, to the extent to which the role expectations attached to women differ from those attached to men, and second, how characteristics typically associated with masculinity or femininity are generally valued in the culture. According to Hofstede, Japan, Germany, Italy and Mexico are markedly masculine cultures, while the Scandinavian countries belong to the more feminine cultures.

One might assume that gender differences are more pronounced in more masculine countries than in more feminine countries. However, this assumption could not be confirmed. Nevertheless, there was a significant correlation with Hofstede's individualism-collectivism dimension (cf. Costa et al. 2001, p. 327): Gender differences are more pronounced in individualist countries than in collectivist ones. Two explanations are used to account for this result: the self-concept and the values associated with the collectivist orientation.

11.4 Gender Differences and Cultural Values

With regard to the *self-concept* it can be argued that the embeddedness of the self in the social context (Chap. 10), which goes hand in hand with the collectivist view, generally reduces the distinctness of personality traits as measured in questionnaires and and thus as well the trait-related gender differences.

Collectivist values seem to alter, i.e. modify, the manifestation of gender differences in the sense of a moderator variable (Box 11.1). Evidence for the effectiveness of *collectivist* values as a moderator variable for gender differences emerges from studies of quasi-natural interaction situations in which both gender and individualism-collectivism orientation were taken into account.

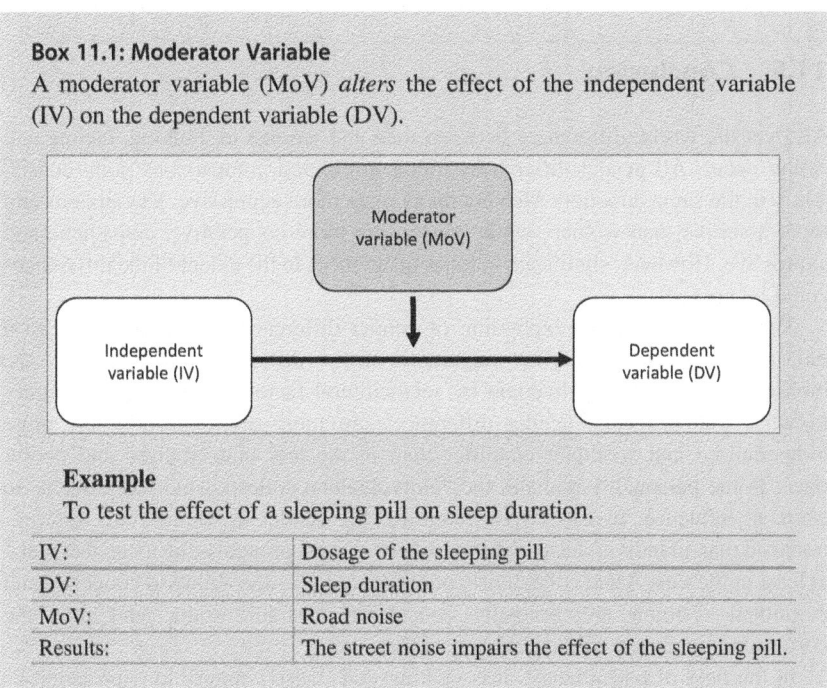

Box 11.1: Moderator Variable
A moderator variable (MoV) *alters* the effect of the independent variable (IV) on the dependent variable (DV).

Example
To test the effect of a sleeping pill on sleep duration.

IV:	Dosage of the sleeping pill
DV:	Sleep duration
MoV:	Road noise
Results:	The street noise impairs the effect of the sleeping pill.

Thus, in a comparison between American and Chinese subjects (Mortenson 2002), no difference between male and female Chinese showed up with regard to the extent of cooperation-oriented expressions (e.g. approving feedback signals), but there was a significant difference between male and female Americans, whereby the Chinese were generally more cooperation-oriented than the Americans according to the degree of collectivism (Sect. 9.7.1). From this it can be concluded that cooperation is generally highly valued in more collectivist oriented cultures and is therefore indiscriminately sought by both sexes, whereas in individualist countries with their stronger factual orientation, cooperation is considered to be the female domain.

The opposite is true of expressivity, which in collectivist cultures tends to be tabooed due to the norm of self-control or restraint (Chap. 10). Here, it was found that American women verbalised their feelings significantly more often than American men, whereas no such difference was observed between Japanese women and Japanese men (Kitayama and Ishii 2002).

11.5 Conclusion

All over the world, differences between men and women in thinking, feeling and acting occur. All gender differences found in cultural comparisons point consistently in the same direction: Men are on average more aggressive, less anxious and more assertive than women, while women are more cooperative, empathetic and expressive. However, significant cultural differences in the extent of the differences could be proved.

The universally equal expression of gender differences argues in favour of a biological basis. The varying magnitude of the differences suggests that the biological conditions are overlaid by sociocultural factors. Surprisingly, contrary to what was expected, gender differences are more pronounced in the more industrialised and wealthier countries than in the less industrialised and poorer ones. In the personality domain, the "individualism-collectivism" factor seems to exert an influence. In collectivist countries, the gender differences are less pronounced than in individualist countries, which is most probably due to the fact that – at least in the East Asian collectivist countries studied – the ability to cooperate and emotional restraint are generally considered desirable traits, and thus the corresponding gender differences are smaller.

In the field of performance, it is striking that – also contrary to expectations – women are more strongly represented in the natural sciences in the less developed countries than in the more developed countries. This can best be explained by the fact that in the less prosperous countries scientific positions – compared to positions in business and administration – are less respected as well as poorly paid and are therefore not particularly attractive to career-minded men, whereas in the more prosperous countries they are associated with comparatively higher prestige and are therefore more sought after by men.

11.6 Questions of Understanding

1. Draw conclusions from research on gender differences in terms of *biological* and *sociocultural* explanations.
2. Explain the role of cultural values as *moderator variables* for gender differences. Give an example.
3. Explain the role of the *reference group* effect with respect to the expression of gender differences.

Further Reading

Matsumoto, D., & Juang, L. (2008). *Culture and psychology* (4th ed.). Thomson Wadsworth (Chapter 6).

Neyer, F. J. & Asendorpf, J. B. (2018). *Psychologie der Persönlichkeit*. Berlin: Springer.

Wood, W. & Eagly, A. H. (2002). A Cross-cultural analysis of the behavior of women and men: Implications for the origins of sex differences. *Psychological Bulletin*, .128 (5), 699–727.

Development in Childhood and Adolescence

12

While in Chap. 3 the phylogenetic development of humans, the so-called *phylogenesis*, was examined, the research interest in the present chapter focuses on the development of the individual within his or her life span, on the so-called *ontogenesis*. Cross-cultural studies have been conducted primarily with regard to development in childhood and adolescence; studies on development in adulthood are rather rare.

12.1 Maturation and Learning in Childhood and Adolescence

If one looks at the expectations that adults in different cultures have of a child of comparable age, one will notice considerable differences: For example, the child may be seen as a schoolchild, a promising offspring, an object of care, a worker, a head of household, or a child soldier. Even when observing the children themselves, striking differences can be found, for example, in the way they interact with adults, in the way they play, in the way they manage everyday tasks and in what they talk about. Despite these obvious differences, however, it should not be ignored that in all cultures people develop from beings who are dependent on comprehensive support at birth to becoming individuals who act relatively independently.

Thus, one can ask whether and to what extent, despite the manifest diversity in all cultures, under the surface of what is different in any case, similar principles of child and adolescent development in thought and action can be discovered, and to what extent the respective culture creates conditions that modify human development in an essential way. The first question is attempted to study in generalisation studies, the second in differentiation studies (Chaps. 1 and 2).

In the Western world, it is generally assumed that before entering adulthood, there is a period of childhood and a period of adolescence. However, quite a few researchers dispute the generality of this division and consider the categories "childhood" and "adolescence" as socio-cultural constructs. For example, the French historian Phillipe Ariès (1962) claimed that in medieval European society the status of childhood did not exist.

In order to clarify the contradiction, it is useful to separate the process of development from the role expectations imposed on the developing individual. With regard to the process of development, it seems to be indisputable that in all cultures the human being undergoes a development that is characterised by *maturation* and *learning* (Box 12.1).

> **Box 12.1: Maturation and Learning**
> *Maturation* is understood to mean those psychophysical changes that arise primarily for internal organismic reasons, such as growth in length and bone nucleus formation, while *learning* is understood to be are those processes that involve an active engagement of the individual with his or her environment.

As we look at the human growth curve, for example using the length growth, we can first note that the overall shape is similar in all cultures, even if the individual age classifications show a certain variability (Bogin 1998, 1999, 2012; Bogin et al. 2018). Irrespective of culture, clear discontinuities in speed (cm/year) can be observed: From a high level at the beginning of the process, the growth rate initially drops rapidly, remains at a relatively constant level for a few years, then shows a renewed short increase, and finally drops off completely (Fig. 12.1). From a biological point of view, the shape of this growth curve provides some justification for the division into at least four stages of development.[1] (1) *infancy* or early childhood, (2) middle and late *childhood*, (3) *adolescence* and (4) *mature adulthood*.

One might ask whether the nature of the learning processes that take place in the three first growth phases also permits a similar classification across cultures. In learning, the individual adapts to the surrounding environment and living world, which is shaped by a variety of ecological, economic, social and cultural conditions.

---

[1] Bogin et al. (2018) distinguish five stages, as they interpret the slight downward trend in the preadolescence stage as a separate stage.

12.1 Maturation and Learning in Childhood and Adolescence

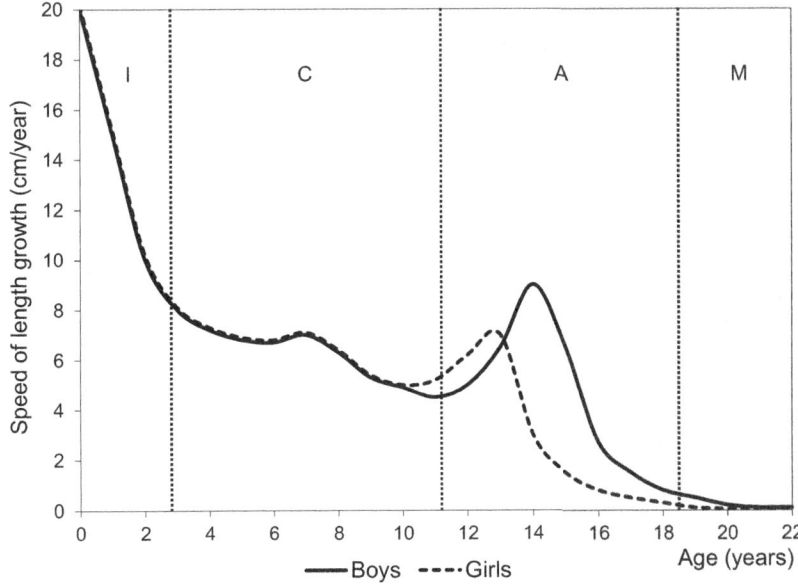

Fig. 12.1 Speed of length growth as a function of age . The developmental stages delimited from each other by the discontinuities are marked as I = infancy, C = childhood, A = adolescence and M = mature adulthood. (Modified after Bogin et al. 2018)

Although learning is tied to certain maturation processes, it cannot be understood without looking at the individual's active engagement with his or her environment. This engagement involves the successful accomplishment of certain requirements or tasks, often referred to as "developmental tasks" (Erikson 1968; Havighurst 1982; Box 12.2). The question thus arises as to whether culturally invariant *developmental tasks* can be found, the delineation of which corresponds to the division into the phases of growth.

Box 12.2: Developmental Tasks
A *developmental task* is a task that an individual has to deal with at a certain point in his or her life.

If the task is successfully performed, happiness and success follow, "whereas failure makes the individual unhappy, meets with rejection from society, and leads to difficulties in coping with later tasks" (Havighurst 1982).

The developmental task of *infancy* (i. e. early childhood) could be cross-culturally that during this phase the child has to acquire certain patterns of satisfying elementary needs such as food intake, excretory processes and social contact as well as its mother tongue. The patterns themselves can differ greatly between cultures, as can the difficulty associated with their acquisition – consider, for example, that food intake must be done by hand, with a spoon, or with chopsticks, depending on the culture. In all cultures, children are given a lot of care and attention during this phase because of their own lack of independence, but there are clear differences in the nature of this care and attention. These mainly concern the type of communication with the child. Thus, in individualist cultures eye contact and verbal address are more frequent than in collectivist cultures, while in the latter physical contact and spatial proximity are more pronounced compared to individualist cultures. Cultures also vary in the importance given to persons other than the mother in caring for the infant. In Western cultures, the mother-child relationship is often exclusive, whereas in many non-Western cultures the child is surrounded by several caregivers – adults and children.

The respective patterns of interaction are at the same time linked to certain predetermined conditions and restrictions which are intended to steer the child's behaviour along certain paths. Thus, in individualist cultures, the child is supposed to achieve autonomy and independence at quite an early age, whereas in collectivist cultures, the prevailing aim is to integrate harmoniously into the social community.

The phase of actual *childhood* is usually characterised by a significantly expanded radius of action, by the widening of social contacts, and by an incipient symbolic understanding. The developmental task here seems to consist in all cultures in acquiring the competencies necessary for adult life. In industrialised societies, the acquisition of these skills is largely formalised institutionally, for example through kindergarten and school, whereas in less industrialised or non-industrialised societies it is more integrated into the concrete context of life and work in the adult world. Accordingly, social interaction can be either more strongly influenced by peers ("peer groups") or rather by age-heterogeneous groups (above all family or kinship). A distinction can also be made between more targeted learning through explicit pedagogical instruction on the one hand and more implicit or incidental (= casual) learning through observation and participation on the other hand. Both take place in all cultures, but the proportions vary, on the one hand, depending on the degree of industrialisation of a society and, on the other hand, between Western and non-Western cultures.

Cultures also differ in the importance attached to children's play. All children in the world play, but there are significant differences in the amount of time children are given to play, the types of toys used (everyday objects versus specialised play materials), and the degree to which play is instutionalised (adult surroundings versus special children's playgrounds).

The phase of *adolescence*, the beginning of which is thought to be puberty, i.e. the development towards reproductive capacity, is relatively easy to pinpoint because of the drastic physical changes that the individual undergoes. The existence of an associated transitional phase between childhood and adult status is hardly disputed in modern Western societies, but is also found among so-called primitive peoples. The developmental task of this phase can be described as a conscious confrontation with one's own identity and becoming an adult.

12.2 Role Expectations in Childhood and Adolescence

Let us now ask whether the role expectations that are imposed on the developing individual also allow for a universally valid division into the aforementioned stages of development. Age-specific role expectations can be expressed in many ways, for example in explicit pedagogical instructions or in withdrawal of maternal love in the case of undesirable behaviour.

The norms of what is expected of an infant, child, or adolescent in a culture can often only be recognised from what is viewed or named as deviance. For example, in cultures with regular compulsory education, a school child who keeps standing up during class and is constantly distracted is often considered to have an attention deficit disorder.

In almost every culture there are "rites of passage" or "*rites de passage*" that mark the transition to a new stage of development, although their number varies considerably from culture to culture. They are most frequently documented as a transition from childhood to adolescence: In traditional cultures they take place in the form of "initiation ceremonies", but they are not unknown in Western industrialised countries either – think of the "confirmation" for the attainment of religious maturity in Europe or the "youth consecration" in the former GDR (German Democratic Republic), which is now being revived in East Germany in a somewhat de-ideologised form.

12.3 Testing the Universal Validity of Cognitive Development Models

An important question within developmental psychology is whether there are universally valid regularities in the cognitive development of the individual or whether the development proceeds qualitatively differently depending on the cultural environment. As follows, the development of thinking and language will be considered.

12.3.1 Piaget's Stage Model of the Development of Childrens' Thinking

A prototypical realisation of the cross-cultural test of cognitive development models is the investigation of the universal validity of Jean Piaget's stage model of children's thinking (cf. Piaget 2003). According to Piaget, thinking develops as an action-like engagement of the individual with the environment. The development takes place in the form of an interrelationship of biological maturation with external environment and progresses in several stages on a path of increasing detachment of action from the respective environment. Each stage involves a qualitative change in thought structures. The four main stages are referred to as *sensorimotor, pre-operational, concrete-operational,* and *formal-operational* (Table 12.1). They follow an internal, an "epistemic" (cognition-based) regularity and are therefore invariant and irreversible in their sequence.

The cultural comparison is intended to examine the extent to which the sequence of the individual stages can claim universal validity. Incompatible with the model are, on the one hand, violations of the sequence of the individual stages, i.e. relapses

Table 12.1 Stages of development according to Piaget

Approximate age	Stage	Description
0–2 years	Sensorimotor stage	Development and coordination of sensorimotor schemes
2–7 years	Pre-operational stage	Thinking is egocentric and one-dimensional
7–11 years	Concrete-operational stage	Use of logical operations to solve concrete problems
From the age of 12 up	Formal-operational stage	Logical thinking also succeeds with fictitious assumptions ("thought experiments")

12.3 Testing the Universal Validity of Cognitive Development Models

into an earlier stage if a higher one had previously been reached, or skipping, i.e. climbing a higher stage while omitting a lower one, and, on the other hand, an early termination of development, i.e. failure to reach the higher stages. Compatible with the model are variations in the age at which the individual stages are reached, i.e. a lower or higher speed of development does not represent a violation of the model.

Most cross-cultural studies have focused on the transition from the pre-operational stage to the concrete-operational stage, which involves the invariance of volume, weight, and quantity. Whether a child is already assigned to the concrete-operational or still to the pre-operational stage depends on the way in which the respective test tasks are answered (Box 12.3).

> **Box 12.3: From Research: Study on Volume Invariance**
> In a typical volume invariance task the child is shown two identical cylindrical glass containers, each containing the same amount of liquid. The liquid is then poured from one of the two containers into a third, which is also cylindrical but has a smaller (or larger) diameter. Children at the pre-operational stage think that the amount of liquid has changed because they only consider one of the two dimensions (height or width) of the column of liquid in the container. Children at the concrete-operational stage recognise that the amount of liquid is the same and also justify it.
>
> Typical volume invariance task
>
>
>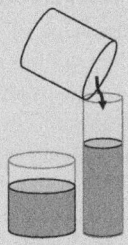
>
>
> Are these the same amounts of liquid or different amounts?
>
> Look what I'm doing now! (Pour the liquid into another container)
>
> Are these the same amounts of liquid or different amounts?

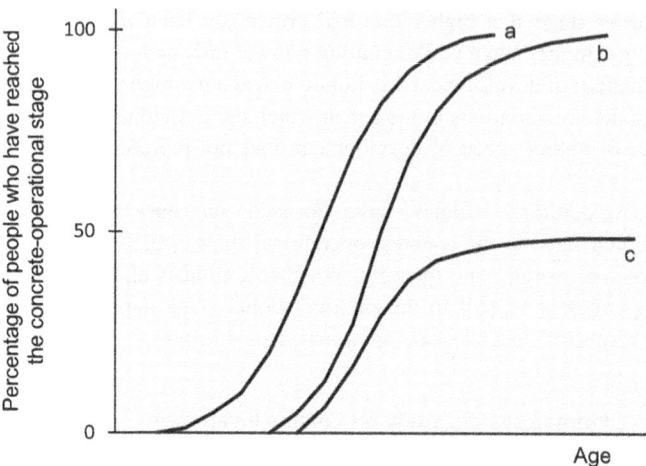

Fig. 12.2 Schematic courses of development until the concrete-operational stage is reached (Dasen and Heron 1981). Curves a and b show hypothesis-compliant courses, curve c represents a nonhypothesis-compliant course

The age of the children serves as the independent variable. The percentage of children in an age group who correctly solve the corresponding tasks forms the dependent variable. According to the model, a monotonically increasing progression of the percentage of correct solutions should result as a function of age (Fig. 12.2). The decisive factor is the shape of the curve and not the specific age value. In fact, in all the cultures studied, within a certain age range, the boundaries of which varied from culture to culture, the hypostasised progression was observed. However, there were cultures where no more than half of the subjects reached the concrete-operational stage, even when higher ages up to adulthood were included (Dasen and Heron 1981, p. 296).

One explanation for this result could be that children from traditional cultures are far less familiar with the type of test items than children from Western industrial nations, i.e. that the postulate of measurement equivalence (Sect. 2.2) is not fulfilled. This explanation is in particular supported by the fact that in most traditional cultures there was considerable training success when the tasks were performed several times in a slightly modified form. After such a training the pattern of results was comparable to that of Western cultures. This was true even when the children had not attended school. Taken together, the cross-cultural comparative studies suggest that the development of *competence* in the Piagetian sense is indeed universal, even if the actual achievement shown (so-called *performance*) is shaped in a culturally specific way.

12.3.2 Cognitive Development as a Gradual Process

Even if the studies proved the validity of Piaget's stage model in principle, it still remains impossible to conclude from this that the development of children's thinking is completely independent of culture. According to Piaget, the postulated sequence of structural changes in thinking should be general, i.e. apply equally to all cognitive phenomena and functions. Thus, a child who has reached a certain stage in one of the sub-areas should also reach the same stage in other sub-areas without too much delay. For example, at the concrete-operational stage, the invariance of quantities, volumes, and weights should be achieved at about the same time as a "structure d'ensemble" (Piaget 2003). However, in empirical studies, one has often found a large temporal gap between the individual subdomains ("horizontal décalage"). The speed and sequence of acquisition of the individual sub-areas could frequently be linked to the experiences in the child's cultural environment (cf. Greenfield 1984, p. 103).

Such findings made some researchers generally doubt the inner logic of the sequence of stages. Many phenomena that Piaget cited as evidence for the structural changes he postulated may also be interpreted in another way (cf. Schneider and Sodian 2008). For example, it is argued that older children are better at solving tasks that younger children fail at, simply because they have already developed efficient problem-solving strategies and automations of elementary thinking operations in certain content areas. The young child, according to this view, is a "universal novice" (Brown and DeLoache 1978). In the course of development, children acquire – either through implicit learning or through explicit instruction – knowledge in the various content areas, whereby the timing and trajectories may vary widely among them.

If this approach were valid, the development of thinking would have to depend to a large extent on the cultural environment. The individuals of those cultures that provide a broad field of experience for the formation of thinking and problem-solving strategies, i.e. cultures with a large number and high quality of stimulating conditions, would have to be at an advantage. One might assume that these are most likely to be cultures with a high level of development (Chap. 5). However, it is also possible to argue the exact opposite: Children from cultures with a high level of development are more often already familiarised with ready-made solutions or at least solution schemes and are therefore not challenged at all to find the actual solution path themselves. They would enrich their factual knowledge but not increase their general information processing capacity and thinking ability. Systematic studies on the appropriateness of these hypotheses have yet to be conducted.

12.3.3 Kohlberg's Stage Model of the Development of Moral Judgement

Certainly even more controversial than Piaget's stage model is the universal validity of the development of moral thinking. Piaget's disciple Kohlberg (cf. Kohlberg 1984) has also postulated a stage model here. He describes the development of moral thought structures as a progression from hedonistic (pleasurable) orientation to general principles of justice. The type of responses to so-called moral dilemmas serves as an indicator for reaching a certain stage (Box 12.4).

> **Box 12.4: From Research: Example of a Moral Dilemma**
> One of the best-known examples of a moral dilemma is the so-called *Heinz dilemma.*.
>
> The following situation is described to the subjects: Heinz's wife is dying. The only hope is a very expensive medicine. Since Heinz cannot afford it, he asks acquaintances and authorities for support. Nevertheless, he cannot raise the required amount and the pharmacist does not want to sell him the medicine cheaper either. Heinz is desperate and plays with the idea of stealing the medicine.
>
> Subsequently, the subjects are asked questions about the dilemma. For example, they are asked whether Heinz should steal the medicine, whether he should also have stolen it for someone else, and whether the subjects judge Heinz's behaviour to be morally wrong, since he is breaking the law with this theft (Kohlberg 1984).

Two conclusions can be drawn from the results of two meta-analyses (cf. Eckensberger 2007), based mostly on longitudinal studies (Sect. 2.3): First, the majority of studies support the cross-cultural validity of the postulated stage sequence, since in most cases neither relapses to earlier stages nor skipping of intermediate stages (except for the very first stage) were observed. Second, the attainment or non-attainment of the higher stages depended on various cultural factors such as industrialisation, opportunity for participation in responsibility, and liberal education, but interestingly did not coincide with the distinction between Western or individualist and non-Western or collectivist cultures.

In other cultures (e.g. India and China) as well stage models of moral development have been designed. From a Chinese perspective, Hing Keung Ma has proposed a model (Ma 1992, 2009) that, like Kohlberg's, involves a progression from a hedonistic orientation to generally binding ethical principles. The lower stages are largely identical to those of Kohlberg, while in the upper stages, in contrast to Kohlberg, less emphasis is placed on the aspect of justice, but rather on humanity ("jen"[2]) and the integration of man into nature.

12.3.4 Language Development

The development of language certainly represents a special case of cognitive development. It is obvious that the individual languages are different (Chap. 9). Nevertheless, one may wonder whether there are structural similarities in the child development of language acquisition. In fact, comparative language development studies suggest certain invariances in the sequence of language acquisition independent of the particular language a child is learning. For example, all children go through a "holophrastic"[3] one-word stage at about 1–2 years of age, followed by a two-word stage at about 2 years of age. Basic principles of grammar are acquired at about 2–4 years of age, after which mastery of grammar is essentially complete (cf. Slobin 1992).

12.4 Achievement Behaviour in Childhood and Adolescence

The examination of developmental models dealt with the question of cultural invariance or variance in the succession of individual developmental steps. However, one can also ask the question about general differences in abilities and achievements depending on the cultural environment. The focus here is not on the progress of development, but on the differential diagnostic investigation of the current status. The preferred method is the psychometric approach (Chap. 2)

---

[2] "jen", in Chinese: "仁", in the pinyin transcription used in mainland China it is written "rén."
[3] "Holophrastic" here means that a single word is representative of an entire sentence.

consisting in test procedures to determine the extent of certain abilities. A cultural comparison with regard to "general intelligence" encounters fundamental methodological difficulties (Chap. 7). In contrast, a cultural comparison can make sense if not general intelligence but specific abilities are tested. The PISA- and TIMSS studies (Box 7.2), which compare the mathematics and science education of students in different countries, can be used as examples of such a comparison.

In those studies, it was assumed that mathematics and science education in all participating countries can be identified by an equivalent core curriculum that anchors the examined skills as normative requirements in the respective curricula in a comparable manner. The test items were selected in such a way that a factor structure applicable to all participating countries resulted, allowing the mapping of ability expression on a common scale.[4] The results show that the performance of German students is in the upper middle range and better than that of the US students. The top group is formed by the East Asian countries Singapore, Taiwan, Hong Kong, Korea and Japan (Sects. 7.2 and 7.3).

One can speculate whether the differences in performance are related to the cultural dimensions listed in Chap. 5. According to Hofstede's research, the East Asian countries would be classified as rather collectivist and hierarchically oriented cultures, while Germany would be classified as individualist and egalitarian. However, the fact that countries with a collectivist and hierarchical orientation can also be found at the lower end of the performance scale (Colombia, Iran and Kuwait) contradicts such a correlation between performance level and culture. Moreover, the direction of the differences is certainly not in line with expectations, since it is precisely in individualist countries that the achievement aspect is more appreciated than in collectivist cultures (Chap. 5). The idea from everyday psychology that East Asian countries are more characterised by diligence, while Western countries are more characterised by their own thinking, also does not apply: The relative weaknesses of the German adolescents lay precisely in the area of conceptual understanding and less in the area of routine procedures.

An additional three-country comparison (Germany, Japan, USA) based on video recordings allows the assumption that the reasons for the differences in performance are rather to be found in the type of school instruction. While mathematics instruction in the USA and Germany tends to focus on knowledge acquisition and procedural mastery, in Japan it tends to focus on problem solving, thereby

---

[4] In this case, the scale was not constructed according to classical test theory as in the case of testing general intelligence, but according to the so-called probabilistic test model (cf. Baumert et al. 2000a, p. 60).

promoting mathematical understanding. Mathematical concepts in Germany are developed in class discussion leading to a single solution. In the USA they are presented by the teacher and applied by the students. In contrast, the open tasks frequently used in Japanese lessons allow solutions of varying quality and also facilitate the transfer of concepts once acquired to new situations. In Japan, too – as in Germany and the USA – the teacher determines what happens in the class, but the pace of interaction is slower (Chap. 5), possibly allowing the young people more time for individual acquisition. In addition, group and partner work is practised more frequently than it is in Germany and the USA.

12.5 Social Behaviour in Childhood and Adolescence

Children in different cultures grow up in different social constellations: The number of caregivers differs, the form of the mother-child relationship varies, interaction with peers is weighted differently, and the ideals of social relationships differ. From the point of view of developmental psychology, therefore, the question arises as to what extent these different social constellations, parenting styles, and parenting ideals are accompanied by different development of social behaviour on the part of the developing young people. Two aspects will be highlighted here: the development of aggressive behaviour and the development of prosocial behaviour. It should not be concealed that this selection is made from a Western perspective: In view of growing violence in schools and the ever-present demand for teamwork in professional life, the question of pedagogical measures to curb aggressive and promote prosocial behaviour seems all too justified. But also against the background of sociobiological approaches, according to which aggression and altruism are essentially motivated by the "selfishness of the genes" (Dawkins 2006), the question of as to what extent cultural factors have a moderating effect gains particular interest.

The majority of empirical studies refer to comparisons between, on the one hand, individualist cultures (predominantly the USA and Germany) and, on the other hand, collectivist cultures (predominantly Asian countries, but also Russia). Put simply, the main difference between educational practices is that individualist cultures emphasise early independence, and thus promote autonomous engagement with the outside world and cultural norms, whereas incollectivist cultures, integration into social ties and norms dominates (Chap. 5).

12.5.1 Aggressive Behaviour

Based on a motivational theory of aggression, Kornadt (cf. Kornadt 2003) investigated the extent to which and why the aggression motive among adolescents in three Asian cultures (Japan, Bali, and Batak) differs in intensity from that in a Western culture (Germany). He distinguished between overt aggression, which is evident in behaviour, and inhibition of aggression, which as a suppressed aggression tendency is expressed only in fantasy. According to Kornadt, these aggressive fantasies can be recorded by means of so-called projective test procedures.[5]

The Asian adolescents showed a significantly lower level of aggression than the Western adolescents (cf. Kornadt 2003, p. 368), not only in terms of overt aggression but also in terms of aggression inhibition (Fig. 12.3).

Thus, the lower behavioural aggressiveness in Eastern cultures, already known from previous studies, apparently cannot be explained simply by the fact that overt aggression is suppressed by the undoubtedly more restrictive social norms.

Based on comparative analyses of mother-child interactions in Germany and Japan, it can be assumed that in the course of socialisation, children learn to deal with frustrating experiences in culturally different ways. Whereas, at the age of two, Japanese children hardly differ from German children with regard to the cause and expression of anger, a considerable divergence occurs at the age of 5 (cf. Kornadt et al. 1994, p. 245). Throughout the learning process, the mother serves as a model for the child's behaviour. The German child learns to perceive frustrations as intentional and unjustified harm to his or her person, whereas in Japan such an interpretation is rather avoided. This is especially evident in the education aiming at complying with norms. The German mother perceives a non-norm-conforming behaviour of the child as an intentional insult, reacts accordingly and thereby challenges a conflict with the child. The Japanese mother, on the other hand, tries to react flexibly and calmly to the non-observance of norms. She makes her demand clear, but if the child is unable or unwilling to comply, she gradually withdraws her demand and avoids open conflict. Thus, on the one hand, she maintains a harmonious relationship with the child while at the same time conveys a depersonalised response to frustrating events. This pattern of behaviour is perceived by the child and learned through imitation.

---

[5] In projective tests, subjects are presented with ambiguous images to which they are asked to express their ideas. It is assumed that the subjects "project" their unconscious wishes and fears into these ideas. The advantage of projective methods is that they are not readily transparent to the subjects.

12.5 Social Behaviour in Childhood and Adolescence

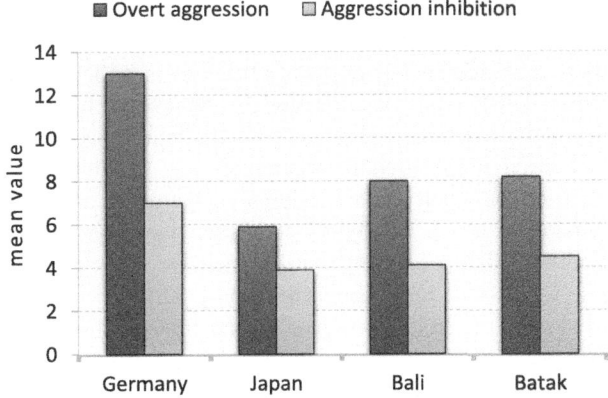

Fig. 12.3 Mean expression of overt aggression and of inhibition of aggression (= aggressive fantasies) among adolescents in different cultures. (Modified after Kornadt 2003, p. 368)

On the other hand, it should not be overlooked that the parenting practices described are not quite as culture-specific as they appear at first glance. An early study by Sears and colleagues (Sears et al. 1957) in the USA investigated the relationship between parental parenting behaviour and child aggressiveness. With regard to norm compliance, they distinguished two dimensions of parental behaviour, which they termed "permissiveness"[6] and "punitiveness".[7] Children's levels of aggression were lowest when parents set clear rules, i.e., were low in *permissiveness,* at the same time, however, punished rule violations only slightly, i.e., they were simultaneously low in *punitiveness.* Similarly, studies by Rohner and colleagues (cf. Rohner et al. 1992; Ajdukovic 1990) show that child-rearing practices vary so widely even within a culture that it is not readily possible to draw a clear distinction between Far Eastern and Western practices.

---

[6] Permissiveness = the extent to which parents allow the child to behave aggressively. High permissive parents set few limits, low permissive parents set many limits. Permissivity refers to parenting behaviour *prior to* an offense.

[7] Punitiveness = the extent to which parents punish an aggressive action by the child. Highly punitive parents punish the child severely for an aggressive act, low punitive parents punish their child less severely. "Punitiveness" thus refers to parental behaviour *following* an offense.

12.5.2 Prosocial Behaviour

Similar attention to aggressive behaviour has been given to helping behaviour or "prosocial"[8] behaviour . Analogous to aggressive behaviour, the question here is whether helping behaviour is more pronounced in children from collectivist cultures compared to children from individualist cultures (cf. Friedlmeier et al. 2011). Research conducted on kindergarten children in Germany, Japan, and Russia involved a scenario in which the child's nonverbal (facial and gestural), verbal, and action reactions to another person's misfortune were observed in a context that was as natural as possible (cf. Kienbaum 1995). Differences resulted in the children's verbal and nonverbal reactions. German children showed their concern about the misfortune of the other person in the form of sympathetic verbal expressions, whereas the Japanese and Russian children reacted more with a "freezing" of facial expressions and gestures (Chap. 8). Within the Russian sample, moreover, there was a clear gender difference: While the boys provided more active assistance, the girls showed a higher degree of concern. The results are not easy to interpret, especially as they may have been confounded by the fact that the 'victim' was an authority figure. Since in collectivist cultures authority figures are generally treated with more respect than in individualist ones, direct assistance may be inappropriate because it would expose the weakness of the authority figure (cf. Kienbaum 1995, p. 102).

12.6 Conclusion

This chapter aimed to show cultural universals and culture-specific features in childhood and adolescence. It was asked whether and to what extent principles of child development in thinking and acting resemble in all cultures and to what extent the respective culture creates specific conditions that influence ontogenetic development in a decisive way.

It can be stated that childhood and adolescence are both biologically shaped and socially constructed. In all cultures, the development from birth to adulthood is divided into specific epochs. The biological changes in maturation are reflected in all cultures in the form of incisions, even if the age limits and age extensions are

---

[8]The term "altruistic" behaviour is deliberately avoided because it implies that prosocial behaviour would be governed exclusively by altruistic motives.

usually only vaguely defined. Often, the basic incisions are supplemented by additional institutional markers (e.g. by "rites of passage").

The period of childhood and adolescence is associated with certain developmental tasks in all cultures. In early childhood, the child must learn culturally appropriate patterns of need satisfaction as well as the mother tongue; in middle and late childhood, he or she must acquire the competencies necessary for adult life; and in adolescence, a confrontation with the adoption of the adult role must take place.

Cognitive development, at least until the end of infancy, shows surprising cultural commonalities. The development of analytical reasoning, for example, reveals universal principles, although the times at which each level is reached and the content areas to which new competencies can be applied vary culturally. Some puzzles surround the role of schooling in cognitive development: Unexpected findings in systematic comparisons of achievement underline a great need for research.

Striking cultural differences are revealed in the development of social behaviour. The extent of aggressive behaviour seems to be significantly lower in collectivist-oriented cultures than in individualist-oriented ones, which can most probably be explained by a culture-specific way of dealing with frustrating experiences.

However, the methodological discussion (Chap. 2) should also have shown that occurring differences cannot unequivocally attributed to cultural factors. In particular, the differences cannot be considered independently of genetic factors, since an interaction between socially mediated information structures and genetic selection must be presupposed (Chaps. 3 and 4).

12.7 Questions of Understanding

1. Explain the difference between *maturation* and *learning*.
2. Explain the term *"developmental task"*.
3. Provide evidence for and objections against the universal validity of *Piaget's stage model of* cognitive development.

> **Further Reading**
> Bogin, B. (2012). The evolution of human growth. In N. Cameron, & B. Bogin (Eds.), *Human growth and development* (2nd ed., pp. 287–324). San Diego: Elsevier Academic Press.

(continued)

Bogin, B., Varea, C., Hermanussen, M., & Scheffler, C. (2018). Human life course biology: A centennial perspective of scholarship on the human pattern of physical growth and its place in human biocultural evolution. *American Journal of Physiological Anthropology, 165*, 834–854.

Trommsdorff, G. (2003). Kulturvergleichende Entwicklungspsychologie. In A. Thomas (Ed.), *Kulturvergleichende Psychologie* (2nd ed., pp. 139–179). Göttingen: Hogrefe.

Working World 13

All over the world, most people spend a large part of their time working. However, work requirements, working environment and working conditions vary widely among countries. In addition, considerable changes have occurred in the course of ongoing industrial globalisation: Modern information and communication technologies have not only fundamentally changed work processes, but have also made distances and national borders disappear as barriers to business transactions. Many domestic firms have branches abroad, jobs are being relocated abroad, and joint ventures or other forms of international business cooperation are being established. However, international cooperation partnerships do not always lead to economic success: At a rough estimate, around 40–70% of all international projects fail. This raises the question of whether it is fundamentally possible to apply general practices and standards in working life, or whether cultural differences instead require different ways of doing things. Industrial and organisational psychology, sometimes also referred to as "human resource management", is concerned with human experience, thought and action in the workplace. Since professional work is typically performed in organisations (companies, social institutions, associations, offices, etc.), the fields of "work" and "organisation" are closely linked. Typical topics in work and organisational psychology are leadership behaviour, work motivation, work performance, decision-making behaviour, and group work. With reference to cross-cultural psychology, the following section will look at similarities and differences in these areas. This cannot be considered without taking organisational framework conditions into account. These are in part culture-dependent, but also depend on other factors such as the degree of industrialisation of a society or the prevailing political system.

13.1 Organisational Structure and Organisational Culture

An essential characteristic of an organisation is the division of labor. The type of activities as well as the type and scope of responsibility are distributed differently among the employees or employee groups. This is reflected in the so-called *organisational structure*. Lammers and Hickson (1979) identified three different types of that structure: the "Latin", the "Anglo-Saxon" and the "Third World" types. The Latin type, found predominantly in Southern and Eastern Europe and Latin American countries, is characterised by a classical bureaucratic structure, centralised distribution of power, and a large number of hierarchical levels. The Anglo-Saxon type, predominantly found in North America and northwestern European countries, shows a more flexible structure, a decentralised distribution of power, and few levels of hierarchy. The Third World type, prevalent in non-industrialised countries but also found in smaller firms and family businesses as well as in rural regions in Western Europe, reveals a low level of formalised rules, a centralised power structure, and a paternalistic style of leadership. Inspired by Hofstede's research (Chap. 5), Lammers and Hickson added a mixed type that is common in Germany and Israel, for example, being characterised by a rigid bureaucracy with a strict rule orientation, but few hierarchical levels.

Technological progress has recently led to some convergence of organisational structures at the country level, but this does not necessarily mean that individual behaviour of employees will converge in a similar way. For example, while high-risk technologies require a great variety of formalised rules everywhere, the extent to which the rules are followed can vary widely across cultures.

While organisational structure refers to the formal structure of an organisation, *organisational culture* refers to values, traditions, symbols, practices and the working climate within an organisation (cf. Hofstede 2011). In analogy to the general concept of culture, which refers to patterns of thinking, feeling and acting at the level of populations (e.g. countries) or sub-populations, organisational culture is to be located at the level of companies. Organisational culture is certainly influenced by factors such as the type of organisation (e.g., manufacturing company or government agency) and company tradition. It is identified either with the help of questionnaires and interviews or through ethnographic descriptions (Sect. 2.3). According to Hofstede (2011), however, the individual behaviour of employees in an organisation is shaped to a much greater extent by cultural tradition than by organisational culture, since cultural tradition, unlike organisational culture, is acquired at an early age.

13.2 Work Attitude and Work Motivation

What motivates people to work at all, and what do they expect from the work they do? Certainly, everywhere in the world, work serves to secure one's own livelihood or that of one's family. But this does not adequately explain, for example, how long people work, how they work, what activities they prefer, and what feelings they experience at work. Even if one may assume that there are universal needs that are satisfied by work, one can nevertheless assume that both the extent of the respective needs and the way in which these needs are satisfied are to a large extent shaped by the respective culture.

First of all, it must be stated that the importance that work has in a person's life can be quite different and is also subject to strong social change (cf. McClelland 1961, 1987). In social science, one speaks of the "*work ethics*" that are rooted in the religious ideas of a culture. The Western world is strongly influenced by the *Protestant ethics* described in detail by Max Weber (1905/1993). According to Weber's "Protestantism thesis", capitalism is based on the Calvinist tradition,[1] the essential element of which is the doctrine of predestination. It states that the fate of every human being is predetermined (predestined) by God independently of the own behaviour. Which fate is assigned to a person is shown in the success of work. Wealth gained through work is seen as a sign of being chosen, failure and poverty are interpreted as a sign of damnation. Accordingly, in the Western world of work, the result of work is more appreciated than its content.

Both Confucian ethics and Orthodox ethics are in contrast to the Protestant ethics. In *Confucian ethics*, which is widespread in the East Asian region, the focus is not on the future result but on the present content of work. The value of present activity is essentially the establishment and maintenance of harmonious relationships. At first glance, the emphasis on the present seems to be in contrast to the long-term orientation that is pronounced in Confucianism (Chap. 5). However, the contradiction is only seeming: The corresponding attitude involves the conviction that the right behaviour in the present also ensures a good future.

The *Orthodox ethics*, which is particularly pronounced in Russia despite the Soviet past (Böhmer 2008), emphasises the spiritual rather the economic attitude when performing work. Work is declared to be a religious service and thus subordinated to higher, spiritual goals. The value of work is measured by the benefit to the spirit and not by material success. Work is to be done for God's pleasure and for charity. The main motivation for work is therefore the inner motivation.

---

[1] Named after the reformer John Calvin (1509–1564).

The most important empirical study on work ethics is the *"Meaning of Working"* study (*"MOW"* study), which is based on a survey of 15,000 people from eight industrialised countries (MOW International Research Team 1987; cf. Rosso et al. 2010). The central question was whether there were differences in the importance of work for one's life between the countries studied. According to the results, work (as compared to other areas of life) occupied the highest importance in Japan and the second highest in former Yugoslavia; it was least important for England and Germany. At the same time, the income earned from work was of little importance to Japanese workers compared to the other countries. The results could be taken as an indication – at least a weak one – that religiously influenced cultural beliefs are indeed reflected in working life. In Japan, in line with Confucian ethics, a high value should be placed on work itself, but less importance should be attached to the result of work in the form of the income it generates. Due to the Protestant ethics, at first glance one would have expected a higher importance to be attached to work in Germany and England, but on closer examination the results obtained do not contradict the Protestantism thesis, since according to the Calvinist view work is only a means to an end and does not embody a value in itself. Moreover, it is consistent with the Orthodox work ethics that in the former Yugoslavia, as an Orthodox country, work itself is highly esteemed. Caution is nevertheless warranted with respect to the interpretations made, as the MOW study addressed the Protestant work ethics but not the Confucian and Orthodox work ethics.

Of particular interest in the cultural comparison are the *motives* or needs that motivate a person to work in the first place, to prefer certain activities over others, and to seek, retain, or leave a particular job. Frequently, the model of the *hierarchy of needs* developed by Maslow (1943, 1987) has been scrutinised (Box 13.1).

> **Box 13.1: Maslow's Model of the Hierarchy of Needs**
> Maslow (1943) developed a model of the *hierarchy of needs*. According to this, human beings have five needs structured (hierarchically) according to levels, whereby the higher-ranking needs (belongingness and love, esteem, and self-actualisation) only come into play when the lower-ranking ones (physiological needs and safety) have been satisfied to some extent.

(continued)

13.2 Work Attitude and Work Motivation

Box 13.1 (continued)

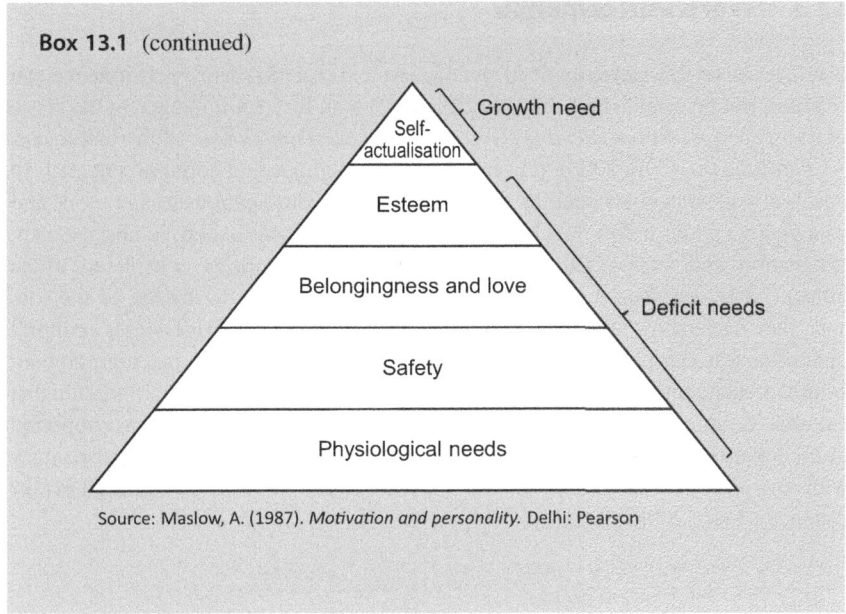

Source: Maslow, A. (1987). *Motivation and personality.* Delhi: Pearson

According to Maslow (cf. Maslow 1987), human beings have five hierarchically structured needs, whereby the higher-ranking needs (belongingness, esteem and self-actualisation) only come into play once the lower-ranking needs (basic physiological needs and safety) have been satisfied to some extent. Ronen (1994, cf. Stumpf and Kammhuber 2003, p. 504) concluded from a survey of work-life goals among workers in Canada, France, England, Germany, Japan, China, and Israel, that the needs specified by Maslow could be found everywhere. Some evidence that the hierarchical structure can also claim universal validity is provided by a study by Hui and Luk (1997): In less developed countries, subsistence needs dominate, while in highly developed countries, immaterial needs gain importance. Also, data from the World Values Survey (Sect. 5.5) suggest, at least in part, that subsistence needs ("survival") predominate in the less developed countries, while the need for self-actualisation is more pronounced in the highly developed countries. Nevertheless, Maslow's model must be viewed critically. For one thing, the separation into the different levels of needs is relatively arbitrary, since overlaps are not taken into account. For example, income can satisfy both physiological needs and the need for self-esteem). Secondly, there is disagreement about the definition of the need for self-actualisation (cf. Yang 2003).

13.3 Work Performance

A direct causal link between need satisfaction and resulting work performance can certainly not be established. As a variable having an indirect influence in the sense of a so-called *mediator variable* (Box 13.2), the *self-commitment* of the employees is often cited (cf. Felfe 2008). It is assumed that a high level of commitment leads to positive work outcomes such as high productivity, conscientiousness at work and collegiality, while a low level leads to negative outcomes such as absenteeism, resignation and stress. The level of commitment in turn is considered to be influenced by the motives and abilities of the employees, the nature of the job, and the leadership style of the supervisors. Based on Hofstede's cultural dimensions, it can be postulated that in vertical-collectivist cultures, commitment is more dependent on the respective supervisor, whereas in horizontal-individualist cultures (Chap. 5), the type of work is more decisive. This hypothesis was supported in a comparison between office workers in Germany (as an individualist country with low power distance) and in China (as a collectivist country with high power distance) (Felfe 2008).

Box 13.2: Mediator Variable
A *mediator* variable (MeV) *arbitrates* the effect of the independent variable (IV) on the dependent variable (DV). If the mediator variable is omitted, there is no longer an effect of IV on DV.

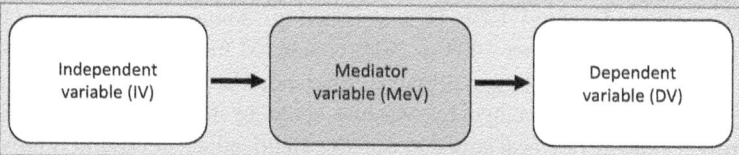

Example:
The effect of work motivation on work performance will be examined.

IV:	Degree of work motivation
DV:	Amount of work
MeV:	Commitment
Results:	Work performance is influenced by work motivation only when work motivation affects commitment

13.4 Leadership Behaviour

"Leadership" is understood as the process of influencing others toward goal achievement (cf. Yukl et al. 2019, p. 26). Based on the so-called Ohio School, it is often assumed that the concrete leadership behaviour of supervisors can be described by two independent dimensions. One dimension can be described as *"concern for people"*, the other as *"concern for production"* (Blake and Mouton 1982, 1985). The former refers to the establishment of a trusting relationship with subordinates, the latter to the accomplishment of the work tasks at hand. The "managerial grid" model derived from this is very popular in Western culture, although not without controversy (Neuberger 2002). Modifications of the model have been developed in India (Sinha 1994) and in Japan (Misumi 1995). According to Sinha, a good leader is characterised by a *"nurturant-task"* style. This style is both employee-oriented and task-oriented, but the employee orientation manifests itself in a different way than in the Western model. The "nurturant-task" leader is authoritative but not authoritarian (Box 13.3). His leadership style is paternalistic in nature, meaning that subordinates are treated with a firm hand, but still with understanding and benevolence. According to Sinha, this type of people-orientation is often appropriate in India because there, most employees are not accustomed to a more participative approach with greater involvement in decision-making.

> **Box 13.3: Authoritarian and Authoritative Leadership Style**
> The *authoritarian* leadership style emphasises the control of employees in the performance of the work tasks at hand.
> The *authoritative* leadership style is paternalistic in nature, i.e. subordinates are treated with a firm hand, but still with understanding and benevolence.
> The *nurturant-task* leader is authoritative but not authoritarian. According to Sinha (1994), this style of leadership is often appropriate in India, since most employees there are unaccustomed to a more participative approach with greater decision participation.

Misumi's (1985) model, which is also two-dimensional, is characterised by its focus on the work group compared to the Western focus on the individual. Both production- and people-orientation ("P = performance" and "M = maintenance" respectively) are related to the work group rather than to individuals. The two dimensions, in contrast to the Western concept, are not conceived as independent of each other, but as dynamically interrelated. The validity of the model was tested not only by means of survey studies, but also in quasi-experimental settings (Chap. 2) and statistics in schools, government agencies, and industrial companies. The dependent variables here included task completion as well as error rates, accident and dismissal rates. It turned out that a company characterised by both high performance orientation (P) as well as by high relationship orientation (M) achieved the best results, with the exception that for low work-motivated employees, a high performance orientation combined with, simultaneously, a low relationship orientation proved most effective. Similar limitations are also claimed in the Western research literature, e.g. Hersey and Blanchard (cf. Blanchard et al. 2015), where the appropriateness of a leadership style depends on the "maturity level" of the employees.

If we look at managers' ideal-typical views about what characterises an efficient management style, there seems to be a certain convergence of ideal concepts irrespective of different cultural traditions in the course of globalisation, which is certainly not least due to the fact that most managers have completed their studies with a strong Western influence. For example, a qualitative survey of Chinese managers who have gone through a Western MBA program shows that characteristics such as communicative competence are highly appreciated, while authoritarian behaviour is viewed negatively (Gao et al. 2011).

13.5 Decision-Making Behaviour

When individuals have to make decisions under uncertain conditions, i.e. when the outcome is uncertain, they do not usually do so from a purely rational point of view (Kahneman 2011). According to classical decision theory (*expected value theory*), a rational approach consists in measuring the value of an alternative according to the weighted sum of its consequences, where each consequence is expressed as the product of the probability of its occurrence and its value:

$$\text{Value of an alternative} = \sum_{\text{All consequences}} (\text{probability} \times \text{value})$$

In studies carried out in the Western cultural area, it has been found that neither the subjectively perceived probability corresponds to the objective probability of occurrence, nor does the subjective value reflect the objective value (e.g. the amount of money). Thus, a small amount of money tends to be overvalued as a gain relative to a large amount of money, i.e., the relative value of a monetary gain decreases as the amount of money increases. Moreover, relative to the same amount of money, the anger about a loss outweighs the joy of a gain (Kahneman and Tversky 1979). Looking at investment decisions associated with a potential gain, we find that a relatively certain low gain (i.e., a low amount with a high probability of occurrence) is preferred over an uncertain high gain (i.e., a high amount with a low probability of occurrence), i.e., a risk-averse risk behaviour dominates over risk- taking behaviour.

However, the regularity found is not universal. Weber and Hsee (2000) compared data of different provenance (quasi-experimental studies, surveys and statistics) from the USA, China, Germany and Poland with regard to the willingness to make investment decisions with different stakes and came to the conclusion that the Chinese were the most willing to take risks and the Americans were, surprisingly, the most risk-averse. The authors explain the result with the so-called "cushion hypothesis", according to which the Chinese are embedded in social networks (family and friends) that provide support and protection against financial losses and thus cushion risks. Risks, therefore, are rather perceived as opportunities than as threats.

However, it cannot be ruled out that risk behaviour is also influenced by the overall economic situation. In an economic environment characterised by growth, such as China, risk appetite is certainly higher than in an environment characterised by stagnation or even recession, such as the USA.

Decisions in organisations differ from the decisions addressed in the studies cited above in at least four respects. First, it should be noted that often there are not any clearly specified alternatives and sometimes there is not even a compulsion to make a decision. Second, a decision is a multi-stage process that includes different phases and types of information gathering and evaluation before the choice to act is actually made. Third, the decision-making process usually involves several people, i.e. it is not a matter of individual decisions but of group decisions. Fourth, usually there are rules about which people are entitled to which types of decisions and which guidelines have to be followed then.

In natural decision-making situations, what is most noticeable is a culturally varying degree of employee participation in operational decisions, ranging from individual decisions made by the respective supervisor to majority decisions with general consensus. Well-known in this context is the *Ringi* system widespread in Japan where a consensus is to be reached before arriving at a decision, regardless of rank and status. At first glance, this seems to contradict the strong hierarchical orientation in Japan. However, the striving for harmony as well as the mutual obligation of superiors and subordinates apparently dominate here.

Whether decisions made are also subsequently implemented seems to depend to a large extent on the support from the superiors in countries with high power distance. However, the extent of control cannot be ignored, because, with inadequate control, "apostate" behaviour seems also to occur more frequently in societies with high power distance.

13.6 Work Behaviour

13.6.1 Use of Time

An important component of work behaviour is the *use of time*. In all cultures, work processes are structured in terms of time, but cultures differ considerably in the way this structuring takes place. This is often not overt, but rather follows unwritten rules – also referred to as "silent language" (Hall and Hall 1990). Ignorance of these unwritten rules gives rise to many misunderstandings and conflicts in international business relationships (Brislin and Kim 2003). A study by Fink and Meyerevert (2004) even suggests that more than half of the conflicts arising in joint ventures between Western European and Russian companies are sparked off by differences in the ways of using time.

Three dimensions of time use are of importance for working life: *time horizon, time allocation* and *tempo*. "Time horizon" refers both to the cultural dimension of *time orientation* identified by Hofstede with its poles of "short-term" versus "long-term", as well as to the dimension of *time orientation* identified by Trompenaars (Chap. 5). "Time allocation" is addressed both in the dimension of *time orientation* by Hall and in Trompenaars' dimension of time *orientation* (Chap. 5). *Tempo* refers to the speeds and durations in working activities, in solving tasks and to making decisions.

- **Time horizon:** Both at the organisational level and at the individual level, work actions are associated with objectives that can extend into the future to varying degrees. They can be located near ("proximal") or far ("distal") relative to the present.
- **Time allocation:** In the execution of work activities, a rather "monochronic" and a rather "polychronic" way of working may be contrasted (Hall 1959; Trompenaars 2012). The former involves a preference for successive processing of individual activities and a tendency to strictly adhere to deadlines once they

13.6 Work Behaviour

Table 13.1 Monochronous versus polychronous time allocation

Monochronicity	Polychronicity
Tasks are accomplished successively	Several things are done at the same time
Deadlines and schedules are taken seriously	Appointments and schedules are handled flexibly
Interruptions are avoided	Interruptions are accepted
Punctuality is important	Punctuality depends on the relationship between the parties to the action

have been set, while in the latter several activities are usually carried out simultaneously and deadlines are handled flexibly (Table 13.1).

- **Tempo:** Work actions can be performed at different *speeds* and can take different *amounts of time*. In terms of the work result, both facets can be subsumed under the term "tempo".

Cross-cultural research on the use of time suggests that differences in the cultural dimensions of *individualism-collectivism* and *power distance* are accompanied by marked differences in the way time is spent. Individualistic cultures with low power distance seem to exhibit a pattern of time use that can be characterised by the metaphor of *"linear time"* (Hassard 1966*)*. Prototypical of this is a focus on long-term goals, a monochronic way of working with precise deadlines, and a fast pace of work. This time pattern reflects the "Protestant work ethics" in the sense of Max Weber (Sect. 13.2) and seems to be particularly characteristic of working life in Germany.

Not uniform to the same extent are the time patterns considered typical of collectivist cultures with high power distance. There seem to be clear differences between East Asian and East European cultures. They are most apparent in the type of goals pursued that tend to be long-term in East Asian societies – in line with the "Confucian ethics" – whereas they tend to be short-term in East European societies – in line with economic instability. However, differences also seem to exist in the adherence to deadlines as well as in the speed of work actions. One may guess that economic circumstances are probably more important than cultural differences. Similarities between different collectivist cultures, on the other hand, can be seen in the allocation of time. A polychronic use of time is generally considered to be a characteristic of collectivist countries, since here, in the sense of the "striving for harmony" interruptions in the work in progress and flexible handling of deadlines are more readily accepted in favour of social interventions than in individualistically oriented countries.

It should not be overlooked that the patterns of time are in the state of changing. Thus, a polychronic use of time depending on activity, gender and personal inclination can also be found in the West and is even growing. However, the seems to be less oriented to the need for social harmony than to the desire to improve efficiency. Once the acceleration mechanisms of a monochronic use of time have been exhausted, this can apparently only be realised by doing several things simultaneously in the form of "multitasking". The new information and communication technologies, such as mobile telephones, video conferencing or computer windows that are open at the same time, make such "time compression" possible and encourage it. However, it must be pointed out that "multitasking" is not synonymous with "polychronicity". In fact, unlike "multitasking", polychronicity is not the simultaneous execution of several activities, but rather a short-term switching between different activities, so that a distinction has recently been made between "polychronicity" and "polytasking" (cf. Leonard 2008).

13.6.2 Incorrect Actions

An important component of work behaviour are also incorrect actions and the way of handling them. Incorrect actions include errors, mistakes, and violations. "Errors" and "mistakes" are the terms used when a work task is not completed, is completed inadequately, or is completed incorrectly. They cannot be completely avoided and sometimes are even necessary when trying to optimise work processes, to acquire functional skills and to arrive at new solutions to problems that have arisen. Thus, it is not exclusively the frequency of errors and mistakes that must be considered, but also the way in which they are tackled: For example, errors may be corrected or covered up by the person acting, and they may be either tolerated or sanctioned by superiors. While "mistakes" and "errors" refer to unintentional wrongdoings, we speak of "violations" when the misconduct is intended. Errors, mistakes, and violations do not always have visible consequences but often lead to losses or even accidents.

Although dealing with errors is mentioned in some cross-cultural studies (e.g. Felfe et al. 2006), systematic studies on this subject have hardly existed to date. In this context, however, a study on the frequency of accidents (Gaygisiz 2010) could be informative. In an analysis of a total of 46 countries, the aim was to find out whether there is a correlation between the rate of fatal road traffic accidents on the one hand and the cultural dimensions according to Hofstede (2001) and

13.6 Work Behaviour

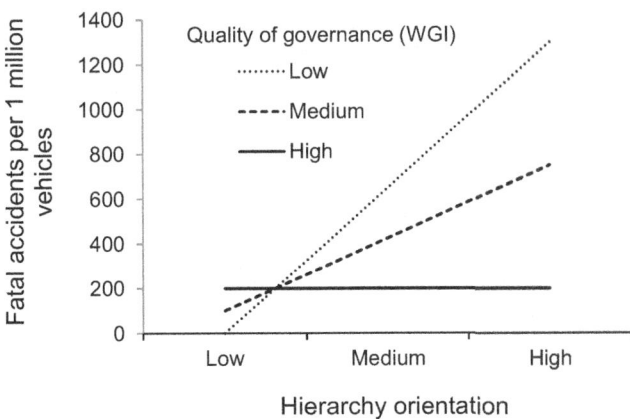

Fig. 13.1 Relationship between quality of governance, hierarchy orientation and fatal accident rate. (Modified after Gaygisiz 2010, p. 1808)

Schwartz (2006) on the other. Initially, significant correlations were found with almost all cultural dimensions. However, later on, most of them turned out to be insignificant as soon as the respective overall political condition of a country was statistically controlled by means of a regression analysis. The overall quality of governance was operationalised by a combined measure derived from the World Bank's *Worldwide Governance Indicators (WGI)*. The measure captures, among other things, control of corruption, political stability, and government effectiveness. Overall, it was found that there is a relationship between Schwartz's dimension of *hierarchy* orientation ("Hierarchy vs. equality", Sect. 5.3) on the one hand and the fatal accident rate on the other, but this merely came into play when the overall quality of governance was low (i.e., high corruption, political instability, and poor government effectivity). When the overall quality of governance was high, the relationship with the cultural variables leveled off. Specifically, in terms of hierarchy orientation, this means that although the accident rate increases with the degree of hierarchy orientation, this is only the case if the country in question suffers from high levels of corruption, poor quality of government and political instability (Fig. 13.1). The overall quality of governance (operationalised as WGI value) thus acted as a moderator variable (Box 13.2) in the relationship between accident rate and hierarchy orientation.

What consequences can be drawn from this with regard to incorrect actions in the workplace? If it was said above that the frequency of "apostate" behaviour – which certainly includes wrongdoing – intensifies with increasing hierarchical orientation, it may be necessary to modify this finding to the effect that the correlation can only be observed under unfavourable organisational and political conditions.

13.7 Group Work

The study of the effectiveness or efficiency of group work compared to individual work has a long tradition in social psychology. Systematic comparisons between work performed in groups (example: five groups of four people each) with aggregated work performed by the same total number of people (in the example: 20 people) in individual work lead to the conclusion that it depends on the type of tasks, the extent of group cohesion, and the group's commitment to the organisation, whether group work is superior or inferior to individual work (cf. Marcus 2011).

Based on Hofstede's cultural dimensions (Chap. 5), one might assume that individuals with an individualist orientation perform better in individual work and individuals with a collectivist orientation perform better in groups. As expected, a comparison of problem solving in a business game between Hong Kong Chinese (collectivist orientation) and US Americans (individualist orientation) revealed that the former performed better in groups and the latter performed better in individual work (Nibler and Harris 2003). However, this only applied if there were no conflicts in the group. Conflicts were perceived as a threat by the Chinese, but as a challenge by the Americans. Accordingly, when conflict occurred, performance deterioration resulted for the Chinese and performance improvement resulted for the Americans. One can draw the conclusion that group cohesion in the Chinese groups is conducive to performance, whereas in the American groups it is rather detrimental.

The strong sense of competition which is evident among East Asian students in everyday life as well as in the PISA- and TIMSS studies (Chap. 7) seems, at first glance, to be opposed to the pronounced groupthink in collectivist cultures. However, the contradiction is resolved when the group is not viewed as a working group but rather as a "reference group". The reference group in this case is one's own family. A good performance or a good degree then serves less as proof of one's own performance but more as an honor for one's family, and is thus consistent with loyalty to one's own group ("in-group collectivism"), as defined by the GLOBE research group (Sect. 5.4).

A special form of group work emerges when the group members come from different cultures (Box 13.4). In the course of globalisation, the number of such "multicultural" working groups is growing. It could be argued that cultural diversity, also referred to as "heterogeneity", improves productivity as the group could benefit from a wider range of experiences and skills compared to culturally homogeneous groups. On the other hand, it is precisely the different cultural backgrounds that can cause friction and hinder productivity. This is especially true for cooperation between members of vertical-collectivist cultures and members of horizontal-individualist cultures. Tensions arise regarding several aspects: as a result of discrepancies in the importance of human relationships, in the type of dividing labour, in hierarchy orientation, in the concept of time and in the appreciation of cooperation and competition.

> **Box 13.4: Multicultural Working Groups**
> *Multicultural working groups* are working groups in which the group members come from different cultures or countries. One then speaks of *cultural heterogeneity*. This special form of group work is increasing in the course of globalisation.

13.8 Conclusion

A cross-cultural comparison of the world of work reveals both cross-cultural similarities and culture-related differences. Commonalities can be seen, for example, in the fact that two dimensions have emerged in leadership behaviour across cultures, which can be characterised as "concern for people" and "concern for production". Nevertheless, the type of people orientation exhibits culture-specific modifications: In cultures characterised by individualism and low power distance, people orientation tends to focus on employee participation, whereas in cultures characterised by collectivism and high power distance, it tends to be displayed in terms of caring for employees. Even greater cultural differences are evident in other areas: work ethics, work behaviour, and group work.

Not all the differences observed between different countries can be traced back to cultural traditions; some of them reflect contrasts in the respective economic, technological and overall political situation rather than in the respective cultural value orientations. However, the interdependence of the individual condition factors must be taken into account, i.e. both multiple conditionality and interactions between the single influencing factors should be used to explain the differences.

13.9 Questions of Understanding

1. Explain the difference between *organisational* culture and *country* culture.
2. Explain the objective of the so-called *MOW study*.
3. Explain similarities and differences between Western and Asian *leadership* models.

Further Reading

Berry, J. W., Poortinga, Y. H., Breugelmans, S. M., Chasiotis, A., Sam, D. M., & Seger, M. (2011). *Cross-cultural psychology* (3rd ed.). Cambridge: Cambridge University Press.

Browaeys, M.-J., & Price, R. (2018). *Understanding cross-cultural management* (3rd ed.). Edinburgh Gate: Pearson Education Limited.

Helfrich, H., Hölter, E., & Arzhenowskiy, I. V. (Eds.). (2012). *Time and management from a cross-cultural perspective*. Cambridge, MA: Hogrefe & Huber.

Helfrich-Hölter, H. (2011). Kultur und Zeit. In W. Dreyer & U. Hößler (Eds.), *Perspektiven interkultureller Kompetenz* (pp. 125–136). Göttingen: Vandenhoeck & Ruprecht.

Smith, P. B. (2011). The cultural contexts of organisational behaviour. In F. J. R. Van de Vijver, A. Chasiotis & S. M. Breugelmans (Eds.), *Fundamental questions in cross-cultural psychology* (pp. 494–517). Cambridge: Cambridge University Press.

Stumpf, S., & Kammhuber, S. (2003). Organisationspsychologische Aspekte im Kulturvergleich. In A. Thomas (Ed.), *Kulturvergleichende Psychologie* (2nd ed., pp. 487–514). Göttingen: Hogrefe.

Mental Disorders 14

When considering mental disorders, the focus is on behaviour, thinking and experience that deviates from the form expected in a society, i.e. from the "norm", to such an extent that it is considered conspicuous and at the same time pathological (= morbid). Three types of information sources are typically taken into account to record these "deviations from the norm": First, the use of clinical counselling or treatment by the person concerned or their relatives; second, statistical data, such as the frequency of suicide or the level of alcohol consumption; and, third, questionnaire data, such as those recorded in a depression scale. Since these sources of information each relate to different samples, it is not surprising that the statements derived from them are not always mutually consistent.

14.1 Cross-Cultural Versus Culture-Specific Diagnostics

In cross-cultural research, the question first arises as to the extent to which there is universal agreement on what is to be described as "abnormal", and to what extent the definition of what is considered deviant is itself culturally determined. From an etic view, it is concretised in terms of whether the standardised diagnostic systems as defined by the World Health Organization (WHO) (2019) in the form of the International Classification of Diseases (ICD-11) and by the American Psychiatric Association (APA) (2022) in the form of the Diagnostic and Statistical Manual of Mental Disorders (DSM-5) can be applied worldwide. However, cultural differences in the diagnosis of the same behaviors or conditions do not necessarily preclude conceptual equivalence (Sect. 2.2.2). A diagnosis communicated to the patient always involves a communication process that may be more or less socially acceptable. In every culture, there are deviations that are more likely to be socially tolerated and those that are more likely to be stigmatised. For example, currently in Germany a "burnout syndrome" is socially tolerated, while a "depression" still tends to be stigmatised. Therefore, it cannot be excluded that the same symptomatology is perceived in the same way by psychiatrists of different cultures, but is named differently in each case. The situation resembles the so-called culture-bound syndromes. Although these may have appeared and been named for the first time in a particular culture – think, for example, of the syndrome *Amok*[1] in the Indonesian cultural sphere – they can also be perceived and described by members of other cultures (Chap. 2).

If disorders can be identified cross-culturally, it must also be asked whether there are cultural differences in the extent and manifestation of certain forms of disorder. Finally, it is asked to what extent universal risk factors or rather cultural factors can be considered as antecedents of certain forms of disorders. The following presentation will be limited to depression, schizophrenia, anxiety disorders and suicide.

14.2 Depression

Cross-cultural studies in which patients seeking psychiatric consultation were classified according to standardised diagnostic procedures suggest that the core symptoms of depression, such as sadness, listlessness, lack of concentration, and feelings of failure, are present in all cultures, although their respective frequency of occurrence varies both intra-culturally and cross-culturally (cf. Draguns and Tanaka-Matsumi 2003). Strong cultural variations were found in the additional occurrence of feelings of guilt as well as in the extent of somatic (= physical) symptoms such as insomnia or heart complaints. Feelings of guilt seem to be more frequent in Western-individualist than in East-Asian-collectivist countries and least frequent in African countries. Somatic symptoms seem to be diagnosed considerably more often in East Asian countries as well as in Turkey compared to Western countries (cf. Draguns and Tanaka-Matsumi 2003).

Overall, depressive disorders appear to be more prevalent in Africa and less prevalent in China compared to Western countries. The low prevalence in China is sometimes attributed to the strong family orientation, which makes depression-triggering losses both less strongly felt and more strongly absorbed socially (Cao et al. 2015; Hsieh 2015; Li et al. 2015). However, it cannot be ruled out that core

---

[1] = sudden violent attack with significant xenodestructive behavior.

symptoms such as listlessness are not assigned to "depression", but to the category of "neurasthenia" (= nervous weakness), which is less stigmatised in China.

14.3 Schizophrenia

In contrast to depression, there is no essential core symptom in schizophrenia – according to established diagnostic procedures. Schizophrenic patients differ more from each other in terms of symptoms than patients with other disorders (cf. Kring et al. 2007). The DSM-5 specifies how many symptoms must be present and to what degree to justify a diagnosis. Cross-cultural studies (cf. Bhugra 2005) suggest that the frequency of each symptom is universally comparable. However, the onset and course of the disease appear to be modified by sociocultural factors. Surprisingly, the long-term prognosis is more favourable in developing countries than in industrialised countries. Responsible for this seem to be the more intensive kinship relations as well as the increased tendency to return to regular work (Matsumoto and Juang 2008, p. 286 f.).

14.4 Anxiety Disorders

Symptoms of anxiety or fear seem to be diagnosable in all cultures, but there is relatively little cross-cultural consensus about what type and degree of anxiety disorders are to be classified as pathological (= morbid). Cultural peculiarities occur primarily in the different forms of anxiety disorders (Table 14.1). Anthropophobia (= fear of people) occurs frequently among adolescents in Japan (there called "kyofusho") and China (there called "taijin kyofusho"). A variant of this, sociophobia (fear of publicity), is often diagnosed in the United States and Western Europe. "Koro" (fear of penis shrinkage) is considered a specific form of anxiety in China, and sudden panic attacks ("ataques de nervios", "susto" or "ufufuyane") are common in Latin America and Africa.

However, cultural differences often already exist in the classification of disorders: When psychiatrists from different countries are asked to classify video recordings of patient intake interviews, they differ both in the extent to which they address the same statements or behaviors as being pathological and also, to which category of anxiety they assign them (cf. Draguns and Tanaka-Matsumi 2003). If one attempts a synthesis of culture-specific characteristics and cross-cultural standards (i.e., a combination of emic with etic approaches), the symptom bundles (syndromes) can be divided into culture-bound conceptions, culture-bound forms of

Table 14.1 Culture-bound forms of fear

Name	Description	Area of occurrence
Kyofusho	Fear of people	Japan
Taijin Kyofusho	Fear of people	China
Sociophobia	Fear of publicity	USA, Western Europe
Koro	Fear of penis shrinkage	China
Ataques de nervios, susto	Sudden panics	Latin America
Ufufuyane	Sudden panics	Africa

coping with anxiety, and culture-bound psychopathological manifestations (cf. Tseng 2001). Of the above examples, "koro" could be assigned to culture-bound conceptions, kyofusho, taijin kyofusho and sociophobia to culture-bound forms of coping with anxiety, and "ataques de nervios" or "ufufuyane" to culture-bound psychopathological manifestations.

14.5 Suicide

The suicide rate is known to show very strong intercultural variations. Korea and the Eastern European countries occupy the top positions. Worldwide, significantly more men than women commit suicide, with China being an exception. Although the suicide rate is lower in adolescents than in older age groups, suicides are the prevailing cause of death in adolescence, along with traffic accidents. The phenomenon of youth suicide has stimulated many cross-cultural studies, although it should be noted that "suicide bombers" are excluded from consideration, so the research focuses on "normal" suicide.

The main motive for suicide seems to be to end an existence that is perceived as unbearable. To actually implement the action, the premises to carry it out (fearlessness, tolerance of pain, and accessibility of means) must also be met.

A wide variety of variables have been examined as possible candidates for risk factors: macroeconomic and political upheavals, socioeconomic conditions, religious beliefs, societal tolerance of suicide, family structures, child-rearing practices, alcohol use, and others.

While in Western countries dysfunctional family structures and excessive alcohol consumption often precede or promote suicide, this does not apply in East Asian countries. The psychoanalytically inspired thesis that the frequency of suicides in a society is compensatory to the frequency of murders also receives little support from cross-cultural research (cf. Tanaka-Matsumi and Draguns 1997, p. 457).

The degree of religiosity is considered the most suitable as a predictor – in the sense that high religiosity reduces the risk of suicide (De Leo 2009; Vijayakumar et al. 2005). Important factors here are religious practice, social support from the faith community, and the intolerance of some religions towards the act of suicide. At least partly in line with this is the so-called anomie theory developed by Emile Durkheim, according to which the loss of value and goal orientation (= anomie) enhances the risk of suicide (cf. Durkheim 1966).

Also compatible with religiosity as a risk-reducing factor is the finding that the frequency of suicide is generally significantly lower among women than among men, since religiosity is more pronounced among women. However, it must be asked why women in China are more likely to commit suicide than men, especially in comparison to the rest of the world. The key to an explanation could be provided by the special value pattern of Confucianism that is pronounced in China (even today and even in Mao times) (Zhang 2014). The basic values are family harmony, reverence for age, and subordination of women. Confucianism thus creates a "man's world" that encourages success and achievement in men, but tends to prevent opportunities for women to develop. Especially in rural areas this can easily lead to a situation of existence for women that is felt to be unbearable. Moreover, since Confucianism does not offer the prospect of a better "life after death", hoping for a turn for the better in the hereafter is also lost.

Finally, it should be noted that the comparability of suicide statistics is hardly guaranteed, since in countries where suicide is highly taboo, suicides are often falsely declared as "accidents".

14.6 Conclusion

In all societies, behaviors and experiences occur that are considered deviations from the "norm". Some of these deviations are socially tolerated, others are stigmatised. Cross-cultural comparison has shown that both the definition of these "norm deviations" as well as their respective degree of tolerance is highly culture-dependent. Phenomenally identical behaviours and experiences can therefore be evaluated in culturally different ways. In the case of psychiatric disorders, there is also the fact that the diagnosis communicated to the patient by the doctor always involves a communication process that can be made more or less socially acceptable.

With regard to psychiatric disorders, it can be stated that if standardised diagnostic systems are used, the corresponding symptoms can be discovered worldwide, but that their frequency varies culturally. Similar to emotions, it also needs to be stated that the triggers for the disorder and its course are influenced by cultural conditions.

Juvenile suicide, the prevalence of which is known to show strong intercultural variations, has received particular interest in cultural comparisons. If we exclude "suicide bombers" from the analysis and restrict ourselves to "normal" suicide, it seems almost impossible to identify universally valid risk factors. The degree of religiosity appears to be the most suitable cross-cultural predictor – in the sense that high religiosity reduces the risk of suicide.

14.7 Questions of Understanding

1. Explain the problem of psychiatric *diagnoses* in cultural comparison.
2. Describe universal and culturally specific aspects of *anxiety disorders*.
3. Assess universal and culture-specific risk factors for *suicide*.

Further Reading

Hook, K. & Vera, E. (2020). Best Practices in Global Mental Health: An exploratory study of recommendations for psychologists. *International Perspectives in Psychology: Research, Practice, Consultation*, 9 (2), 67–83.

Kirmayer, L. J. (2013). 50 years of Transcultural Psychiatry. *Transcultural Psychiatry, 50,* 3–5.

Kirmayer, L. J., & Swartz, L. (2014). Culture and global mental health. In V. Patel, H. Minas, A. Cohen, M. J., Prince, V. Patel, H. Minas, ... M. J. Prince (Eds.), *Global mental health: Principles and practice* (pp. 41–62). Oxford: Oxford University Press.

Matsumoto, D., & Juang, L. (2008). *Culture and psychology* (4th ed.). Belmont (CA): Thomson Wadsworth (Chapter 12).

Final Remarks 15

This textbook aimed to focus on similarities and differences between people of different cultures. It was guided by the following questions: Are people of other cultural origins different from us? Or are similar deep structures of thinking, feeling, and acting hidden beneath the surface of the exotic or threatening foreign? But why do conspicuous differences in behaviour occur, and how can they be explained? To clarify these questions, the textbook introduced the most important contents, perspectives and methods of cross-cultural psychology. What should be highlighted is the relationship between culture and individual behaviour.

15.1 Possibilities and Limits of Cross-cultural Psychology

The fundamental question of cross-cultural psychology is to what extent mental processes and structures are universal and to what extent they undergo culturally specific modifications. The answer to this question also has consequences for the future of psychology in general. Cultural comparison serves as a touchstone for existing psychological theories by examining their core statements for validity in a new context. Whereas in these so-called generalisation studies "culture" forms the background within which individual behaviour occurs (Munroe and Munroe 1997, p. 173), in so-called differentiation studies "culture" is specifically considered an antecedent for individual behaviour (Lonner and Adamopoulos 1997) by testing certain cultural factors as "independent variables" in their "impact" on certain dependent variables. As the latter, the researcher is particularly interested in individual thinking, perception or memory skills, feelings and emotions, attitudes or social actions. Among the independent variables, especially the dimension *individualism-collectivism* was examined in its possible influence on certain forms of thinking and acting as dependent variables.

This "variable-oriented" comparison of cultures (Eckensberger and Plath 2002) has been criticised from various sides (cf. e.g. Oyserman et al. 2002). In its milder form, the criticism is directed against Hofstede's cultural value dimensions, which were obtained in a secularised working world shaped by Western thinking and thus largely omit important cultural components such as religious aspects. Religious values and attitudes would only be taken into account in their secularised form, e.g. as Protestant work ethics or Confucian dynamics, and thereby deprived of their genuinely religious content (cf. e.g. Tarakeshwar et al. 2003; Van Ess 2003). An example of this neglect would be the dynamics of Islam. For example, one could ask to what extent suicide attacks reflect Islamic thought and to what extent factors of an individual and social nature that are independent of the concrete religious system should be taken into account. The fact that suicide attacks have also been carried out in other historical constellations – think of the Japanese kamikaze pilots and the German suicide missions in the Second World War – speaks in favour of their inclusion.

The criticism is even more fundamental: With regard to the countries, it is true that due to the affiliation with the multinational company studied by Hofstede, only countries with a relatively high degree of industrialisation were involved, i.e. members of so-called primitive peoples virtually do not appear. With regard to the subjects studied, it is true that the parallelisation of the samples (in each case employees of the same multinational corporation) is accompanied by a different representativeness of the single country samples: Being an employee of the corporation studied (IBM) implies a different social class affiliation in emerging countries than in highly developed countries.

In a more rigorous form of criticism, it is argued that the factor "culture" is not suitable being used as an independent variable because its different levels cannot be manipulated experimentally (Sect. 2.3). Instead, "cultural factors" are "organismic" variables. This means that the individuals cannot be arbitrarily assigned to the respective factor levels by the researcher (e.g., by randomisation), but can only be selected according to their "natural" affiliation to a particular factor level. "Culture" thus is precisely not an independent variable in the sense of an experimental manipulation. It is not an inescapable "treatment", but rather delineates a framework of possibilities for action (cf. Boesch 1980), which can be individually shaped and autonomously further developed, thus controlling the cultural offer oneself in an independent way. This interaction between the individual and culture would have to be, in future, taken more into account as a research goal by pursuing the emergence and change of cultural forms of life as a function of the thoughts and actions of individuals or groups (cf. Straub and Thomas 2003). One step towards achieving this should be to supplement the hitherto rather statically oriented experimental settings and methods with more dynamically oriented ones, e.g. the analysis of temporal patterns of development (cf. Helfrich 1999; Hong 2001). This is all the more important as there are increasingly fewer homogeneous cultural communities and the contemporary world is sometimes dominated rather by cultural change than by cultural tradition.

In the most radical form of criticism, from an "emic" view, the split into "independent" and "dependent" variables, as undertaken in the "etic" approach, is generally criticised. According to this view – as advocated in particular by the line of research known as "cultural psychology" (Chap. 1) – psychological phenomena cannot be understood at all outside their cultural context, so that every psychology without exception is cultural psychology.

However, it should have become clear that "etic" and "emic" views do not constitute absolute opposites but complement each other. To overcome the contradiction, a mutual adoption of perspectives is inevitable. It can only be realised through increased cooperation between researchers from different cultures and thus allows for a supplementation of previous research strategies through a "transcultural consensual validation" (Shweder and Sullivan 1990), i.e. through a research process that, in all phases of investigation – from the development of the research question to the interpretation of the findings, is realised cooperatively by researchers from each of the cultures concerned (cf. Eckensberger and Plath 2002). By including the perspective of "indigenous" researchers (Serpell 1990), there may even be an opportunity for a "paradigm shift" (Kuhn 2012) or at least a paradigm modification.

Overall, it must be noticed in cultural psychological research that cultural differences are overemphasised and similarities tend to be neglected (cf. Van de Vijver 2006). This "bias" in favour of cultural differences applies to both the emic and etic approaches. Thus, from an emic view, as is typical of indigenous psychology and cultural psychology, the focus is predominantly on "otherness" or "uniqueness" of the culture under consideration, whereas parallels to other cultures are largely ignored. The otherness is often justified by pointing out that there are phenomena which can only be understood by recurring to their culturally specific symbolic meaning. An example of this would be the eating of a wafer as part of a ceremonial ritual in a Catholic church, which is to be understood as a religious act that would be completely misunderstood as food intake (cf. Straub and Chakkarath 2010). However, from the perspective of functional equivalence (Sect. 2.2.2), one might look at ritual acts in other cultures that serve a similar purpose, even if they are realised by different kinds of behaviour. With reference to the above example of eating a wafer, one could ask, for example, to what extent cultures are similar or different in terms of which everyday activities are preferably used to perform ritual acts.

With regard to the etic approach, it should first be noted that the proportion of generalisation studies is significantly lower than the proportion of differentiation studies (cf. Van de Vijver 2006), i.e. the research interest is primarily directed towards differences than towards similarities between different cultures. Particularly in bilateral differentiation studies, as explicitly realised in quasi-experimental designs to uncover cultural differences, the bias is partly favoured by the type of statistical analysis: If the hypothesised differences turn out not to be statistically significant, the null hypothesis (i.e. that no differences exist) must be maintained, but its validity is by no means proven. In scientific practice, this often means that the insignificant findings obtained in this way are not published at all. A way out of this dilemma can be to use research designs – such as a multi-level analysis – that explicitly take into account factors other than cultural affiliation (e.g. school education or parenting style).

15.2 Consequences for Intercultural Cooperation

It can be assumed that cultural differences have consequences with regard to intercultural encounters. This applies to encounters with people of other cultural origins on an international level, be it in a foreign host country or also in one's own country. Knowledge of different ways of thinking and different norms of behaviour and communication styles can be of great practical importance in the currently ongoing process of globalisation. Success in political meetings, business negotiations, teaching situations, social consultations and personal relationships depends to a large extent on whether the culturally prescribed or expected communicative "rules of the game" are observed.

Such consequences with regard to intercultural encounters are dealt with by the application-oriented "Intercultural Psychology" (Chap. 1) which is geared towards the practice of communication. One might now think that this is simply given in the application of the insights gained in cross-cultural psychology to the intercultural field of action. In fact, however, the intercultural situation of action differs in multiple respects from a cross-cultural view.

First, cross-cultural psychology starts from a scientific observation in which the observer takes a standpoint outside of the cultures being examined. However, the person standing in the midst of a concrete intercultural encounter situation is precisely not an uninvolved observer, but is part of an *action process* into which his or her wishes, goals and expectations enter as important components. It is known from social psychology that the assessment of behaviour of others and the

15.2 Consequences for Intercultural Cooperation

attribution of intentions to act, are influenced both by the identification with the self-group (Tajfel 1982) and by the importance of the respective action situation (Jones and Davis 1965).

Second, knowledge of foreign cultural peculiarities can encourage overgeneralisation and stereotyping in the intercultural encounter situation, since inter-individual and situational variation within the foreign culture can easily be overlooked. For example, not all individuals of a collectivist culture behave according to the collectivist behaviour pattern in all situations.

Third, none of the interaction partners involved will behave in exactly the same way in an intercultural encounter situation as in the intracultural communication situation (Chap. 9), since the interaction partners know that they are in an unusual situation. This *knowledge* can lead to mutual adaptation, e.g. in the use of English as a "lingua franca", or in granting an "idiosyncrasy credit" (Hollander 1992) to the foreign partner, which means that inappropriate behaviour patterns are tolerated more readily than with partners from one's own culture.

Fourth, the intercultural encounter situation is also shaped by the *status relation* of the partners taking part in the interaction. For example, many international co-operations are characterised by the dominance of the Western partner which can easily provoke resistance reactions from the non-Western side. Moreover, the intercultural status relationship may also be influenced by the internal organisational conditions, for example, by the fact that at the personal level as well a status relationship acts as a "confounding variable" – for instance, if a superior-subordinate situation exists.

Fifth, the intercultural encounter situation often involves a *new* situation, especially when all participants are confronted with a previously unknown problem for which they have to find a solution together by possibly having to use new techniques. Think, for example, of the situation in Fukushima (Japan) after the reactor disaster in March 2011.

As a consequence, intercultural cooperation needs more than just the application of cross-cultural psychology to the field of intercultural psychology. In the context of intercultural cooperation, new situations arise which cannot be derived solely from the comparison of cultures. The novelty results from new work tasks, global challenges and new technologies, but also from the knowledge of the actors that they participate in an exchange with people from cultures which are different from their own culture. From this, intercultural psychology can develop practical recommendations for shaping communication. Even without such recommendations, however, an "intercultural learning process" can be expected to some extent throughout the encounter itself.

15.3 Conclusion

The merit of cross- cultural psychology can be seen above all in its contribution to raising awareness of the range of variation in human ways of thinking and acting. This has consequences with regard to intercultural cooperation. However, the results cannot be transferred to concrete action situations without being checked, since the acting persons are not "objective" observers, but are integrated in an interaction process into which their goals, wishes and expectations enter as important components.

Although cross-cultural psychology has undoubtedly provided important insights into differences and similarities between cultures, the limits of previous research are also becoming visible. A fundamental criticism is raised by the line of research known as "cultural psychology". Here it is argued that "culture" is not an inescapable "treatment", but rather delineates a framework of action possibilities, which can be individually shaped and independently further developed through by controlling the cultural offer oneself. This interaction between the individual and culture should be given more attention in future research.

Further Reading

Shiraev, E. B., & Levy, D. A. (2017). *Cross-cultural psychology: Critical thinking and contemporary applications* (6th ed.). New York: Routledge.

Straub, J., & Thomas, A. (2003). Positionen, Ziele und Entwicklungslinien der kulturvergleichenden Psychologie. In A. Thomas (Ed.), *Kulturvergleichende Psychologie* (2nd ed., pp. 29–80). Göttingen: Hogrefe.

References

Ajdukovic, M. (1990). Differences in parent's rearing style between female and male predelinquent youth. *Psychologische Beiträge, 32*, 7–15.
Amelang, M., & Bartussek, D. (2006). *Differentielle Psychologie und Persönlichkeitsforschung* (6th ed.). Stuttgart: Kohlhammer.
American Psychiatric Association (APA) (2022). *Diagnostic and statistical manual of psychiatric disorders (DSM-5-TR)*. New York: APA.
Ames, D. L., & Fiske, S. T. (2010). Cultural neuroscience. *Asian Journal of Social Psychology, 13*, 72–82.
Ariès, P. (1962). *Centuries of childhood: A social history of family life*. New York: Vintage Books.
Baddeley, A. D. (2007). *Working memory, thought and action*. Oxford: Oxford University Press.
Barinaga, M. (1994). Surprises across the cultural divide. *Science, 263*, 1468–1470.
Barkow, J. H. (1989). *Darwin, sex, and status. Biological approaches to mind and culture*. Toronto: University of Toronto Press.
Barry, H., Child, I. L., & Bacon, M. K. (1959). Relation of child training to subsistence economy. *American Anthropologist, 61*, 51–63.
Baumert, J., Artelt, C., Klieme, E., Neubrand, M., Prenzel, M., Schiefele, U., Schneider, W., Tillmann, K.-J., & Weiß, M. (2002). *Pisa 2000: Die Länder der Bundesrepublik Deutschland im Vergleich*. Opladen: Leske & Budrich.
Baumert, J., Bos, W., & Lehmann, R. (eds.). (2000a). TIMSS/III., *Dritte Internationale Mathematik- und Naturwissenschaftsstudie – Mathematische und naturwissenschaftliche Bildung am Ende der Schullaufbahn*. Band 1. Mathematische und naturwissenschaftliche Grundbildung am Ende der Pflichtschulzeit. Opladen: Leske & Budrich.
Baumert, J., Bos, W., & Lehmann, R. (eds.). (2000b). TIMSS/III., *Dritte Internationale Mathematik- und Naturwissenschaftsstudie – Mathematische und naturwissenschaftliche Bildung am Ende der Schullaufbahn*. Band 2. Mathematische und naturwissenschaftliche Grundbildung am Ende der gymnasialen Oberstufe. Opladen: Leske & Budrich.
Berlin, B., & Kay, P. (1969). *Basic color terms*. Berkeley: University of California Press.
Berry, J. W. (1969). On cross-cultural comparability. *International Journal of Psychology, 4*, 119–128.

Berry, J. W. (1989). Imposed etics, emics and derived etics: The operationalization of a compelling idea. *International Journal of Psychology, 24*, 721–735.
Berry, J. W., Poortinga, Y. H., Seger, M., Breugelmans, A., Chasiotis, D., & Sam, D. L. (2011). *Cross-Cultural Psychology: Research and Applications* (3rd ed.). Cambridge: Cambridge University Press.
Bhugra, D. (2005). The global prevalence of schizophrenia. *PLoS Medicine, 2*, e151.
Bickerton, D. (1999). Creole languages, the language bioprogram hypothesis, and language acquisition. In W. C. Ritchie & T. K. Bhatia (eds.), *Handbook of child language acquisition* (pp. 195–220). San Diego, CA: Academic Press.
Blake, R. R., & Mouton, J. S. (1982). Management by grid principles or situationalism. Which? *Group and Organization Studies, 7*, 207–210.
Blake, R.; Mouton, J. (1985). *The Managerial Grid III: The Key to Leadership Excellence.* Houston: Gulf Publishing.
Blanchard, K., Zigarmi, P., & Zigarmi, D. (2013). *Leadership and the one minute manager.* New York: HarperCollins.
Böhmer, A. (2008). About the impact of traditional ethical principles on Western and Russian working Life. In H. Helfrich, A. V. Dakhin, E. Hölter & I. V. Arzhenovskiy (Eds.), *Impact of culture on human Interaction: Clash or challenge?* (pp. 257–267). Cambridge, MA: Hogrefe & Huber.
Boesch, E. E. (1980). *Kultur und Handlung: Einführung in die Kulturpsychologie.* Bern: Huber.
Bogin, B. (1998). Evolutionary and biological aspects of human growth. In C. Panter-Brick, *Biosocial perspectives on children* (pp. 10–44). Cambridge: Cambridge University Press.
Bogin, B. (1999). *Patterns of human growth.* Cambridge: Cambridge University Press.
Bogin, B. (2012). The evolution of human growth. In N. Cameron & B. Bogin (eds.), *Human growth and development* (2nd ed., pp. 287–324). San Diego: Elsevier Academic Press.
Bogin, B., Varea, C., Hermanussen, M., & Scheffler, C. (2018). Human life course biology: A centennial perspective of scholarship on the human pattern of physical growth and its place in human biocultural evolution. *American Journal of Physiological Anthropology, 165*, 834–854.
Brislin, R. W., & Kim, E. S. (2003). Cultural diversity in people's understanding and use of time. *Applied Psychology: An International Review, 52*, 363–382.
Bronfenbrenner, U. (1979). *Two worlds of childhood: U.S. and U.S.S.R.* New York: Sage.
Brown, A. L., & DeLoache, J. (1978). Skills, plans, and self-regulation. In R. Siegler (Ed.), *Children's thinking: What develops?* (pp. 3–35). Hillsdale, N.J.: Erlbaum.
Brown, R. W., & Lenneberg, E. H. (1954). A study in language and cognition. *Journal of Abnormal and Social Psychology, 49*, 454–462.
Brunswik, E. (1956). *Perception and the representative design of psychological experiments.* Berkeley: University of California Press.
Bühler, K. (1990). *The Theory of Language.* Amsterdam: John Benjamin's Publishing Company..
Cao, W., Li, L., Zhou, X., & Zhou, C. (2015). Social capital and depression: Evidence from urban elderly in China. *Aging & Mental Health, 19*, 418–429.
Cattell, R. (1987). *Intelligence: Its structure, growth and action.* Amsterdam: North Holland.
Cavalli-Sforza, L. L. (2000). *Genes, Peoples, and Languages.* New York: North Point Press.

References

Cheung, F. M. (2004). Use of Western and Indigenously Developed Personality Tests in Asia. *Applied Psychology: An International Review, 53*, 173–191.

Cheung, F. M. (2006). A combined emic–etic approach to cross-cultural personality test development: The case of the CPAI. In Q. Jing, H. Zhang & K. Zhang (Eds.), *Psychological science around the world* (vol. 2, pp. 91–103). London: Psychology Press.

Cheung, F. M., & Leung, K. (1998). Indigenous personality measures: Chinese examples. *Journal of Cross-Cultural Psychology, 29*, 233–248.

Cheung, F. M., Leung, K., Zhang, J. X., Sun, H. F., Gan, Y. Q., Song, W. Z., & Xie, D. (2001). Indigenous Chinese personality construct: Is the Five Factor Model complete? *Journal of Cross-Cultural Psychology, 32*, 407–433.

Child, D. (2006). *The essentials of factor analysis* (2nd ed.). London: Continuum International Publishing Group.

Chomsky, N. (1998). *Aspects of the theory of syntax*. Cambridge, MA: MIT Press.

Chomsky, N. (1999). On the nature, use, and acquisition of language. In W. C. Ritchie, & T. K. Bhatia (Eds.), *Handbook of child language acquisition* (pp. 33–54). San Diego, CA: Academic Press.

Church, A. T. (2000). Culture and personality: Toward an integrated cultural trait psychology. *Journal of Personality, 68*, 651–703.

Church, A. T., & Lonner, W. J. (1998). The cross-cultural perspective in the study of personality: rational and current research. *Journal of Cross-Cultural Psychology, 29*, 32–62.

Clark, C. M., Lawlor-Savage, L., & Goghari, V. M. (2016). The Flynn effect: A quantitative commentary on modernity and human intelligence. *Measurement: Interdisciplinary Research and Perspectives, 14*, 39–53.

Cosmides, L., & Tooby, J. (2002). Unraveling the enigma of human intelligence: Evolutionary psychology and the multimodular mind. In R. J. Sternberg & J. C. Kaufman (Eds.), *The evolution of intelligence* (pp. 145–198). Mahwah, NJ: Erlbaum.

Costa Jr., P. T., Terracciano, A., & McCrae, R. R. (2001). Gender differences in personality traits across cultures: Robust and surprising findings. *Journal of Personality and Social Psychology, 81*, 322–331.

Cox, J. L. (ed.). (2018). *Transcultural psychiatry*. London: Rotledge.

Crane, D. R., & Heaton, T. B. (eds.). (2008). *Handbook of families and poverty*. Los Angeles: Sage.

D'Andrade, R. G. (1995). *The development of cognitive anthropology*. Cambridge: Cambridge University Press.

Darwin, C. (1859). *On the origin of species by means of natural selection*. London: John Murray.

Darwin, C. (1872). *The expression of the emotions in man and animals*. London: John Murray.

Dasen, P. R., & de Ribaupierre, A. (1988). Neo-Piagetian theories: cross-cultural and differential perspectives. In A. Demetrion (ed.), *The Neo-Piagetian theories of cognitive development: toward an integration* (pp. 287–326). Amsterdam: North Holland.

Dasen, P. R., & Heron, A. (1981). Cross-cultural tests of Piaget's theory. In H. C. Triandis & A. Heron (eds.), *Handbook of cross-cultural psychology* (vol. 4, pp. 295–341). Boston: Allyn & Bacon.

Dawkins, R. (2006). *The selfish gene*. Oxford: Oxford University Press.

De Leo, D. (2009). Cross-cultural research widens suicide prevention horizons (Editorial). *Crisis, 30,* 59–62.
Diamond, J. (2012). *The world until yesterday. What can we learn from traditional societies.* New York: Penguin Books.
Dickens, W. T., & Flynn, J. R. (2001). Heritability estimates versus large environmental effects: The IQ paradox resolved. *Psychological Review, 108,* 346–369.
Doi, T. (1981). *The anatomy of dependence.* Tokyo: Kodansha International.
Draguns, J. G., & Tanaka-Matsumi, J. (2003). Assessment of psychopathology across and within cultures: Issues and findings. *Behaviour Research and Therapy, 41,* 755–776.
DuBois, C. (1944). *The people of Alor.* New York: Harper and Row.
Durham, W. H. (1990). Advances in evolutionary culture theory. *Annual Review of Anthropology, 19,* 187–210.
Durkheim, E. (1966). *Suicide: A study in sociology.* New York: Free Press, 1966.
Ebbinghaus, H. (1908). *Abriss der Psychychologie.* Leipzig: Veith.
Ebner-Priemer, U. W., Kubiak, T., & Pawlik, K. (2009). Ambulatory Assessment. *European Psychologist,* 14(2), 95–97.
Eccles, J. C. (1989). *Evolution of the brain: creation of the self.* London: Routledge.
Eckensberger, L. (1992). Agency, action and culture: three basic concepts for psychology in general, and for cross-cultural psychology in specific. *Proceedings of the IACCP-Conference, Catmandu, 1992.* Lisse: Swets & Zeitlinger.
Eckensberger, L. (2003). Kultur und Moral. In A. Thomas (ed.), *Kulturvergleichende Psychologie* (2nd ed., pp. 310–345). Göttingen: Hogrefe.
Eckensberger, L. H. (2007). Werte und Moral. In J. Straub, A. Weidemann & D. Weidemann (Hrsg.), *Handbuch Interkulturelle Kommunikation und Kompetenz* (S. 505–515). Stuttgart: Metzler.
Eckensberger, L. H., & Plath, I. (2002). Möglichkeiten und Grenzen des „variablenorientierten" Kulturvergleichs. In H. Kaelble & J. Schriewer (Eds.), *Vergleich und Transfer – Komparatistik in den Sozial-, Geschichts-und Kulturwissenschaften.* Frankfurt a.M.: Campus.
Edwards, A. L. (1971). *Versuchsplanung in der psychologischen Forschung.* Weinheim: Beltz.
Ekman, P. (1984). Expression and the nature of emotion. In K. R. Scherer & P. Ekman (eds.), *Approaches to emotion* (pp. 319–344). Hillsdale, NJ: Erlbaum.
Ekman, P. (1993). Facial expression and emotion. *American Psychologist, 48,* 376–379.
Ekman, P., & Friesen, W. V. (1971). Constants across cultures in the face and emotion. *Journal of Personality and Social Psychology, 17,* 124–129.
Elfenbein, H. A., & Ambady, N. (2002). On the universality and cultural specificity of emotion recognition: A meta-analysis. *Psychological Bulletin, 128,* 203–235.
Elias, N. (1994). The *civilizing process.* Oxford: Blackwell.
Erikson, E. H. (1968). *Identity: Youth and crisis. New York:* Norton.
Eysenck, H. J., & Eysenck, M. W. (1985). *Personality and individual differences.* New York: Plenum Press.
Fahrenberg, J., Myrtek, M., Pawlik, K., & Perrez, M. (2007). Ambulatory assessment – Monitoring behavior in daily life settings: A behavioral-scientific challenge for Psychology. *European Journal of Psychological Assessment,* 23(4), 206–213.

Felfe, J., Schmook, R., & Six, B. (2006). Die Bedeutung kultureller Wertorientierungen für das Commitment gegenüber der Organisation, dem Vorgesetzten, der Arbeitsgruppe und der eigenen Karriere. *Zeitschrift für Personalpsychologie, 5,* 94–107.

Felfe, J. (2008). The impact of supervisor commitment on OCB and turnover intention in different cultural contexts. In H. Helfrich, A. V. Dakhin, E. Hölter & I. V. Arzhenovskiy (Eds.), *Impact of culture on human Interaction: Clash or challenge?* (pp. 269–286). Cambridge, MA: Hogrefe & Huber.

Fink, G., & Meyerevert, S. (2004). Issues of time in international, intercultural management. East and Central Europe from the perspective of Austrian managers. *Journal for East European Management Studies, 9,* 61–84.

Flynn, J. R. (1987). Massive IQ gains in 14 nations: What IQ tests really measure. *Psychological Bulletin, 101,* 171–191.

Flynn, J. R. (1994). IQ gains over time. In R. J. Sternberg (Ed.), *Encyclopedia of human intelligence* (pp. 617–623). New York: Macmillan.

Freud, S. (1940). *Gesammelte Werke.* London: Imago, Frankfurt a.M.: Suhrkamp.

Friedlmeier, W., Corapci, F., & Cole, P. M. (2011). Emotion socialization in cross-cultural perspective. *Social and Personality Psychology Compass, 5,* 410–427.

Gallois, C., & Callan, V. (1997). *Communication and culture: A guide for practice.* Chichester: Wiley.

Gao, J., Arnulf, J. K., & Kristoffersen, H. (2011). Western leadership development and Chinese managers: Exploring the need for contextualization. *Scandinavian Journal of Management, 27,* 55–65.

Gardner, H. (1993). *Multiple intelligences.* New York: Basic Books.

Gaygisiz, E. (2010). Cultural values and governance quality as correlates of road traffic fatalities: A nation level analysis. *Accident Analysis and Prevention, 42,* 1894–1901.

Goleman, D. (1995). *Emotional intelligence.* New York: Bantham.

Goodall, J. (2010). *50 Years at Gombe.* New York: Stewart, Tabori & Chang.

Gordon, M., & Heath, J. (1998). Sex, sound symbolism, and sociolinguistics. *Current Anthropology, 39* (4), 421–442.

Gould, S. J. (1991). Exaptation: A crucial tool for an evolutionary psychology. *Journal of Social Issues, 47,* 43–65.

Grammer, K., & Eibl-Eibesfeldt, I. (1993). Emotionspsychologische Aspekte im Kulturenvergleich. In A. Thomas (Ed.), *Kulturvergleichende Psychologie* (S. 298–322). Göttingen: Hogrefe.

Graumann, C. F. (1972). Interaktion und Kommunikation. In C. F. Graumann, L. Kruse & B. Kroner (eds.), *Sozialpsychologie. 2. Halbband: Forschungsbereiche* (pp. 1109–1262). Göttingen: Hogrefe.

Greenfield, P. M. (1984). Kulturvergleichende Forschung und Piagets Theorie: Paradox und Fortschritt. In T. Schöfthaler & D. Goldschmidt (Eds.), *Soziale Struktur und Vernunft: Jean Piagets Modell entwickelten Denkens in der Diskussion kulturvergleichender Forschung* (pp. 96–111). Frankfurt a. M.: Suhrkamp.

Greenwald, A. G., McGhee, D. E., & Schwartz, J. L. K. (1998). Measuring individual differences in implicit cognition: The Implicit Association Test. *Journal of Personality and Social Psychology, 74,* 1464–1480.

Günthner, S. (1996). Male-female speaking practices across cultures. In M. Hellinger, & U. Ammon (Eds.), *Contrastive sociolinguistics* (pp. 447–473). Berlin: Mouton de Gruyter.

Hagemann, R. (2009). Epigenetik und Lamarckismus haben nichts gemeinsam! *Laborjournal, 4*, 12.

Hall, E. T. (1959). *The silent language.* New York: Doubleday.

Hall, E. T., & Hall, M. R. (1990). *Understanding cultural differences. Germans, French and Americans.* Yarmouth, ME: Intercultural Press.

Hammer, S., Reiss, C., Lehner, M. C., Heine, J. H., Sälzer, C., & Heinze, A. (2016). Mathematische Kompetenz in PISA 2015: Ergebnisse, Veränderungen und Perspektiven. In Reiss, K., Sälzer, C., Schiepe-Tiska, A., Klieme, E., & Köller, O. (Eds.), *PISA 2015: Eine Studie zwischen Kontinuität und Innovation* (pp. 219–247). Münster: Waxmann.

Hassard, J. (1966). Images of time and work in organisation. In S. R. Clegg, C. Hardy & W. R. Nord (Eds.), *Handbook of organisation studies* (pp. 581–598). London: Sage.

Havighurst, R.J. (1982). *Developmental tasks and education* (3rd ed.). New York: Basic Books.

Hedden, T., Park, D. C., Nisbett, R., Ji, L.-J., Jing, Q., & Jiao, S. (2002). Cultural variation in verbal versus spatial neuropsychological function across the life span. *Neuropsychology, 16*, 65–80.

Heine, S. J., Lehmann, D. R., Peng, K., & Greenholtz, J. (2002). What's wrong with cross-cultural comparisons of subjective Likert scales?: The reference-group effect. *Journal of Personality and Social Psychology, 82*, 903–918.

Hej, A. (2001). Ist Liebe Frauensache? Über die stammesgeschichtlichen Wurzeln geschlechtsspezifischer Emotionen. In H. Helfrich (Ed.), *Patriarchat der Vernunft – Matriarchat des Gefühls?* (pp. 83–122). Münster: Daedalus.

Helfrich, H. (1999). Beyond the dilemma of cross-cultural psychology: Resolving the tension between etic and emic approaches. *Culture & Psychology, 5*, 131–153.

Helfrich, H. (2003). Methodologie kulturvergleichender Forschung. In A. Thomas (Ed.), *Kulturvergleichende Psychologie* (2nd ed., pp. 111–139). Göttingen: Hogrefe.

Herder, J. G. (1887). In B. Suphan (Ed.), *Herders Sämtliche Werke.* Berlin: Deutsche Buch-Gemeinschaft.

Herrmann, T., & Grabowski, J. (1994). *Sprechen.* Heidelberg: Spektrum Akademischer Verlag.

Hermstein, R., & Murray, C. (2010). *The bell curve: Intelligence and class structure in American life.* New York: Free Press.

Hofstätter, P. R. (1966). *Einführung in die Sozialpsychologie.* Stuttgart: Kröner.

Hofstede, G. (1980). *Culture's consequences: International differences in work-related values.* Beverley Hills, CA: Sage.

Hofstede, G. (1986). Cultural Differences in Teaching and Learning. *International Journal of Intercultural Relations, 10* (3), 301–305.

Hofstede, G. (2001). *Culture's Consequences: Comparing Values, Behaviors, Institutions, and Organizations across Nations.* Thousand Oaks, CA: SAGE.

Hofstede, G. (2010). The GLOBE debate: Back to relevance. *Journal of International Business Studies, 41*, 1339–1346

Hofstede, G. (2011). Dimensionalizing cultures: The Hofstede model in context. *Online Readings in Psychology and Culture, 2* (1)

Hofstede, G., & Bond, M. H. (1988). The Confucius connection: From cultural roots to economic growth. *Organizational Dynamics*, 16 (4), 4–21.

Hofstede, G., Hofstede, G. J., & Minkov, M. (2010). *Cultures and Organizations: Software of the Mind* (3rd ed.). New York: McGraw Hill.

Hollander, E. P. (1992). Leadership, followership, self, and others. The Leadership Quarterly, 3 (1),43–54.

Hong, Y. (2001). Toward a paradigm shift: from cross-cultural differences in social cogntion to social-cognitive mediation of cultural differences. *Social Cognition, 19*, 181–196.

Horn, R. (2009). *Standard Progressive Matrices (SPM). Deutsche Bearbeitung und Normierung nach J. C. Raven* (2nd. ed.). Frankfurt a.M.: Pearson Assessment.

House, R. J., Hanges, P. J., Javidan, M., Dorfman, P. W., & Gupta, V. (2004). *Culture, leadership, and organizations: The GLOBE study of 62 societies.* New York: Sage.

Hsieh, N. (2015). Economic security, social cohesion, and depression disparities in post-transition societies: A comparison of older adults in China and Russia. *Journal of Health and Social Behavior, 56*, 534–551.

Hui, C. H., & Luk, C. L. (1997). Industrial/organizational psychology. In J. W. Berry, M. H. Segall & C. Kagitçibasi (Eds.), *Handbook of cross-cultural psychology, vol. 3: Social behavior and applications* (2nd ed., pp. 371–411). Boston: Allyn & Bacon.

Huntington, S. P. (1996). *The clash of civilizations and the remaking of the world order.* New York: Simon & Schuster.

Jacob, F. (1977). Evolution and tinkering. *Science, 196*, 1161–1166.

Jensen, A. R. (1998). *The g factor: The science of mental ability.* Westport, CT: Praeger.

Jones, E. E., & Davis, K. E. (1965). From acts to dispositions: The attribution process in person perception. In L. Berkowitz (Ed.), *Advances in experimental social psychology* (vol. 2, pp. 219–266). New York: Academic Press.

Jung, C. G. (2011). *Ausgewählte Schriften.* Ostfildern: Patmos.

Kagitcibasi, C. (1997). Individualism and collectivism. In J.W. Berry, M.H. Segall & C. Kagitcibasi (Eds.), *Handbook of cross-cultural psychology.* Vol. 3. Social behavior and applications. 2nd edition (pp. 1–49). Boston: Allyn & Bacon.

Kahneman, D. (2011). *Thinking, fast and slow.* London: Penguin.

Kahneman, D., & Tversky, A. (1979): Prospect theory: An analysis of decision making under risk. *Econometrica, 47*, 263–291.

Kardiner, A. (1939). *The individual and his society.* New York: Columbia University Press.

Kay, P., Berlin, B., Maffi, L., & Merrifield, W. (1997). Color naming across languages. In C. L. Hardin & L. Maffi (Eds.), *Color categories in thought and language* (pp. 21–56). Cambridge: Cambridge University Press.

Kay, P., & Kempton, W. (1984). What is the Sapir-Whorf hypothesis?. *American Anthropologist, 86*, 65–79.

Kemmelmeier, M. (2016). Cultural differences in survey responding: Issues and insights in the study of response biases. *International Journal of Psychology, 51*, 439–444.

Keenan, E. (1993). Normen kreieren – Normen variieren. Männliches und weibliches Sprechen in einer madadassischen Gemeinschaft. In: S. Günthner, & H. Kotthoff (Eds.), *Von fremden Stimmen: weibliches und männliches Sprechen im Kulturvergleich* (2nd ed.; pp. 75–100). Frankfurt (M.): Suhrkamp.

Kienbaum, J. (1995). Sozialisation von Mitgefühl und prosozialem Verhalten. Ein Vergleich deutscher und sowjetischer Kindergartenkinder. In G. Trommsdorff (Ed.), *Kindheit und Jugend in verschiedenen Kulturen* (pp. 83–107). Weinheim: Juventa.

Kim, H. S., Sherman, D. K., & Taylor, S. E. (2008). Culture and social support. *American Psychologist*, *63*, 518–526.

Kitamura, C., Thanavishuth, C., Chulalongkorn U., Burnham, D., & Luksaneeyanawin, S. (2002). Universality and specificity in infant-directed speech: Pitch modifications as a function of infant age and sex in a tonal and non-tonal language. *Infant Behavior and Development*, *24*, 372–392.

Kitayama, S., & Ishii, K. (2002). Word and voice: Spontaneous attention to emotional utterances in two languages. *Cognition and Emotion*, *16*, 29–59.

Klieme, E., Artelt, C., Hartig, J., Jude, N., Köller, O., Prenzel, M., Schneider, W., & Stanat, P. (Eds.). (2010). *PISA 2009. Bilanz nach einem Jahrzehnt*. Münster: Waxmann.

Kluckhohn, C. (1949). Mirror for Man, New York: Fawcett.

Kluckhohn, C., & Murray, H. A. (1948). *Personality in nature, society, and culture*. New York: Knopf.

Kohlberg, L. (1984). *The psychology of moral development: The nature and validity of moral stages (Essays on Moral Development, Volume 2)*. New York: Harper & Row.

Kornadt, H.-J. (2003). Beiträge des Kulturvergleichs zur Motivationsforschung. In A. Thomas (Ed.), *Kulturvergleichende Psychologie* (2nd ed., pp. 348–383). Göttingen: Hogrefe.

Kornadt, H.-J., Trommsdorff, G., & Kobayashi, R. B. (1994). „Mein Hund hat mich bestorben" – sprachlicher Ausdruck von Gefühlen im deutsch-japanischen Vergleich. In H.-J. Kornadt, J. Grabowski & R. Mangold-Allwin (Eds.), *Sprache und Kognition* (pp. 233–250). Heidelberg: Spektrum Akademischer Verlag.

Kring, A. M., Davison, G. C., Neale, J. M., & Johnson, S. L. (2007). *Abnormal psychology* (10th ed.). New York: Wiley.

Kroeber, A. L., & Kluckhohn, C. (1952). *Culture: A critical review of concepts and definitions*. Vol. 47, No. 1., Cambridge, MA: Peabody Museum.

Kühnen, U., Hannover, B., Röder, U., & Schubert, B. (2000). *Procedural consequences of semantic priming: The role of self-knowledge for context-bounded versus context-independent modes of thinking*. Unpublished Manuskript. University of Michigan.

Kuhn, T. (2012). *The structure of scientific revolutions*. Chicago: University of Chicago Press.

Labov, W. (1972). Hypercorrection by the lower middle class as a factor in linguistic change, In W. Bright (Ed.), *Sociolinguistic patterns* (pp. 122–142). Philadelphia: University of Pennsylvania Press.

Lam, M., Chan, G., Marcet, M. M., Wong, W., Wong, J., & Wong, D. (2014). Spontaneous self-concept among Chinese undergraduates in Hong Kong. *Social Behavior and Personality*, *42*, 1353–1364.

Lammers, C. J., & Hickson, D. J. (1979). *Organizations alike and unlike: International and interinstitutional studies in the sociology of organizations*. London: Routledge.

Langenmayr, A. (1997). *Sprachpsychologie: Ein Lehrbuch*. Göttingen: Hogrefe.

Lass, U., Lüer, G., Becker, D., Fang, Y., Chen, G., & Wang, Z. (2000). Kurzzeitgedächtnisleistungen deutscher und chinesischer Probanden mit verbalen und figuralen Items: Zur Funktion von phonologischer Schleife und visuell-räumlichem Notizblock. *Zeitschrift für Experimentelle Psychologie, 47*, 77–88.

Laux, L. (2003). *Persönlichkeitspsychologie*. Stuttgart: Kohlhammer.

Lazarus, R. S., & Folkman, S. (1984). *Stress, appraisal, and coping*. New York: Springer.

Lazarus, M., & Steinthal, H. (Ed). (1860). Zeitschrift für Völkerpsychologie und Sprachwissenschaft.

LeDoux, J. (1996). *The emotional brain*. New York: Schuster & Schuster.

LeDoux, J. (2000). Emotion circuits in the brain. *Annual Review of Neuroscience, 23* (1), 155–184

Lévy-Bruhl, L. (1910). *Les functions mentales dans les sociétés inférieures*. Paris: Alcan.

Li, H. Z. (2001). Cooperative and intrusive interruptions in inter- and intracultural dyadic discourse. *Journal of Language & Social Psychology, 20*, 259–284.

Li, W., Leonhart, R., Schaefert, R., Zhao, X., Zhang, L., Wei, J., & Fritzsche, K. (2015). Sense of coherence contributes to physical and mental health in general hospital patients in China. *Psychology, Health & Medicine, 20*, 614–622.

Liang, Y. (2003). Sprachroutinen und Vermeidungsrituale im Chinesischen. In A. Thomas (Ed.), *Psychologie interkulturellen Handelns* (2nd ed., pp. 247–268). Göttingen: Hogrefe.

Lien, N. M., Meyer, K., & Winick, M. (1977). Early malnutrition and later adoption into American families. *American Journal of Clinical Nutrition, 30*, 1734–1739.

Lin, E. J.-L. (2003). Are indigenous Chinese personality dimensions culture-specific? An investigation of the Chinese Personality Assessment Inventory in Chinese American and European American samples. *Dissertation Abstracts International: Section B: The Sciences & Engineering, 63(7-B)*, 3505.

Lin-Huber, M. A. (1998). *Kulturspezifischer Spracherwerb: Sprachliche Sozialisation und Kommunikation im Kulturvergleich*. Bern: Huber.

Lonner, W. J., & Adamopoulos, J. (1997). Culture as antecedent to behavior. In W. Berry, Y. H. Poortinga & J. Pandey (Eds.), *Handbook of cross-cultural psychology, vol. 1: Theory and method* (2nd ed., pp. 43–83). Boston: Allyn & Bacon.

Lorenz, K. (1998). *Das sogenannte Böse. Zur Naturgeschichte der Aggression*. München: Deutscher Taschenbuch Verlag.

Lüer, G., Becker, D., Lass, U., Yunqiu, F., Guopeng, C., & Zhongming, W. (1998). Memory span in German and Chinese: Evidence for the phonological loop. *European Psychologist, 3*, 102–112.

Lynn, R., & Vanhanen, T. (2002). *IQ and the wealth of nations*. Westport, CT: Praeger.

Ma, H. K. (1992). The moral judgement development of the Chinese people: A theoretical model. *Philosophica, 49*, 55–82.

Ma, H. K. (2009). Moral development and moral education: An integrated approach. *Educational Research Journal《教育研究學報》, 24*, 293–326.

MacLaury, R. E. (1997). Skewing and darkening: Dynamics of the Cool category. In: C. L. Hardin & L. Maffi (eds.), *Color categories in thought and language* (pp. 261–282). Cambridge: Cambridge University Press.

Magala, S. J. (2007). *From minding your steps to minding diversities*. Presentation at the conference „Economic globalisation, cultural diversity and cross-cultural competence". Cologne.

Magnus, H. (1877). *Die geschichtliche Entwicklung des Farbensinnes*. Leipzig: Viet.

Malinowski, B. (1927). *Sex and repression in savage society*. London: Kegan Paul.

Marcus, B. (2011). *Einführung in die Arbeits- und Organisationspsychologie*. Wiesbaden: VS Verlag für Sozialwissenschaften.
Markus, H. R., & Kitayama, S. (1991). Culture and the self: Implications for cognition, emotion, and motivation. *Psychological Review*, 98, 224–253.
Markus, H. R., & Kitayama, S. (1998). The cultural Psychology of personality. *Journal of Cross-Cultural Psychology*, 29, 63–87.
Marsella, A. J., Dubanoski, J., Hamada, W. C. & Morse, H. (2000). The measurement of personality across cultures. *American Behavioral Scientist*, 44, 41–62.
Maslow, A. H. (1943). A theory of human motivation. *Psychological Review*, 50, 370–396.
Maslow, A. H. (1987). *Motivation and personality* (3rd ed.). Delhi: Pearson education.
Matsumoto, D. (1999). Culture and self: An empirical assessment of Markus and Kitayama's theory of independent and interdependent self-construals. *Asian Journal of Social Psychology*, 2, 289–310.
Matsumoto, D., & Juang, L. (2008). *Culture and Psychology* (4th ed.). Belmont (CA): Thomson Wadsworth.
McCrae, R. R., Chan, W., Jussim, L., De Fruyt, F., Löckenhoff, C. E., De Bolle, M., Terracciano, A. et al. (2013). The inaccuracy of national character stereotypes. *Journal of Research in Personality*, 47, 831–842.
McCrae, R. R., & Costa, P. T., Jr. (1997). Personality trait structure as a human universal. *American Psychologist*, 52, 509–516.
McCrae, R. R., & Costa, P. T., Jr. (2008). The five-factor theory of personality. In O. John, R. W. Robins & A. Lawrence (eds.), *Handbook of personality: Theory and research* (3rd ed., pp. 159–181). New York: Guilford Press.
McCrae, R. R., Terracciano, A., De Fruyt, F., De Bolle, M., Gelfand, M. J., & Costa, P. J., Jr. (2010). The validity and structure of culture-level personality scores: Data from ratings of young adolescents. *Journal of Personality*, 78, 815–838.
Mead, M. (1928). *Coming of age in Samoa*. New York: Wiley.
Mervis, C. B., & Rosch, E. (1981). Categorization of natural objects. *Annual Review of Psychology*, 32, 89–115.
Mischel, W. & Shoda, Y. (1995). A cognitive-affect system theory of personality: Reconceptualizing situations, dispositions, dynamics, and invariance in personality structure. *Psychological Review*, 102, 246–268.
Misumi, J. (1995). The development in Japan of the performance-maintenance (PM) theory of leadership. *Journal of Social Issues*, 51, 213–228.
Morgan, C. L. (1903). *An introduction to comparative psychology* (2nd ed.). London: Walter Scott.
Morgan, L. H. (1877). *Ancient society*. New York: Henry Holt.
Mortenson, S. T. (2002). Sex, communication values, and cultural values: Individualism-collectivism as a mediator of sex differences in communication values in two cultures. *Communication Reports*, 15, 57–71.
Moscovici, S. (1981). On social representations. In J. P. Forgas (Ed.), *Social cognition* (pp. 181–209). London: Academic Press.
Munroe, R. L., & Munroe, R. H. (1997). A comparative anthropological perspective. In W. Berry, Y. H. Poortinga & J. Pandey (Eds.), *Handbook of cross-cultural psychology, vol. 1: Theory and method* (2nd ed., pp. 171–213). Boston: Allyn & Bacon.
Myers, D. G. (2004). *Psychology* (7nd ed.). New York: Worth Publishers.

Neuberger, O. (2002). *Führen und geführt werden* (6th ed.). Stuttgart: Lucius & Lucius.
Newson, L., & Richerson, P. (2018). Dual inheritance theory. *The International Encyclopedia of Anthropology, 12*, 1–5.
Nibler, R., & Harris, K. L. (2003). The effects of culture and cohesiveness on intragroup conflict and effectiveness. *Journal of Social Psychology, 143*, 613–631.
Nisbett, R. E. (2003). *The geography of thought: How Asians and Westerners think differently ... and why.* New York: The Free Press.
Nisbett, R. E., Peng, K., Choi, I., & Norenzayan, A. (2001). Culture and systems of thought: Holistic versus analytic cognition. *Psychological Review, 108*, 291–310.
Nisbett, R. E., Peng, K., Choi, I., & Norenzayan, A. (2008). Culture and systems of thought: Holistic versus analytic cognition. In J. E. Adler & L. J. Rips (eds.), *Reasoning: Studies of human inference and its foundations* (pp. 956–985). New York: Cambridge University Press.
Ogbu, J. U. (2002). Cultural amplifiers of intelligence: IQ and minority status in cross-cultural perspective. In J. M. Fish (Ed.), *Race and intelligence: Separating science from myth* (pp. 241–278). Mahwah, NJ: Lawrence Erlbaum.
Orne, M. (1962). On the social psychology of the psychological experiment: With particular reference to demand characteristics and their implications. *American Psychologist, 17*, 776–783.
Osgood, C. E., Suci, G. J., & Tannenbaum, P. H. (1957). *The measurement of meaning.* Urbana, IL: University of Illinois Press.
Oyserman, D., Coon, H. M., & Kemmelmeier, M. (2002). Rethinking individualism and collectivism: Evaluation of theoretical assumptions and meta-analyses. *Psychological Bulletin, 128*, 3–72.
Qu, Y., & Telzer, E. H. (2017). Cultural differences and similarities in beliefs, practices, and neural mechanisms of emotion regulation. *Cultural Diversity and Ethnic Minority Psychology, 23*, 36–44.
Panter-Brick, C. (1988). *Biosocial perspectives on children.* Cambridge: Cambridge University Press.
Piaget, J. (1966). Nécessité et signification des recherches comparatives en psychologie génétique. *Journal International de Psychologie, 1*, 3–13.
Piaget, J. (2003). *The psychology of intelligence.* London: Routledge.
Pike, K. L. (1967). *Language in relation to a unified theory of the structure of human behavior.* Den Haag: Mouton.
Pinker, S. (1994). *The language instinct.* New York: Monroe.
Pohl, R. (2022). What are cognitive illusions? In R. Pohl (ed.), Cognitive Illusions: Intriguing phenomena in thinking, judgment, and memory (3rd ed.). London: Routledge.
Poortinga, Y. H., & Van Hemert, D. A. (2001). Personality and culture: Demarcating between the common and the unique. *Journal of Personality, 69*, 1033–1060.
Rasmussen, J. (1986). *Information processing and human-machine interaction.* Amsterdam: North Holland.
Raven, J. (1987). *Manual for the Raven's Progressive Matrices and Vocabulary Scales.* London: Lewis.
Reifman, A. (2000). Revisiting the bell curve. *Psycoloquy, 11*, 1–13.
Reinhold, F., Reiss, K., Diedrich, J., Hofer, S., & Heinze, A. (2019). Mathematische Kompetenz in PISA 2018 – aktueller Stand und Entwicklung. In K. Reiss, M. Weis,

E. E. Klieme, & O. Köller (eds.), *Grundbildung im internationalen Vergleich* (pp. 187–209). Münster: Waxmann.

Rohner, R. P., Hahn, B. C., & Koehn, U. (1992). Occupational mobility, length of residence, and perceived maternal warmth among Korean immigrant families. *Journal of Cross-Cultural Psychology, 23*, 366–376.

Rosso, B. D., Dekas, K. H., & Wrzesniewski, A. (2010). On the meaning of work: A theoretical integration and review. *Research in Organizational Behavior, 30*, 91–127.

Ryan, A. M. (2001). Explaining the Black-White test score gap: The role of test perceptions. *Human Performance, 14*, 45–76.

Sapir, E. (1933). *Language*. New York: Macmillan Company.

Sarrazin, T. (2012). *Deutschland schafft sich ab: Wie wir unser Land aufs Spiel setzen*. München: DVA.

Schachter, S., & Singer, J. E. (1962). Cognitive, social, and physiological determinantes of emotional state. *Psychological Review, 69*, 379–399.

Scherer, K. (1997). The state of art in vocal communication: A partial view. In A. Wolfgang (Ed.), *Nonverbal behavior: Perspectives, applications, intercultural insights* (pp. 335–349). Seattle: Hogrefe & Huber.

Scherer, K. R. (2001). Appraisal considered as a process of multilevel sequential checking. In K. R. Scherer, A. Schorr & T. Johnstone (Eds.), *Appraisal processes in emotion* (pp. 92–120). Oxford: Oxford University Press.

Scherer, K. R. (2009). The dynamic architecture of emotion: Evidence for the component process model. *Cognition and Emotion, 23*, 1307–1351.

Schneider, W., & Sodian, B. (2008). *Kognitive Entwicklung in der Kindheit*. Stuttgart: Kohlhammer.

Schulz von Thun, F. (1999). *Miteinander reden: Psychologie der Kommunikation. Sonderausgabe*. Reinbek bei Hamburg: Rowohlt TB.

Schwartz, S. H. (1994). Are there universal aspects in the structure and contents of human values? *Social Issues, 50*(9), 19–45.

Schwartz, S. H. (2006). A theory of cultural value orientations: Explication and applications. *Comparative Sociology, 5*, 137–182.

Searle, J. R. (1969). *Speech acts*. Cambridge: Cambridge University Press.

Sears, R. R., Maccoby, E. E., & Levin, H. (1957). *Patterns of child rearing*. Evanston.

Segall, M. H., Campbell, D. T., & Herskovits, M. J. (1966). *The influence of culture on visual perception*. Indianapolis: Bobbs-Merr.

Segall, M. H., Dasen, P. R., Berry, J. W., & Poortinga, Y. H. (1999). *Human behaviour in global perspective*. Boston: Allyn & Bacon.

Semin, G., & Zwier, S. (1997). Social cognition. In J. W. Berry, M. H. Segall & C. Kagitcibasi (Eds.), *Handbook of cross-cultural psychology, vol. 3: Social behavior and applications* (2nd ed., pp. 51–75). Boston: Allyn & Bacon.

Shweder, R. A., & Sullivan, M. A. (1990). The semiotic subject of cultural psychology. In L. A. Pervin (Ed.), *Handbook of personality theory and research* (pp. 99–416). New York: Guilford.

Sims, T., Koopmann-Holm, B., Young, H. R., Jiang, D., Fung, H., & Tsai, J. L. (2017). Asian Americans respond less favorably to excitement (vs. calm)-focused physicians compared to European Americans. *Cultural Diversity and Ethnic Minority Psychology*, Advance online publication.

References

Sinha, D. (1990). Interventions for development out of poverty. In R. W. Brislin (ed.), *Applied cross-cultural psychology* (pp. 77–97). Newbury Park, CA: Sage.

Sinha, J. B. P. (1994). *The cultural context of leadership and power.* New Delhi: Sage.

Slobin, D. I. (1992). Introduction. In D. I. Slobin (Ed.), *The crosslinguistic study of language acquisition* (vol. 3, pp. 1–13). Hillsdale, NJ: Erlbaum.

Spearman, C. (1904) „General intelligence", objectively determined and measured. *American Journal of Psychology, 15*, 72–101.

Serpell, R. (1990). Audience, culture and psychological explanation. *The Quarterly Newsletter of the Laboratory of Comparative Human Cognition, 12*, 99–132.

Spencer, H. (1876). *Principles of sociology.* New York: Appelton.

Sternberg, R. J. (1985). Beyond IQ: A triarchic theory of human intelligence. New York City: Cambridge University Press.

Sternberg, R. J. (2012). The triarchic theory of successful intelligence. In D. P. Flanagan, & P.L. Harrison (eds.). Contemporary Intellectual Assessment: Theories, tests, and issues (3rd ed., pp. 156–177). New York (NY): Guilford Press.

Straub J., & Chakkarath P. (2010) Kulturpsychologie. In G. Mey, & K. Mruck (Eds.), *Handbuch Qualitative Forschung in der Psychologie* (pp. 195–209). Wiesbaden: VS Verlag für Sozialwissenschaften.

Strohschneider, S. (2001). *Kultur – Denken – Strategie. Eine indische Suite.* Bern: Huber.

Stumpf, S., & Kammhuber, S. (2003). Organisationspsychologische Aspekte im Kulturvergleich. In A. Thomas (Ed.), *Kulturvergleichende Psychologie* (2nd ed., pp. 487–514). Göttingen: Hogrefe.

Tanaka-Matsumi, J., & Draguns, J. (1997). Culture and psychopathology. In J. W. Berry, M. H. Segall, & C. Kagitçibasi (Eds.), *Handbook of cross-cultural psychology, vol. 3: Social behavior and applications* (pp. 449–491). Boston: Allyn & Bacon.

Tajfel, H. (1982). *Social identity and intergroup relations.* Cambridge: Cambridge University Press.

Tarakeshwar, N., Stanton, J. & Pargament, K.I. (2003). Religion: An overlooked dimension in cross-cultural psychology. *Journal of Cross-Cultural Psychology, 34*, 377–394.

Thomas, A. (2003). Psychologie interkulturellen Lernens und Handelns. In A. Thomas (Ed.), *Kulturvergleichende Psychologie* (2nd ed, pp. 433–485). Göttingen: Hogrefe.

Triandis, H. C. (1995). *Individualism and collectivism.* Boulder: Westview Press.

Trommsdorff, G. (2003). Kulturvergleichende Entwicklungspsychologie. In A. Thomas (Ed.), *Kulturvergleichende Psychologie* (2nd ed., pp. 139–179). Göttingen: Hogrefe.

Trompenaars, F. (2012). *Riding the waves of culture: Understanding cultural diversity in business* (3rd ed.). London: Brealey.

Tseng, W.-S. (2001). *Handbook of cultural psychiatry.* San Diego, CA: Academic Press.

Tylor, E. B. (1865). *Researches into the early history of mankind and development of civilization.* London: John Murray.

United Nations (2022). *Human development report 2021/2022. Overview.* New York: United Nations Development Programme.

Van de Vijver, F. J. R. (2006). Culture and psychology: A SWOT analysis of cross-cultural psychology. In Q. Jing, H. Zhang & K. Zhang (Eds.), *Psychological science around the world* (vol. 2, pp. 279–298). London: Psychology Press.

Van de Vijver, F. J. R., & Leung, K. (2000). Methodological issues in psychological research on culture. *Journal of Cross-Cultural Psychology, 31*, 33–51.

Van Ess, H. (2003). *Der Konfuzianismus*. München: Beck.
Vijayakumar, L., John, S., Pirkis, J., & Whiteford, H. (2005). Suicide in developing countries (2): Risk factors. *Crisis: The Journal of Crisis Intervention and Suicide Prevention, 26*, 112–119.
Vogel, C., & Eckensberger, L. (1988). Arten und Kulturen – Der vergleichende Ansatz. In K. Immelmann, K. R. Scherer, C. Vogel & P. Schmook (Eds.). *Psychobiologie – Grundlagen des Verhaltens* (pp. 563–606). Jena: Gustav Fischer; Weinheim: Psychologie Verlags Union.
Von Helversen, O., & Scherer, K. R. (1988). Nonverbale Kommunikation. In K. Immelmann, K. R. Scherer, C. Vogel & P. Schmoock (Eds.), *Psychobiologie – Grundlagen des Verhaltens* (S. 609–647). Stuttgart: Gustav Fischer, Weinheim: Psychologie Verlags Union.
Von Humboldt, W. (1906). Grundzüge des allgemeinen Sprachtypus. In A. Leitzmann (Hrsg.), *W. v. Humboldts Werke. Fünfter Band* (S. 364–475). Berlin: Behr.
Von Humboldt, W. (1988). Ueber die Verschiedenheit des menschlichen Sprachbaues und ihren Einfluß auf die geistige Entwicklung des Menschengeschlechtes. In A. Flitner & K. Giel (Hrsg.), *W. von Humboldt, Werke in fünf Bänden, Schriften zur Sprachphilosophie* (6. Aufl.). Darmstadt: Wissenschaftliche Buchgesellschaft.
Von Neumann, J. (1958). *The computer and the brain*. New Haven, CT: Yale University Press.
Vygotsky, L. S. (1978). *Mind in society: The development of higher psychological Processes*. Cambridge, (MA): Harvard University Press.
Vygotsky, L. S. (1981). The genesis of higher mental functions. In J. V. Wertsch (Ed.), *The concept of activity in Soviet psychology* (pp. 144–188). Armonk (NY): Sharpe.
Watzlawick, P., Beavin, J. H., & Jackson, D. D. (2015). Some Tentative Axioms of Communication. In P. Watzlawick, W. J. Lederer, & D. D. Jackson (eds.), *Pragmatics of Human Communication - A study of interactional patterns, pathologies and paradoxes*. New York: Norton.
Weber, M. (1993). *Die protestantische Ethik und der „Geist" des Kapitalismus*. Textausgabe auf der Grundlage der ersten Fassung von 1904/05 herausgegeben und eingeleitet von K. Lichtblau und J. Weiss. Bodenheim: Athenaeum.
Weber, M. (2000). Die protestantische Ethik und der „Geist" des Kapitalismus. In J. Winkelmann (Ed.), *Max Weber: Die protestantische Ethik I. Eine Aufsatzsammlung* (9th ed., pp. 27–277). Gütersloh: Gütersloher Verlagshaus.
Weber, E. U., & Hsee, C. K. (2000). Culture and individual judgement and decision making. *Applied Psychology: An International Review, 49*, 32–61.
Weinert, A. (2004). *Organisations- und Personalpsychologie*. Weinheim: Psychologie Verlags Union.
Welzel, C., & Inglehart, R. (2010). Agency, values, and well-being: A human development model. *Social Indicator Research, 97*(1), 43–63.
Wendt, H., Bos, W., Selter, C., Köller, O., Schwippert, K., & Kasper, D. (Eds.). (2016). *TIMSS 2015. Mathematische und naturwissenschaftliche Kompetenzen von Grundschulkindern in Deutschland im internationalen Vergleich*. Münster: Waxmann.
Whiting, B. B. (1963). *Six cultures: Studies of child rearing*. New York: Wiley.
Whiting, B. B., & Edwards, C. P. (1988). *Children of different worlds*. Cambridge, MA: Harvard University Press.

References

Whiting, B. B., & Whiting, J. W. M. (1975). *Children of six cultures: A psychocultural analysis*. Cambridge, MA: Harvard University Press.

Whorf, B. L. (1956). *Language, thought and reality*. Cambridge, MA: M.I.T. Press.

Whorf, B. L. (2008). *Sprache, Denken, Wirklichkeit: Beiträge zur Metalinguistik und Sprachphilosophie*. Reinbek bei Hamburg: Rowohlt TB.

Wierzbicka, A. (1991). *Cross-cultural pragmatics*. Berlin: Mouton de Gruyter.

Woodley of Menie, M. A., Peñaherrera-Aguirre, M., Fernandes, H. F., & Figueredo, A. (2017). What causes the Anti-Flynn effect? A data synthesis and analysis of predictors. *Evolutionary Behavioral Sciences*, doi:https://doi.org/10.1037/ebs0000106 Accessed: 13.03.2023

Wong, W.-C. (2009). Retracing the footsteps of Wilhelm Wundt: Explorations in the disciplinary frontiers of psychology and in Völkerpsychologie. *History of Psychology*, 12 (4), 229–265.

World Health Organization *(2019)*. *ICD-11: International classification of diseases*. 11th Revision. Geneva: WHO.

Wundt, W. (1913). *Elemente der Völkerpsychologie – Grundlinien einer psychologischen Entwicklungsgeschichte der Menschheit*. Leipzig: Kröner.

Yang, K.-S. (2003). Beyond Maslow's culture-bound linear theory: A preliminary statement of the double-Y model of basic human needs. In J. Berman, & J. Berman (Eds.), *Cross-cultural differences in perspectives on the self, Vol. 49 of the Nebraska Symposium on Motivation* (pp. 157–305). Lincoln, Nebr.: University of Nebraska Press.

Yukl, G., Gardner, W., III, & Gardner, W. (2019). Leadership in organizations (9th ed.). Harlow: Pearson.

Zhang, J. (2014). The gender ratio of Chinese suicide rates: An explanation in Confucianism. *Sex Roles, 70*, 146–154.

Index

A
Accident frequency, 168
Acculturation, 6
Adaptation, 8, 27, 32, 41, 43–46, 94, 132, 183
Adolescence, 139–155, 176
Adulthood, 7, 139–141, 146, 154
Affectivity, 16, 61, 115, 132
Aggression, 3, 8, 15, 16, 20–22, 101, 132, 151–153
Agreeableness, 125, 126, 128, 132
Ajase complex, 124
Alternative hypothesis (H_1), 36–38
Amae, 19, 21, 124
Ambulatory measurement, 127
Antecedent, 2, 9, 15, 81–90, 95, 118–121, 174, 179
Anthropophobia, 175
Anti-Flynn effect, 79
Anxiety disorder, 174–176
Appeal function, 117
Appraisal, 38, 100–103
Approach
    anthropological, 4, 6, 28, 33
    ecocultural, 8
    ecological, 8, 30
    emic, 14, 17–19, 38, 77, 93
    empiricist, 67
    ethological, 32
    ethnographic, 25
    etic, 13, 14, 18, 19, 38, 77, 93
    idiographic, 14, 18, 38
    interactionist, 67
    nativist, 67
    nomothetic, 14, 18, 38
    psychometric, 19, 25, 78, 125, 149
    universalist, 61, 72
Archetype theory, 124
Assertiveness, 55, 58
Autonomy *vs.* embeddedness, 57
Auxiliary language, 115

B
Baby talk, 115
Baddeley's memory model, 85, 86
Behavioral differential, 127
Behaviour
    aggressive, 23, 37, 151, 154, 155
    decision, 165, 166
    expressive, 101, 103
    measurement, 9, 24
    observations, 32, 182
    practices, 3, 53, 153, 158
    prosocial, 151, 154
    risk-averse, 165
    risky, 165
Behavioural biology, 32
Behaviourism, 10
Bias (distortion), 102
Big Five model (Five Factor model of personality), 128
Black and White gap, 89
Body language, 110
Brunswik's theory of transactional functionalism, 68–70
Bühler's organon model, 116

C

Calvinism, 159, 160
Cannon's theory of emotion, 99
Carpentered world, 69
Causal *vs.* final, 32
Causes *vs.* reasons, 17
Childhood, 7, 90, 92, 133, 139–155
Chinese Personality Assessment Inventory (CPAI), 127
Civilisation, 6, 7, 64
Cluster analysis, 57
Code, 109, 110
Cognition, 8, 14, 73, 77, 81, 84, 90–95
　See also Thinking
Collectivism
　horizontal, 57
　in-group, 58, 63, 170
　institutional, 58
　vertical, 57
Colour
　perception, 72–74
　spectrum, 72–74
　vocabulary, 73
Commitment, 17, 132, 162, 170
Communication
　animal, 110
　functions, 116
　linguistic, 109–112, 116, 121
　models, 116–118
　non-verbal, 110
　paralinguistic, 112
　verbal (linguistic), 110, 112, 118, 142
Comparability, 13, 20–23, 112–113, 177
　See also Equivalence
Comparative behavioural science, 32
Competence, 78, 146
Competence *vs.* performance, 78, 146
Concern
　for people, 163, 171
　for production, 163, 171
Conformity, 20, 128, 129, 133
Confucian dynamics, 55, 84, 180
Confucianism, 159, 177
Conscientiousness, 125, 126, 128, 162
Construct, 20–25, 35, 78, 82, 112, 127, 129, 130, 140

Content
　aspect, 20, 117, 180
　vs. value, 159
Context factor, 54, 62
Contextual reference, 60
Conversation control, 112
Coping, 3, 68, 77, 100, 101, 105, 141, 175, 176
Correlation analysis, 28, 29, 49
Correlation coefficient, 28, 49
Creole language, 114
Criterion, 27, 28, 37, 69, 74, 94
Critical interaction situations, 28, 33
Cross-Cultural (Chinese) Personality Assessment Inventory (CPAI-2), 127
Cross sectional study, 32
Cultural
　anthropology, 129
　dimensions, 25, 26, 54–61, 65, 77, 84, 123, 128, 150, 162, 166–171, 179, 180
　psychology, v, vii, 1, 2, 8, 9, 14, 16, 18, 25, 34, 47, 53, 75, 123, 129, 144, 150, 151, 157, 179, 181, 184
　relativism, 17, 124
Culture
　areas, vi, vii, 1, 53, 58, 59
　comparative psychology, 2, 3
　differentiating factors, 54
　fair, 79
　genesis, 92, 94
　groups, 34, 58, 60, 146, 180
　national, 5
　regional, 5
　standards, 3, 116
　terms, 88, 98, 173, 181
Culture and Personality School, 8, 123, 129, 133
Cumulative deficit syndrome, 89
Cushion hypothesis, 165

D

Decision making behaviour, 157, 164–166
Deep structure, v, vii, 1, 104, 114, 179
Deficit

cumulative, 89
model, 77, 78, 95
syndrome, 89
Demarcation factor (context factor), 54, 66
Dependence, 8, 18, 21, 85, 124
Depression, 132, 173–175
Derived etics, 19
Development
   cognitive, 16, 32, 77, 78, 89–91, 95, 132, 144–149, 155
   level, 45, 51, 65, 73, 78, 92, 95, 132, 147, 155, 180
   stage, 7, 10, 16, 73, 77, 92, 144–149
   studies, 27, 32, 73, 77, 80, 89, 90, 98, 114, 139, 146–149
Developmental task, 141–143, 155
Diagnostic and Statistical Manual of Mental Disorders (DSM-5), 173, 175
Difference model, 77–78, 95
Differentiation study, 15, 25, 26, 32, 34–36, 139, 179, 182
Dimension, 26, 54, 55, 58–62, 64, 68, 84, 91, 98, 123, 125, 128, 134, 145, 153, 163, 166, 169
Display rules, 104, 107
Disposition, 47–49, 51, 52, 97, 125, 127, 130
   See also Trait
Distortion, *see* Bias
Do-it-yourself principle (tinkering), 45

E
Ecological, 68, 106, 133, 140
Economic form, 8, 34, 133
Education
   level, 31, 64, 89
   style, 182
Effect size (magnitude of effect), 38, 131
Egalitarianism (gender equality), 58, 63
Emotion
   dimensions, 98, 99, 102, 105
   expression, 105
   other-related, 102
   recognition, 105
   self-related, 102
   theories, 98, 99
   two-factor theory, 99
Emotional stability, 125, 126
Empathy, 132
Employee orientation, 163
Enculturation, 5, 6
Epigenetics, 48
Equivalence
   conceptual, 20, 21, 79, 95, 98, 127, 173
   functional, 22–24, 112, 113, 116, 181
   material, 22, 112, 113, 116
   measurement, 22, 24, 95, 127, 146
   metric, 23, 25
   operational, 22, 24
   postulates, 20–24, 59, 127, 146
   scale, 23–25, 28, 80, 116
   structural, 21, 59
   See also Reliability; Validity
Error probability, 37
Ethnopsychiatry, 28, 33
Etic *vs.* emic, 13–19, 38, 77, 94, 175, 181
Evolution, 10, 41–43, 45, 46, 98, 132
Evolutionary
   biology, 27, 42–44
   theory, 46, 132
Exaptation, 43–46
Experience
   with right angles, 69, 70
   with spatial depth, 69, 70
Ex post facto studies, 30
Expression function, 16
Expressivity, 136
Extraversion, 36, 37, 125, 128, 132

F
Facial expressions, 97, 101, 104, 154
Factor, 2
   analysis(factor analytical studies), 26
   condition, 15, 29, 30, 34, 171
   context (demarcation), 54, 62, 65, 66, 88
   control, 70
   cultural, 15, 26, 29, 34, 53, 54, 66, 90, 95, 118–121, 128, 148, 151, 155, 174, 179, 180

Factor (*cont.*)
  g- (general), 78
  hormonal, 132
  random, 15, 34
  structure, 23, 80, 128, 130, 150
  See also Variable
Family orientation, 174
Feature
  culture-specific, 154
  linguistic, 112, 115, 116
  paralinguistic, 112, 113
  personality, 128
  species-specific, 110–112
Feedback signals, 112, 120, 135
Femininity, 54, 55, 63, 120, 134
Field studies
  anthropological, 33
  ethnographic, 25, 33
Fitness, 42–45
Five-factor model, *see* Big Five model
Flynn effect, 79
Frustration, 152
Future orientation, 55, 58, 63

G
Gender
  biological (sex), 131–133, 136
  egalitarianism, 58, 63
  social (gender), 30, 55, 61, 111, 120, 121, 131–136, 154, 168
Generalisability, 15, 33
Generalisation study, 15, 26, 28, 34–36, 139, 179, 182
Generation comparison, 95
G-factor, 78
Global Leadership and Organizational Behaviour Effectiveness Research Program (GLOBE), 58
Group
  cohesion, 170
  collectivism, 170, 171
  reference, 157, 170
  work, 102, 151, 157, 163, 170–171

H
Hardy-Weinberg law of genetic equilibrium, 42
Harmony, 57, 63, 105, 119, 120, 165, 167, 168, 177
Heinz Dilemma, 148
Hermeneutics, 14, 17
Hierarchy orientation, 53, 169, 171
Hopi Indians, 84
Horizontal décalage, 147
Horizontal-vertical illusion, 69, 70
Human development index (HDI), 62–65
Human Relation Area Files (HRAF), 27, 30
Human Resource Management, 157
Hunter gatherer culture, 133
Hypothesis, 8, 18, 36–38, 68, 70, 72–74, 83–85, 115, 119, 120, 148, 162
Hypothetical construct, 20, 125

I
Iconic meaning, 110
Illusion
  cognitive, 88
  optical, 68
Impact, 14, 15, 26, 91, 105, 121, 179
Implicit Association Test (IAT), 103
Imposed etics (pseudo-etics), 19
Incest taboo, 27, 32
Income, 62, 64, 160, 161
Indicator, 20–22, 24, 25, 35, 59, 64, 84, 148
Indigenous psychology, 3
Individualism
  horizontal, 57
  vertical, 57
Indulgence, 55, 63
Infancy, 104, 140–142, 155
Information
  exchange, 109
  factual, 117, 118, 148
  processing, 148
  speeds, 61
Initiation ceremonies, 143
Intelligence

crystallized, 79, 88
emotional, 79
fluid (liquid), 79
general, 25, 78–81, 94, 149
general factor model, 78
kinesthetic-motor, 79
triarchic, 94
Intelligence quotient (IQ), 25, 79
International Classification of Diseases (ICD-11), 173
Interpersonal relatedness, 127
Interrelationship analyses, 26, 28
Invariance of quantity, volume and weight, 145
Item selection, 127

J
James Lange theory of emotion, 99

K
Kohlberg's stage model of the development of moral judgment, 148–149

L
Language
  ability, 7, 45, 75, 110
  acquisition, 114, 115, 149
  auxiliary, 115
  body, 110
  creole, 114
  pidgin, 114, 115
  routines, 116
  spoken, 84, 114
  usage rules, 111, 112
  women's, 120
Lateralisation (asymmetry of the cerebral hemispheres), 133
Lazarus and Folkman's stress model, 101
Leadership, 27, 132, 157, 158, 162–164, 171
Learning
  implicit, 142, 147
  incidental, 142
  targeted, 142

Length growth, 140, 141
Life expectancy, 64
Lifeworld, 4, 5, 33, 62, 64, 68
Likert scale, 129
Lingua franca, 89, 112, 183
Linguistics, 7, 13, 33, 67, 72, 73, 84, 89, 110–116, 120, 121
Longitudinal study, 32, 148

M
Maintenance *vs.* performance, 163
Managerial grid model, 163
Masculinity, 54, 55, 63, 120, 121, 134
Maslow's model of the hierarchy of needs, 160
Ma's stage model of moral development, 149
Mastery *vs.* harmony, 57
Matrilinear, 16
Maturation, 139–144, 154
Meaning of Working study (MOW study), 160
Memory
  capacity, 80, 85, 86
  long-term, 86
  model, 85, 86
  short term, 86
  span, 85, 86, 115
  working, 86
Meta analysis, 38, 106, 148
Migration, v, 43, 89
Minority, 5, 54, 88–89
Mistake, 168
Monochronicity, 167
Moral dilemma, 148
Mother-child, 8, 22, 24, 142, 151, 152
  attachment, 24
  interaction, 152
  relationship, 22, 142, 151
Mother tongue, 84–87, 112, 115, 142, 155
Motiv, 154, 160, 162
Müller Lyer illusion, 69, 70
Multilevel analysis, 25, 27, 30, 31
Multitasking, 168
Mutation, 42, 43

N

Naming strategy, 74
National character, 8, 129
Native psychology, 67, 72, 75
Nativism, 67, 72, 75
Nature
    differential, 48
    nature *vs.* nurture, 47–52
    universals, 97, 107
Need, 19, 24, 77, 87, 91, 102, 109, 116, 124, 132, 142, 155, 159–162, 168, 178, 183
Neurasthenia, 175
Neurophysiological, 103
Neuroticism, 126, 132
Neutrality *vs.* affectivity, 61
Null hypothesis (H_0), 36, 37, 182
Nurturant-task leadership, 163

O

Obedience, 20, 133
Objectivity, 13, 14, 21–23
Oedipus complex, 15, 16, 124
Ohio School, 163
Ontogenesis, 5, 6, 27, 32, 42, 67, 111, 121, 139
Openness to experience, 125, 126, 128
Organisational
    cultures, 109, 158
    structure, 109, 158
Otherness, v, 1, 7, 77, 78, 181

P

Parallelisation, 35, 36, 62, 180
Participation, 64, 142, 149, 163, 165, 171
Particularism, 63
Partner selection, 42
Path analysis, 27, 31
Peer group (peers), 142
Peoples psychology, 10
Perception illusion (optical illusion), 68
Performance, 25, 27, 29, 32, 36, 37, 44, 45, 58, 68, 73, 77–95, 102, 106, 136, 147, 150, 157, 162, 163, 170
    See also Competence vs. performance
Performance orientation, 58, 63, 164
Permissiveness, 8, 55, 153
Personality
    dimensions, 128
    factor, 25, 125, 127–130, 136
    factor models, 125–128
    psychology, 97, 125
    trait, 18, 20, 25, 30, 97, 125–127, 129, 135, 136
Perspectivity, 13, 14
Phenomenon, 13, 14, 16, 18–20, 22–24, 33, 34, 62, 68, 78, 89, 112, 115, 147, 176, 181
Phonemics, 13
Phonetics, 13, 87, 110, 112
Phonological loop, 85, 86
Phylogenesis, 41, 42, 45, 139
Piaget's stage model of cognitive development, 16, 144–147, 155
Pidgin language, 114, 115
PISA study, 26, 80, 81, 84, 89, 90, 150, 170
Polychronicity, 167, 168
Polytasking, 168
Population, 25, 33–35, 42–44, 47, 48, 64, 88, 89, 158
Poverty, 54, 62, 66, 89–90, 159
Power distance, 26, 31, 55–58, 63, 118–121, 162, 166, 167, 171
    See also Hierarchy orientation
Predestination, 159
Predictor, 27, 28, 31, 177, 178
Prestige, 51, 134, 136
Principle
    of communicative relativity, 115
    of linguistic relativity (Sapir-Wolf hypothesis), 71–75
    maternal, 124
    paternal, 124
    resonance, 94
    tinkering, 45
    of triarchic resonance, 93, 94
Probability of error, 37
Progressive Matrices Test (RPM, SPM), 79
Projective tests, 152
Protestantism thesis, 159, 160

Proximate *vs.* ultimate influencing variables, 32
Psychoanalysis, 7, 124, 129
Psychology
  cross-cultural, v, vi, 1–5, 9, 13, 25, 34, 47, 51, 125, 129, 157, 179, 182–184
  culture-comparative, 2, 3
  developmental, 42, 144
  differential, 3, 47, 52, 123, 125
  folk, 7
  indigenous psychology, 2, 9, 181
  intercultural (psychology of intercultural action), 2, 3, 9, 182–184
  local, 2, 18
  native, 67, 72, 75, 77
  social, 2, 9, 10, 130, 157, 179, 182
Punitivity, 153

Q
Quality criteria, 20–23
Quasi-experiment, 19, 25, 26, 29, 30, 49, 51, 68, 70, 82, 86, 103, 105, 119, 164, 165, 182

R
Random
  factor, 15, 16, 34, 87
  sample, 33, 34, 78
Randomisation, 29, 180
Raven's Progressive Matrices Test (RPM, SPM), 79
Reading literacy, 89
Reasons *vs.* causes, 17
Regional culture, 5
Regression analysis, 26–31, 169
Relationship
  aspects, 151
  orientation, 34, 118
  towards environment, 61, 63
Reliability, 21, 23
Religiosity, 177, 178
Representation function, 117
Representativeness, 34, 35, 62, 78, 180
Research methods

qualitative, 17
quantitative, 17
Resonance, 90–92, 94, 95
Response set, 129
Retinal pigmentation, 70
Ringi system, 165
Rites de passage (rites of passage), 143
Role
  differentiation, 55, 120, 133
  expectation, 134, 140, 143
Rules
  communicative, 182
  linguistic, 111
  morphological, 110, 111, 114
  phonological, 110, 111, 114
  pragmatic, 111, 114
  semantic, 110, 111
  syntactic, 110, 111, 114

S
Sample
  random, 34, 78
  selection, 34, 37, 62, 78
  standard, 25
  typical, 34, 35
Sapir-Whorf hypothesis (linguistic relativity principle), 8, 72–74, 84, 85, 115
Scale
  bipolar, 55
  common, 20, 23, 25, 80
  equivalences, 23, 25, 79, 116
  interval, 23
  ordinal, 23, 25
  ratio, 23
Schizophrenia, 28, 174, 175
Schulz von Thun's communication model, 117, 118
Searle's speech act theory, 117
Secondary analysis, 30
Secularised rationality, 59
Selection
  genetic, 42–44, 51, 132, 155
  natural, 41–44
  partner, 42, 43, 132
Self

Self (cont.)
  actualisation, 160, 161
  assertion, 63, 132
  centeredness, 128
  concept, 134, 135
  control, 17, 136
  description, 19, 125, 127
  disclosure, 117, 128
  esteem, 161
  interest of genes, 44
  interpretation, 94
  reflection, 127
Selfishness of genes, 151
Semantic differential, 98
Sex
  biological, 132
  differences, 131, 133
  roles, 132, 133
  social, 132
  See also Gender
Significance level, 37
Similarity, 2, 20, 55, 59, 62, 66, 73, 94, 98, 104, 112, 123, 128, 149, 157, 167, 171, 179, 181, 182, 184
Situationism debate, 127
Six Cultures Study, 8
Social
  behaviour, 2, 3, 9, 127, 142, 151–155, 157, 159, 179, 182
  desirability, 102, 129
  evolutionism, 77
  psychology, 170, 182
Socialisation, 5, 152
Sociobiology, 43
Sociophobia, 175, 176
Speech
  acts, 114, 117
  interruptions, 112, 118, 120
  pauses, 110, 112
  register, 115
  style, 115, 118
  See also Language
Stage
  of cognitive development, 144, 149
  of moral development, 149
Standard
  deviation, 173
  of comparison, 20, 23, 116
  samples, 25
State *vs.* trait, 97
Status relation, 183
Stereotypes, 129
Stroop test, 119
Structure d'ensemble, 147
Subculture, 33–35, 54
Suicide, 17, 173, 174, 176–178, 180
Surface structure, 114, 115
Survival, 42, 43, 59, 63, 161
Susceptibility to deception, 70, 71

T
Tarahumara Indians, 73, 74
Task orientation, 163
Tempo, 166, 167
Thinking
  abstract, 88
  analytic, 26
  deductive, 81, 87
  formal logic, 87
  holistic, 26, 82–84
  math, 89
  maths and science, 81, 87, 89
  moral, 148
  prelogical, 7
  spatial, 133
Time
  allocation, 166, 167
  concept, 84, 151, 171
  division, 140
  horizon, 55, 166
  linear, 167
  orientation, 55, 60, 166
  setting, 61
  use, 45, 55, 166–168, 173
Tinkering principle, 45
Traditionality, 59
Training, 3, 36, 82, 90, 146
Trait (property, characteristic), 29, 34, 97, 125
  See also State vs. trait
Transcultural psychiatry, 33

Index

Transfer, 49, 86, 88, 151
Trends in International Mathematics and Science Study (TIMSS), 80, 81
Triarchic, 90, 94, 95
Trobriander, 16
Twenty statements test (TST), 127
Twin method, 48–50

U

Uncertainty avoidance, 55, 58, 62–64, 101
Uniqueness, 14, 15, 18–19, 110, 181
Universal Grammar, 114
Universalism, 63
Universality, 7, 14, 18–19, 26, 28, 115, 131–132
Universals, 1–4, 7, 9, 16, 18, 27, 32, 35, 41–43, 46–48, 62, 73, 82, 94, 99, 101, 104, 105, 114–115, 123, 124, 129, 131, 144–149, 154, 155, 159, 161, 165, 173, 174, 179
Unpackaging, 15

V

Validity, 9, 16, 20–23, 27, 32, 70, 106, 123–129, 144–149, 161, 164, 179, 182
  construct, 21, 22
  ecological, 106
  indicator, 21, 22
  instrument, 21
  scale, 21
  universal, vi, 9, 16, 32, 144–149, 161
Value aspect, 20
Vantage theory, 73
Variable
  confounding, 34, 70, 112, 183
  control, 30
  dependent, 15, 16, 29, 30, 38, 106, 120, 146, 164, 181
  independent, 9, 14–16, 29, 30, 38, 135, 179, 180
  mediator, 162
  moderator, 135, 137, 169
  organismic, 29, 50, 52, 180
  random, 16
Violation, 144, 145, 153, 168
Voice, 21, 22, 24, 44, 101, 106, 110, 112, 115, 119
Völkerpsychologie, 7
Volume invariance, 145

W

Watzlawick's communication theory, 117
Work
  ethics, 159, 160, 167, 171, 180
  motivation, 157, 159, 160, 162
  performance, 102, 157, 162
World Values Survey (WVS), 59, 60, 63, 161
Worldwide Governance Indicators (WGI), 169
Wrongdoing, 168, 169

Y

Youth, 5, 143, 176

Z

Zone of proximal development, 94

SPRINGER NATURE

GPSR Compliance

The European Union's (EU) General Product Safety Regulation (GPSR) is a set of rules that requires consumer products to be safe and our obligations to ensure this.

If you have any concerns about our products, you can contact us on ProductSafety@springernature.com

In case Publisher is established outside the EU, the EU authorized representative is:

Springer Nature Customer Service Center GmbH
Europaplatz 3
69115 Heidelberg, Germany

The manufacturer's authorised representative in the EU is Springer Nature Customer Service Centre GmbH, Europaplatz 3, 69115 Heidelberg, Germany. If you have any concerns regarding our products, please contact ProductSafety@springernature.com

Printed and bound by CPI Group (UK) Ltd, Croydon, CR0 4YY
25/03/2026
02078172-0002